Mathematics Children Use and Understand

Mathematics Children Use and Understand

Preschool Through Third Grade

Wilbur H. Dutton

University of California, Los Angeles

Ann Dutton

Modesto Junior College

MAYFIELD PUBLISHING COMPANY

Mountain View, California

London • Toronto

Library of Congress Cataloging-in-Publication Data

Dutton, Wilbur H.
    Mathematics children use and understand : preschool through third
grade / Wilbur H. Dutton and Ann Dutton.
        p.   cm.
    Includes bibliographical references and index.
    ISBN 0–87484–968–3
    1. Mathematics — Study and teaching (Elementary)   2. Mathematics —
Study and teaching (Preschool)   I. Dutton, Ann.
II. Title.
QA135.5.D893   1991
372.7 — dc20   90–47524
                                                                   CIP

Manufactured in the United States of America
10 9 8 7 6 5 4 3 2

Mayfield Publishing Company
1240 Villa Street
Mountain View, California 94041

Sponsoring editor, Franklin C. Graham; managing editor, Linda Toy; production editor, Sondra Glider; developmental editor, Carol Dondrea; text and cover designer, Joan Greenfield; illustrators, Rose Sheifer, Alan Noyes. Cover illustration by Rose Sheifer.

The text was set in 11/13 Times Roman by Thompson Type and printed on 50# Butte des Morts by Banta Company.

The photo on p. 44 was provided by Modesto Jr. College Child Development Laboratory Preschool. The photo on p. 56 was provided by Capistrano Elementary School, Modesto. All other photos were provided by Corrine Seeds Elementary School, University of California, Los Angeles.

CONTENTS

CHAPTER 3 *Mathematics for Four-Year-Old Children*   38

CHAPTER 4

Mathematics for Five-Year-Old Children   60

CHAPTER 7   *Mathematics for Eight-Year-Old Children*   159

CHAPTER 10

Planning for Instruction, Classroom Organization, and Resource Materials   264

Appendix A

Physical, Cognitive, Social-Emotional Traits, and Needs of Children Four Through Eight Years of Age   301

PREFACE

This book has been written for teachers of young children four through eight years of age. We have used basic data from studies of child growth and development to prepare a sequential arrangement of mathematical learnings that are appropriate for young children. We emphasize a developmental approach. Such an approach stresses that, when selecting, organizing, developing, and presenting new mathematical content, teachers and educators must keep the individual child in mind. They must consider the sequence of developing cognitive structures.

The delivery of instruction is organized around both Piaget's theories of intellectual development and modern principles of learning. These include using hands-on materials and models to help children develop an understanding of math concepts; guiding learning activities so that children will act (mentally) on what is being learned to make their own meaning for each new concept; organizing and presenting learning activities (sequencing) according to the cognitive structures available as children mature and interact with their environment; providing for the learning of basic skills along with each new aspect of mathematics; and developing positive attitudes toward mathematical learning and an appreciation of the contributions of mathematics to the children's world.

The mathematical content in this book has been selected from three main sources: (1) the structure of mathematics; (2) *Essential Mathematics for the 21st Century,* prepared by the National Council of Supervisors of Mathematics; and (3) the components of children's environment that identify their need for math in *their own real-world activities*. The content for each age group (four through eight) has been identified and sequenced to form a continuum for each aspect of the mathematics program.

Three strands run through each learning level and help to synthesize the elements that make up the content of the math program:

1. Problem solving, centering around the components of children's environment and providing opportunities for exploration and for acquiring new skills
2. Number work, sequentially presented and appropriate for the development of children at each learning level
3. Evaluation, an integral part of instruction to guide each learning activity and to assess cognitive and affective development.

Teachers are given guidance in using instructional materials in the following areas:

1. Use of hands-on materials to introduce and develop new math concepts as well as to enable children to relate previous experiences with the new learnings
2. Selection and construction of teaching devices and models appropriate for the development of understanding math concepts
3. Preparation and use of appropriate follow-up activities, including the use of hands-on materials, provision for desirable practice, and children's assessment of their own work.

The major contributions of this book to the teaching of mathematics for young children are the following:

1. It recognizes the classroom teacher as the major component in curriculum change and in the improvement of instruction.
2. It identifies the basic cognitive and social-emotional traits and needs of children as the basis for selecting content and presenting instruction.
3. It provides a sequence of mathematical concepts for each learning level that is appropriate for children's age and cognitive development.
4. It uses the components of children's environment to provide meaningful problem-solving situations for applying mathematics.
5. It makes suggestions for teachers to establish learning environments that enable pupils to develop their own understanding of mathematics through hands-on materials, models, calculators, and computers.
6. It makes evaluation an integral part of the teaching-learning process as well as the basis for determining children's achievement in mathematics.
7. It provides a variety of resource materials and suggestions for lesson planning, classroom organization, conducting individual interviews, preparing test items, and measuring children's attitudes toward mathematics.
8. It provides selected references for teachers to use in obtaining background information and in extending their understanding of mathematics.

We have striven to prepare a book that will help primary-level teachers make mathematics instruction for young children developmentally appropriate, meaningful, and useful.

ACKNOWLEDGMENTS

To all who helped us in the preparation of this book, we express our heartfelt thanks and appreciation. The creative suggestions, support, and encouragement of these people helped us to write a book that we hope is practical and challenging for beginning primary-level teachers and a useful source for in-service classes for experienced teachers.

For reviewing the first draft of the book, we want to thank Mary M. Rogers, Consultant in Education and Lead Reviewer, State of California School Improvement Program, Thousand Oaks, California; Gail D. Lowe, Principal of Acacia Elementary School, Conejo Valley Unified School District, Thousand Oaks, California, assisted by Carol Berger (kindergarten) and Christina Myren (primary levels).

We also wish to thank the Brentwood Unified Science Magnet School and Beverly Tietjin, Principal, for providing computer lab instruction and sharing their classroom organization design.

Instructional guides and classroom visitations were provided by Cynthiana Brown, Assistant Principal of Corrine A. Seeds Elementary School, UCLA. Joe Lucero, a Media Specialist, also photographed children in math-related activities for the book.

Bob Foster, a Media Specialist at Modesto Junior College, photographed children at Capistrano Elementary School and Fremont Elementary School in Modesto, California.

Graphic art and illustrations in the manuscript were done by William W. Dutton and Gloria Fu Dutton.

Assistance in explanations of computer functions was given by Dr. Robert W. Dutton, Professor and Director for Design at the Center for Integrated Systems, Stanford University.

TRIAD Mathematics Laboratory materials and evaluation components were provided by Dr. R. W. Rawlinson, Dr. R. D. Phillips and Dr. Kathy B. Yaksley at the Center for Research in Learning and Instruction, New South Wales, Sydney, Australia.

Information about math for gifted learners was provided by Dr. and Mrs. Norman J. Mirman of The Mirman School for Gifted Children, West Los Angeles, California.

We thank Sara Gwen Kincaid, Senior Word Processor at the Graduate School of Education, UCLA, for her creative and professional preparation of the manuscript.

We appreciate the help of the editorial staff of Mayfield Publishing Company, especially Franklin C. Graham, Sondra Glider, and Carol Dondrea.

We give a special thanks to our "in-home" editor and proofreader, Roberta Holden Dutton. She is an inspiration to both authors.

Our efforts have been stimulated and guided by all the experiences we have had with the children we have reared, taught, and worked with.

Wilbur H. Dutton, Professor Emeritus
University of California, Los Angeles

Ann Dutton
Modesto Junior College

Mathematics Children Use and Understand

CHAPTER 1

Reform in Arithmetic, New Mathematical Content, and Structure of Mathematics

CURRENT REFORM IN ARITHMETIC

During the past few decades, the content, methods of teaching, and organization of arithmetic for young children have undergone many changes. Now, for example, arithmetic, geometry, and measurement are all being described by the term *mathematics*. The name change is part of a reform movement in mathematics that is concerned with presenting high-quality mathematics programs to children in a safe and nurturing environment that promotes their physical, social, emotional, and cognitive development. This emphasis on child growth and development derives from two important sources: (1) the work of the National Association for the Education of Young Children (NAEYC), especially *Developmentally Appropriate Practice in Early Childhood Programs Birth through Age 8* (1988); and (2) the theories of Jean Piaget, which describe children's intellectual development and their need to explore and manipulate concrete materials as aids in discovering and understanding mathematical concepts (Copeland, 1974; Kamii, 1985; Lavatelli, 1978). Both contributions are discussed in Chapter 2.

The movement is also interested in identifying mathematical skills that children need in daily life. The National Council of Supervisors of Mathematics (NCSM), in its position paper entitled "Essential Mathematics for the 21st Century" (1988), defines the mathematical competencies students need for both responsible adulthood and daily living. In Chapter 2, we list and discuss the 12 mathematical competencies identified in this work.

Use of the computer in the classroom beginning in the primary grades is another important part of the mathematical revolution now underway. Computers provide geometric displays; organize data; graph; generate numerical sequences, patterns, and programs; and simulate a great variety of problem situations. Software has been developed to help children explore and experiment with mathematical concepts, enrich mathematical learning experiences, and support curriculum for new mathematics programs. We will discuss computers in Chapters 3–7 in connection with mathematics programs for children ages four through eight.

THE REFORM MOVEMENT IN MATHEMATICS EDUCATION

The reform movement in mathematics education was brought on to a large extent by social, economic, and political forces all focused on the need to improve mathematics programs and instruction. As part of the reform trend, mathematics educators have been identifying the goals of mathematics education, defining appropriate mathematics content, and developing appropriate instructional practices for young children.

Underlying all this are several basic assumptions. First, the classroom teacher is the major component in curriculum change and improvement of instruction. Second, we must tailor mathematics programs to meet the needs of children rather than expecting children to adjust to the demands of a special program. Third, the major determinant of program quality in mathematics for young children is the degree to which the program is developmentally appropriate.

These three assumptions comprise the main themes of this book. They direct our efforts toward helping dedicated, qualified teachers create environments in which children can learn mathematics through their own discovery, using hands-on materials and interaction with other children. [To this end, teachers can use the guidelines cooperatively prepared by NCSM (1988) and NAEYC (1988).] They encourage teachers to provide mathematical learning activities based on children's needs and to encourage children to actively participate in using mathematics in their daily activities. They direct teachers to select the important characteristics of child growth and development for each age group in order to develop instruction that is age-appropriate and that enables children to learn and achieve optimum results in their own unique ways. Finally, they encourage us to make evaluation an integral part of the teaching-learning process, replacing antiquated and invalid achievement measures based on standardized tests.

We also consider the content of mathematics programs for children four through eight years of age: what teachers should teach. We have used three sources to determine this content: (1) the recommendations of the National Council of Supervisors of Mathematics and their statement on essential mathematics for the 21st century; (2) the organization and structure of mathematics itself; and (3) the components of children's environment that necessitate the use of mathematics operations in exploring and solving problems involved in daily living.

TWELVE COMPONENTS OF ESSENTIAL MATHEMATICS

In 1988, in its paper, "Essential Mathematics for the 21st Century," the National Council of Supervisors of Mathematics prepared a list of twelve components of essential mathematics to guide curriculum development and teaching in elementary schools. Essential mathematics is defined as the mathematical competencies students will need to function adequately as adults in our society and in daily living. Although not all of these skills are taught in early childhood mathematics programs, students will eventually need to develop competence in all of these essential areas.

The following list does not imply an instructional sequence or order of priority — all areas are interrelated.

- *Problem solving* — Problem-solving strategies include posing questions, analyzing situations, translating results, illustrating results, drawing diagrams, and using trial and error. Students should have experience with problems involving more than a single solution.
- *Communicating mathematical ideas* — Students should learn the language and notation of mathematics. They should understand place value and scientific notation; learn to receive mathematical ideas through listening, reading, and visualizing; be able to present mathematical ideas by speaking, writing, drawing pictures and graphs, and demonstrating with concrete models; and be able to discuss and ask questions about mathematics.
- *Mathematical reasoning* — Students should be able to investigate mathematical ideas independently. They should be able to identify and extend patterns and use experiences and observations to make conjectures (tentative conclusions); learn to use a counterexample to disprove a conjecture and to use models, known facts, and logical arguments to validate a conjecture; and be able to distinguish between valid and invalid arguments.
- *Applying mathematics of everyday situations* — Students should be encouraged to translate everyday situations into mathematical representations (graphs, tables, diagrams, or mathematical expressions), process the mathematics, and interpret the results in light of the initial situation.
- *Alertness to the reasonableness of results* — In solving problems, students should question the reasonableness of a solution or conjecture. They must develop the number sense to determine if results of calculations are reasonable.

- *Estimation* — Students should be able to use mental arithmetic and a variety of computational estimation techniques to make rapid approximate calculations. An estimate can be used to check reasonableness, examine a conjecture, or make a decision in a problem or in a consumer setting.
- *Appropriate computational skills* — Students should gain facility in using addition, subtraction, multiplication, and division with whole numbers and decimals.
- *Algebraic thinking* — Students should learn to use variables (letters) to represent mathematical quantities and expressions. They should be able to represent mathematical functions and relationships using tables, graphs, and equations.
- *Measurement* — Students should learn the fundamental concepts of measurement through concrete experiences. They should be able to measure distance, mass (weight), time, capacity, temperature, and angles; learn to calculate simple perimeters, areas, and volumes; and be able to measure in both the metric and English systems using the appropriate tools and levels of precision.
- *Geometry* — Students should understand the geometric concepts necessary to function effectively in the three-dimensional world. They should have knowledge of concepts such as parallelism, perpendicularity, congruence, similarity, and symmetry.
- *Statistics* — Students should plan and carry out the collection and organization of data to answer questions in their everyday lives. Students should know how to construct, read, and draw conclusions from simple tables, maps, charts, and graphs.
- Students should understand elementary notions of probability to determine the likelihood of future events. They should be able to identify situations where immediate past experience does not affect the likelihood of future events, and become familiar with how mathematics is used to help make predictions such as election results, business forecasts, and outcomes of sporting events.

State departments of education and local school districts use this list to help them prepare curriculum guides for teaching mathematics to young children. The California State Department of Education, for example, has prepared two publications — *Mathematics Framework for California Public Schools, K–12* (1985) and *Mathematics — A Model Curriculum Guide, K–8* (1987) — based on NCSM recommendations.

THE ORGANIZATION AND STRUCTURE OF MATHEMATICS

A knowledge of the framework of mathematics — unifying ideas of the properties of the number field, sets, functions, and relations — is important to a knowledge of how children learn the subject. Children come to understand each new mathematical idea or concept as it relates to what they already know about the framework of mathematical ideas and relationships. Learning the structure of mathematics helps young children to:

1. Use fundamental principles and ideas in practical situations and in problem solving
2. Store ideas and information in their memory
3. Better understand all aspects of mathematics
4. Compare new concepts to fundamental ideas taught earlier

In the next few sections we outline the basic structure of arithmetic, measurement, and geometry. Although we discuss these areas separately, teachers must understand that they are interrelated. For example, in learning to tell time the child will use basic arithmetic operations, measurement concepts (units of time), and geometric concepts (space defined for the face of a clock and divided into measurable units).

In Chapters 3–7 we discuss these same concepts according to age. Because children learn mathematics based on their age-related developmental level, we describe in these chapters the sequence in which concepts should be taught and make instructional suggestions for doing so for children ages four to eight. Some children in each age group will not be developmentally ready to learn all the concepts for that age. Each chapter focuses on a separate age — Chapter 3, for example, discusses mathematics for four-year-olds.

Arithmetic

Arithmetic involves the use of numbers, numeration, and basic operations $(+, -, \times, \div)$ and their properties. The four fundamental operations of arithmetic are meaningfully introduced at appropriate times for each age group. The facts, skills, and concepts are introduced gradually. Children use hands-on materials and practical problems to learn how the decimal system, with its ideas of **place value** and **notation,** provides the rationale for the four fundamental operations of arithmetic.

NUMBERS Number theory is explained to help teachers better understand what they teach. The concepts of number and numeration are based on the ten **digits,** 0 through 9, what they mean, and how to use them. These digits are used to express: the set of **whole numbers; counting** or **natural numbers; integers** (positive and negative whole numbers); and **rational numbers,** which include fractions, decimals, and percents.

What numbers mean and how they are used raise questions concerning the terms *number, numeral,* and *numeration.* **Number** is used to express a mathematical idea. **Numeral** is used to identify the symbol for the idea or the use made of a number. **Numeration** is the term applied when one names or uses numbers. Teachers should take a practical, meaningful approach to teaching these terms. They should model correct language and demonstrate the use of these terms so that children understand the differences and use them correctly to communicate their mathematical thinking.

Whole numbers

$$0, 1, 2, 3, 4, 5, \ldots$$

Counting numbers or natural numbers

$$1, 2, 3, 4, 5, 6, \ldots$$

Integers (positive and negative whole numbers)

$$-3, -2, -1, 0, +1, +2, +3, +4, \ldots$$

Rational Numbers

Fraction: a numeral that represents a rational number; a common fraction such as $\frac{1}{2}$ or $\frac{1}{4}$

Decimal: a fraction whose denominator is some power of 10, indicated by a dot (.), such as .05 for five-hundredths

Percent: a ratio between some number and 100, meaning "per centum," one one-hundredth part, 1%, or .01

NUMERATION   The numeration system we use was invented by the Hindus. They developed the decimal place-value system of whole numbers, probably during the second century A.D. The numerals 1, 2, 3, 4, 5, 6, 7, 8, 9 were developed first, whereas the symbol for zero wasn't developed until around A.D. 876. The system was carried to the Western world by Arab traders. For these reasons, we call the numeration system used in the United States the "Hindu-Arabic numeration system" and the numerals are called **Hindu-Arabic numerals**.

The invention of zero and the use of place value are two characteristics that set our number system apart from earlier systems used by the Greeks, Romans, and Egyptians. The properties of zero and place values are discussed in detail in Chapters 6 and 7 in connection with the four fundamental operations — for example $6 + 0 = 6$, $6 - 0 = 6$, $6 \times 0 = 0$, $0 \div 6 = 0$, and $6 \div 0$ is undefined. Zero is also used on number lines, thermometer scales, and charts; it is used for keeping records and scores; and it is the basis for the concept of place value.

Each of the first nine numerals can be written with a single symbol. To write the numeral following 9, two symbols must be used: 1 and 0 are used to make 10. Because we use the ten numerals in a place-value scheme based on powers of ten, we call the system a "decimal numeration system." The base of our number system is ten. For example, each numeral in the number 154 has a cardinal value (how many) and a positional or place value. The numeral 1 shows one and holds the hundreds position. The numeral 5 shows five and holds the tens place. The numeral 4 shows four in the ones place. Beginning with the ones place, each position to the left of the ones place is ten times greater than that preceding:

	10^2	10^1	
	Hundredths	*Tens*	*Ones*
	1	5	4

BASIC ARITHMETIC OPERATIONS AND PROPERTIES

As we noted earlier, the decimal system, with its ideas of place value and notation, provides the rationale for the fundamental operations of arithmetic. The history of the development of these basic operations is interesting. Around the year 825, an Arab mathematician, Mohammed ibu Musa al-Khowarizmi, wrote a book describing the Hindu computation system. This textbook was translated and used in Europe during the twelfth century. The followers of al-Khowarizmi used his systems of computation and were called "algorists." The name **algorism,** thus, grew out of the name of this mathematician, and today we use the word **algorithm** to describe the operations of addition, subtraction, multiplication, and division.

■ ADDITION ALGORITHM The addition algorithm is a special computational system for working with base ten to find the **sum** of two or more numbers (or **addends**) without counting. Three fundamental postulates (assumptions) apply to addition:

The commutative law $a + b = b + a$ (addend + addend = sum)
$4 + 2 = 2 + 4$

The associative law $(a + b) + c = a + (b + c)$
$(4 + 2) + 3 = 4 + (2 + 3)$

The closure law For every pair of numbers a and b, there exists a unique number $(a + b)$ that is called the sum of a and b.

The addition algorithm is introduced and developed in Chapter 5 in the discussion of mathematics for six-year-old children.

■ SUBTRACTION ALGORITHM The subtraction algorithm describes the process of finding one of two numbers when their sum and one number are given. Thus, $6 - 2$ indicates that 6 is the sum of two numbers, one of which is 2, and the other is the number we are attempting to find. Six minus two means that we are trying to find the number that must be added to 2 to give 6. In this sense, subtraction is the **inverse** of addition:

$$4 + 2 = 6$$
$$6 - 2 = 4$$
$$6 - 4 = 2$$

Inverse processes are usually more difficult to understand than direct processes. Subtraction can be applied in three situations: to find a remainder, to find a missing addend, and to find the difference between two numbers. These situations are described for different age levels in Chapters 4–7.

■ MULTIPLICATION ALGORITHM Multiplication is based on addition. In the process of addition, addends may be different numbers, as in $2 + 3 + 5 = 10$. In multiplication, the addends are the same number repeated a certain number of times. For example, 4×2 means four 2s, or 2 four times:

$$
\begin{array}{cc}
2 & 2 \\
\times\ 4 & 2 \\
\hline
8 & 2 \\
 & 2 \\
 & \underline{} \\
 & 8
\end{array}
$$

The inverse fact is 2×4, which means two 4s, or 4 two times:

$$
\begin{array}{cc}
4 & 4 \\
\times\ 2 & 4 \\
\hline
8 & 8
\end{array}
$$

Since multiplication is based on addition, and addition is based on counting, it follows that multiplication is based indirectly on counting.

Multiplication of whole numbers can be defined as an operation that begins with two numbers (**multiplicand** and **multiplier,** or **factors**) and produces a unique number called the **product**. The operation is characterized completely by the closure law, identity law, commutative law, associative law, and distributive law. These are defined as follows:

The closure law	The product of two natural numbers is a natural number. This is the law of closure for multiplication. Thus, $2 \times 3 = 6$. The product 6 is a natural number. We say that the set of natural numbers is closed with respect to multiplication. This law also applies to addition, as we showed earlier.
The identity law	The product of any whole number and 1 is that whole number ($2 \times 1 = 2$, $10 \times 1 = 10$, and so on), and the product of 1 and any whole number is that whole number ($1 \times 5 = 5$, $5 \times 1 = 5$, $1 \times 25 = 25$, $25 \times 1 = 25$, and so on). Thus, $a \times 1 = a$ and $1 \times a = a$ for all numbers a.
The commutative law	The product of two numbers is the same regardless of which number is given first: $a \times b = b \times a$, or $2 \times$

5 = 10 and 5 × 2 = 10. The facts have different meanings but the product is the same.

The associative law   The product of three numbers is the same no matter how the numbers are grouped:

$$(4 \times 5) \times 3 = 4 \times (5 \times 3)$$
$$20 \times 3 = 4 \times 15$$
$$60 = 60$$

To generalize using a, b, and c:

$$(a \times b) \times c = a \times (b \times c)$$

The distributive law   The distributive property is the basis for the multiplication algorithm. Distributing one factor (multiplier) over the terms of the other factor (multiplicand) is called the distributive property of multiplication with respect to addition.

For example, in multiplying 2 × 124, the operations include multiplying to find the products of ones, tens, and hundreds. Then the separate products are added to find the sum: $2[(100) + (20) + (4)] = 200 + 40 + 8 = 248$. Generalizing the process using letters, we see that

$$a(b + c + d) = (a \times b) + (a \times c) + (a \times d)$$

For example,

$$
\begin{array}{rcr}
124 = & & 100 + 20 + 4 \\
\times\ \ 2 & \times & 2 \\
\hline
& & 200 + 40 + 8 = 248
\end{array}
$$

■   DIVISION ALGORITHM   Division assigns to a product and a factor, the other factor: product ÷ factor = factor, or 8 ÷ 2 = 4. Children should learn that division is related to multiplication. In this example, children should learn to think, "By what number must I multiply the given factor in order to get the product?" That is, $2 \times ? = 8$.

For each multiplication statement with different factors, there are two related division facts. For example,

$$5 \times 6 = 30 \quad \text{and} \quad 6 \times 5 = 30$$

It follows from this that

$$30 \div 6 = 5 \quad \text{and} \quad 30 \div 5 = 6$$

$$
\begin{array}{cc}
5 & 6 \\
6\overline{)30} & 5\overline{)30}
\end{array}
$$

Division may be interpreted in three ways: (1) as the inverse of multiplication; (2) as a process of partition, telling the "size of each part," such as: "With 12 feet of ribbon divided into four streamers, how long will each streamer be?" (3 feet each); and (3) as successive subtraction.

As subtraction is the inverse of addition, so division is the inverse of multiplication. And since multiplication is successive addition, it is logical that division is successive subtraction. Calculators divide by treating division as successive subtraction.

Division is difficult for young children because the algorithm uses the operations of multiplication and subtraction, as well as skills in estimating quotient figures; it also requires an understanding of place values. Much of the work in division is held off until children are eight or nine years of age.

Measurement

Measurement, as we noted earlier, is one of the major areas of mathematics, and several of its attributes are important to components of the children's environment. For example, children learn how to count discrete things and to measure the continuous attributes of geometric figures such as area, as well as how to measure attributes of temperature, money, and time. In order to show the structure of measurement, we identify in the following list the attribute to be measured and the system or process used in measuring it. The main concepts and skills involved in measuring these attributes are presented in Chapters 3–7 for each learning level and connected with the relevant components of the children's environment.

Attribute to be measured	Examples
Length	Nonstandard and standard units and line segments — the distance along one dimension
Time	School time, intervals of time, seasons — the continuous measurement of change
Money	A medium of exchange, debts, goods and services, place values, coins, notes — the worth of things
Area	Coverage of surface — two-dimensional shapes
Volume	Interior of a shape — three-dimensional objects
Capacity	The amount an object can hold — liquids, grain, sand
Mass	A body of coherent matter, indefinite shapes, size — the amount of matter an object has
Temperature	Heat — warm, cold, body temperature, liquids, Fahrenheit, Celsius (F or C)

SYSTEMS OF MEASUREMENT   Two systems of measurement are introduced in mathematics programs for young children: the customary (English) system, with irregular relationships among and within units, and the metric system (meters, grams), which is based on the decimal system, with regular and consistent relationships among and within units. The main topics introduced in kindergarten and extended throughout each learning level are

Linear measurement	Centimeter ruler and inch ruler
Liquid measurement	Liter, cup, pint, quart
Weight	Kilogram, pound

In the process of learning to measure, young children go through several stages. They must first recognize certain attributes so they can describe, talk about, compare, classify, and then measure. They must also have experiences that will enable them to understand conservation. For example, they must understand the concept of quantity and know that the quantity of a substance, such as clay, has not changed when separated into several pieces. Nonstandard measurement, such as measuring a cabinet by shoe length, should be used so that children can discover the need for standard measurement. Direct measurement will precede indirect measurement such as the use of computation, mechanical, and electronic measurement. These learning stages are discussed in Chapter 2. Learning sequences for measurement are given in Chapters 3–7 for each age group.

Geometry

Geometry involves shapes of varied dimensions, transformation of shapes, and the properties of shapes. Nonmetric rather than metric geometry is studied. Metric geometry involving measurement is used in junior high school and above.

Geometric models are used to help children understand basic concepts. The main concepts of geometry that are taught to young children are as follows:

Dimensions

    Three dimensions — objects with length, width, and depth (cups, blocks, balls)

    Two dimensions — shapes with length and width (figures small enough to trace to make lines, curves, angles)

    One dimension — models of line segments (a drawing, kite string, parts of letters such as N,W,T)

    Zero dimension — models for a "point" (vertices and angles)

Transformations

    Transformations help children observe changes in the environment as well as things that may not change. Experiences with transformations encourage children to be creative and flexible in their thinking and in the use of language to describe changes. Children observe likenesses and differences.

Topological transformations — deal with the irregular stretching and shrinking of objects and materials (facial features such as a smile, body movements, rubber gloves, a sweat shirt, inflated balloons). What stays the same? What changes?

Projective transformations — deal with changes of shape and size that occur through changes of perspective (shadows in the light of a projector, airplanes in the sky seeming to shrink in size or grow larger depending on distances, mountains close by or at a distance).

Euclidean transformations — deal with things that do not change while in the process of evolving. This is the geometry of shape and size. Topological and projective properties are subsumed in Euclidean geometry.

Slides — Objects sliding up, down, right, or left require a direction (which is shown with the use of an arrow, a vector) and a length.

Flips — Objects flipping over require a direction and a length. Direction of a flip is determined by the position of a line about which the flip is made (the line of symmetry), and length is shown by the distance between the line and the object flipped.

Turns — Objects that are turning require direction, length, and the center of the turn (center of rotation), which is given by a point.

Constructions

Construction activities provide many opportunities for children to create, to enjoy building and rebuilding, and to explore making new shapes and forms. Use paper cutting and folding, clay, straws, rods, geoboards. The children make and share constructions with a friend or the class.

MATHEMATICAL COMPONENTS OF CHILDREN'S ENVIRONMENT

The mathematical components of children's environment are important determinants of program content. Every child should be actively involved in mathematical learning through experiences that are meaningful, natural, part of everyday living, and enjoyable.

Using the components of children's environment provides opportunities to motivate children through learning activities; to engage them in meaningful problem-solving activities; and to introduce them to mathematical skills and concepts through the interaction of their own thinking with their experiences in the external world.

Using these environmental components gives us access to the immediate, daily lives of children, and makes it easier to adjust for differences in background and for differences in the way children process and use mathematics skills and concepts.

To help children learn the basic concepts and skills of arithmetic and to use the four fundamental operations of arithmetic, we have described components that all children use to some degree each day as they live, play, and grow toward maturity at home and at school. They are: time, length, shape, mass, capacity, money, and the need to handle and manipulate objects so that structures or patterns are made. There will also be opportunities to measure geometric shapes and to introduce experiences in logical thinking. Concepts and skills are sequenced for each age group.

The definitive studies of C. Kamii support our use of the components of children's environment as an appropriate and major source for determining mathematical content and experiences for young children. Kamii's studies involve group games in early childhood math education (1980); the need for young children to reinvent arithmetic (1985); and how children learn math best when handling objects (1988).

SUMMARY

In this chapter we discussed the reform movement in mathematics education that is now under way. Changes brought about by this movement have helped to clarify the goals of mathematics education; identified the importance of appropriate, developmental instructional practices; defined a larger, richer mathematical content; ushered in the use of the latest technology, with many implications for mathematics education; promoted evaluation procedures; and recognized the classroom teacher as the main component in curriculum improvement.

Recommendations for selecting mathematical content for young children came from three sources: (1) the social aspects of mathematics (NCSM, 1988); (2) the structure and organization of mathematics; and (3) the mathematical components of children's environment.

We discussed the 12 areas of mathematical competence the NCSM (1988) suggests be woven into mathematics programs. Not all of these are appropriate for young children. However, such competencies as problem solving, communicating math ideas, reasoning, applications of math, estimating, using statistics, and notions of probability are important at each learning level. With young children, these are integrated into daily mathematical activities rather than developed as separate topics.

We also showed the structure and organization of mathematics (arithmetic, measurement, geometry), including the basic concepts, algorithms, and skills that must be sequenced and learned in order to understand and use mathematics effectively. These factors are cumulative; children learn simple concepts and skills first, and then, building on what they have already learned, they extend their understanding to more complex forms.

Finally, we discussed the importance of using the components of children's environment to determine program content and to guide instruction. This idea was established and has been supported by leading research workers in mathematics education. Using these components provides opportunities to motivate children through learning activities, engage them in meaningful problem-solving work, and introduce them to mathematical skills and concepts through the interaction of their own thinking with their experiences in everyday living. Children are able to discover and use meaningful mathematical concepts and skills appropriate for their developmental levels.

In the next chapter, we discuss the importance of teachers' understanding child growth and development and of using this knowledge to guide desirable learning activities in mathematics.

ACTIVITIES FOR TEACHER INSIGHT

1. Identify some of the problems generated by the "new math." Read references such as Labinowicz (1985) or talk to teachers who were involved in using the new math.
   a. Who determined what was to be taught?
   b. Who determined how the new math was to be learned?
2. If we accept the premise that the classroom teacher should be the major component in curriculum change and improving instruction, what should we do about the use of textbooks and workbooks?
3. Identify some mathematics learning activities related to the components of children's environment that are important to children in your neighborhood.
   a. How would you introduce and use these with one age group, such as six-year-olds?
   b. What advantages does this approach have over the use of a textbook or workbook? How could these activities be used in connection with a textbook?

REFERENCES

BROWNELL, W. A. (1941). *Arithmetic in grades I and II: A critical summary of new and previously reported research*. Durham, NC: Duke University Press.

————. (January 1947). The place of meaning in the teaching of arithmetic. *Elementary School Journal*.

California State Department of Education. (1985). *Mathematics framework for California public schools K–12*. Sacramento, CA: Bureau of Publications.

California State Department of Education. (1987). *Mathematics—Model curriculum guide K-8*. Sacramento, CA: Bureau of Publications.

COPELAND, R. W. (1974). *How children learn mathematics: Teaching implications research*. New York: Macmillan.

CROWLEY, M. L. (1987). The Van Hiele model of the development of geometric thought. In M. M. Lindquist (Ed.), *Learning and teaching geometry, K-12, 1987 yearbook*. Reston, VA: National Council of Teachers of Mathematics.

DUTTON, W. H. (1945). *G. Stanley Hall and the child study movement in America*. Unpublished doctoral dissertation, Stanford University, Stanford, CA.

———. (1964). *Evaluating pupils' understanding of arithmetic*. Englewood Cliffs, NJ: Prentice-Hall.

HANNA, P. (1935). Opportunities for the use of arithmetic. In *The teaching of arithmetic*. Washington, DC: National Council of Teachers of Mathematics.

HOLLIS, L. Y. (1981). Mathematical concepts for very young children. *Arithmetic Teacher, 29*(2), 24–27.

KAMII, C. (1985). *Young children reinvent arithmetic*. New York: Teachers College Press, Columbia University.

KAMII, C., & DE VRIES, R. (1980). *Group games in early education: Implications of Piaget's theory*. Washington, DC: National Association for the Education of Young Children.

KAMII, C., & WILLIAMS, C. K. (1988). How children learn by handling objects. *Young Children, 42*(1), 23–26.

LABINOWICZ, E. (1985). *Learning from children: New beginnings for teaching numerical thinking—A Piagetian approach*. Menlo Park, CA: Addison-Wesley.

LAVATELLI, C. S. (1978). *Piaget's theory applied to an early childhood curriculum*. Boston: Center for Media Development.

MUELLER, D. W. (1985). Building a scope and sequence for early childhood mathematics. *Arithmetic Teacher, 33*(2), 8–11.

National Advisory Committee on Mathematics Education. (1975). *Overview and analysis of school mathematics: Twenty-first yearbook*. Washington, DC: National Council of Teachers of Mathematics.

National Association for the Education of Young Children (NAEYC). (1988). *Developmentally appropriate practice in early childhood programs birth through age 8*. Washington, DC: Author.

National Council of Supervisors of Mathematics (NCSM). (1988). Essential mathematics for the 21st century. (A position paper.)

National Council of Teachers of Mathematics. (1953). *The learning of mathematics: Twenty-first yearbook*. Washington, DC: Author.

OLSON, W. C. (1959). *Child development*. Boston: D. C. Heath.

CHAPTER 2

Child Development and Applications of Piaget's Theories to Mathematics Teaching and Learning

A review of the reform movement in mathematics education reveals how programs have changed in response to social, economic, and political forces. These changes, up to the current mathematics revolution now under way, have not taken into account the basic developmental needs of young children. We believe, however, that the main determinant of the quality of mathematics programs for young children is the extent to which child growth and development are defined and implemented in these programs. In this regard, *Developmentally Appropriate Practice in Early Childhood Programs Birth Through Age 8* put out by the National Association for the Education of Young Children (1988) is both timely and authoritative. The statement provides a framework for setting up developmentally appropriate programs and instructional practices.

CHILD DEVELOPMENT

When we talk about child development, we are concerned with an emerging self, slowly opening up, expanding, tentatively reaching out into new and higher forms of behavior (Hymes, 1981). Development concerns the sequences of related changes in a child from birth throughout life. As the child develops, he or she advances to a higher degree of differentiation and complexity. Educators, psychologists, pediatricians, and those who work in areas relating to the education of young children recognize certain principles of development (M. Dopyera-Lay & J. Dopyera, 1987). The most important of these principles are

1. The child acts and learns as a whole, involving mental, physical, and social-emotional characteristics and traits.

2. The child's response to instruction is influenced by previous learnings, maturity, and cognitive development.
3. Children develop mental, physical, and social-emotional traits at different rates according to a unique pattern for each child.
4. Development is continuous and is influenced by the interaction of heredity and environment.
5. The differences within and among individuals must be considered. Not only do the rates of development of different children vary, but each child's rate may vary from one time to another.
6. There are many acceptable patterns of behavior at each age level.
7. Sex differences exist, but children are also alike in many ways.

These principles are important to all learning and instruction for children. However, they have specific implications for teaching mathematics, and we will point these out throughout the book.

At school, young children are grouped into classes according to age and, in many schools, according to achievement within these classes. Age and individual differences, therefore, are important factors in learning and in the delivery of instruction, and they must be taken into consideration. NAEYC's position statement (1988) discusses the importance of these two dimensions — age appropriateness and individual appropriateness — in defining developmental appropriateness.

Age appropriateness studies show that universal, predictable sequences of growth and change occur in children during the first nine years of life (Hymes, 1981; Labinowicz, 1985). These changes occur in all aspects of development (physical, emotional, social, and cognitive). Teachers need to know the typical development pattern of children within each age span served by the mathematics program. With this information, they can arrange a suitable environment and plan appropriate learning experiences. (See the outlines of children's physical, cognitive, and social-emotional traits and needs in Appendix A.)

Individual appropriateness refers to the uniqueness of each child. Each child has an individual growth pattern and rate, as well as a unique personality, learning style, and home background. These individual differences are important in curriculum development and important to the way adults interact with children. Young children learn through the interaction of their own thoughts and experiences with materials and with adults. Providing for the range of developmental abilities and interests of each learning group is difficult. However, many primary-level teachers have altered the curriculum provided by the school to meet individual child needs without school support. Thus, to be able to arrange desirable learning activities for each child, teachers must take into account both age and level of growth and development.

In this book we stress the importance of total interrelated growth in all areas: physical, social, and emotional. Properly conceived and presented mathematics can make significant contributions to each of these areas. The contributions of mathematics to children's intellectual (or mental) development are apparent. But teachers should also consider how mathematics can help in developing the social and moral realms (Piaget, 1965; Kamii, 1985).

James Hymes refers to *basic growth tasks* — children's learnings that make up the meaning they take from all that happens to them.

> Children search for trust in adults, they search for joy in their age mates, they search for confidence in themselves . . . the development of self-concept. . . . The whole point of their living, its very significance, lies in the movement toward self-concept. (1981, pp. 105f)

If a task given a young child is too difficult, the child feels inadequate and often makes up false answers to please the teacher. This can affect self-esteem and the trust relationship necessary between teacher and child. In order to feel confident, a young child needs to be able to do many things on his own, to be autonomous.

In her discussion of the long-term effects of developing autonomy, Constance Kamii identifies three aspects: (1) children's relationships with adults (authority, rules, affection, trust); (2) their relationship with peers (leadership, acceptance, community feelings); and (3) their relationship to learning (curiosity, confidence, alertness) (Kamii, 1985, p. 243).

As we discuss intellectual development, we must consider as well the other important aspects of total growth and development in children. Social and emotional factors affect mental development. Young children are reluctant to try any new material or mental task unless they think they can succeed. Piaget pointed to approaching the child as an autonomous whole.

PIAGET'S CONTRIBUTIONS TO MATHEMATICS EDUCATION

For several decades researchers have debated the relative importance of heredity and environment in stimulating intellectual growth. Is intelligence a fixed product of heredity or is environment the crucial factor in intellectual development? Today, most educators agree that intellectual development is the result of an *interaction* between heredity and environment.

Eminent Swiss psychologist Jean Piaget studied intellectual development in children. His theories help explain the continuous changes that occur in the organization and development of intelligence. They emphasize the importance of developing the child's curiosity and eagerness to learn through the active exploration of meaningful components in the environment. The development of mathematical concepts, which are built up through maturation and experience, is closely related to the way Piaget believed intellectual development takes place.

Piaget's Background

Piaget's research was not originally intended for education and teaching. Only a small part of his work dealt with these topics. People first read his writings on language and moral development during the 1930s and early 1940s (Lavatelli, 1978). By the 1960s, however, his work was being studied by a variety of research workers and educators.

Paul Rosenbloom (1962), reporting at a conference of the Science and Mathematics Center and the National Science Foundation stated that "it is imperative that teachers and curriculum workers understand children's development and such theories as conservation. . . . American mathematics educators have neglected the work of Piaget." Rosenbloom summarized Piaget's work on education and nurtured a movement to study and research his theories.

In 1978, Lavatelli wrote,

> Piaget is recognized as one of the great theorists in developmental psychology. He has given us a model of processes involved in the acquisition of knowledge and the development of logical intelligence (birth through adolescence). Many disciplines are using his theories: psychology, education, sociology, anthropology and mathematics.

In order to understand Piaget's theories we must examine his early background. He was born in 1896 in Neuchatel, Switzerland. At a very early age he showed a keen interest in nature and published a small paper on his observations of an albino sparrow. These interests led him to biology, where he wrote his doctoral dissertation on mollusks. This background provided Piaget with his unique biological conception of knowledge and the development of intelligence.

Piaget was also interested in philosophy, especially epistemology, the branch of philosophy concerned with the nature of knowledge. He examined knowledge from a biological perspective, asking: How does knowledge come about? According to Furth (1969), this approach "implied an attempt to explain knowledge through its formation and development. Because of this approach, Piaget has been referred to as a genetic epistemologist" — one who attempts to get at the problem of the origin and development of knowledge. Bruner (1967) stated that

> unquestionably he [Piaget] is the most impressive figure in the field of cognitive development today. . . . His principal mission is not psychological but epistemological . . . and concerned with the nature of knowledge as it exists in different points in the development of the child.

In 1905, Piaget worked under Binet in Paris on standardizing intelligence test items for children. Binet had been given a commission by the French government to prepare tests to identify children with low mental abilities. These children were to be excluded from French schools because, it was felt, they would not be able to profit from the regular instructional program. During this work, Piaget began asking the children to explain the answers — both correct and incorrect — that they had given to test items. He felt the children had reasons and logic for their answers. Later he studied similar behavior in his own children. His observations provide evidence to support his evolving theory of how intelligence developed.

Piaget believed that studying individuals would reveal the underlying processes of thinking common to all people. Thus, in his early work, his samples were small: "If all human beings had this underlying logical system of thinking which evolved over time, it would be necessary to examine only a small number of individuals to discover the structure and function of intelligence" (McNally, 1978). His studies are called *ontogenetic* because their concern is to discover what is common to the sample rather than what is different.

Piaget's Theory of Intellectual Development

Mental growth, according to Piaget, is the result of interaction between the maturing organism and the environment in accord with fundamental biological principles. A baby does not inherit ready-made behavioral patterns. However, certain reflexes, such as sucking, grasping, and ocular movements, which are inherited, can be modified through interaction with the environment. For example, a mother holds a bottle for her baby while the baby sucks; over a period of time, as he matures, the child gradually learns how to accept the bottle and hold it himself while sucking. The baby has adapted to a new way of feeding. This ability to adapt is common to all life and is fundamental to Piaget's conception of the development of intelligence. Piaget saw adaptation to the environment as a fundamental principle that applies as much to the development of intelligence as to any other aspect of development.

In addition to adaptation, Piaget postulates another basic biological principle involved in the development of intelligence: the tendency of an organism toward organization. Each adaptive act takes place as part of organized behavior because all actions are coordinated within the brain.

Piaget believed that we inherit ways of intellectual functioning that interact with the environment to bring about the progressive development of intellectual structures. These structures are ways of dealing with the environment. We touch, watch, listen, and experiment with the environment to take in information and process it. Our understanding of that information gradually increases in complexity. A structure, the general form of coping with the environment, is available at each developmental level. The structures for a young child will be different from those of an older child.

A baby will put a toy in his mouth, a two-year-old will bang it against a solid object, a four-year-old will experiment with various uses, an adult assesses the toy by looking or by touching it. But the fundamental process (the function) underlying the progressive development of each child is identical. Piaget believed that the fundamental properties of intellectual functioning remain the same throughout life.

The two basic functions that always operate are adaptation and organization. Piaget called these two complementary principles "functional invariants" — functions that do not vary.

Piaget's Stages of Intellectual Development

Intellectual functioning, as we noted, depends on the **cognitive** structures available at any one time. These structures develop continually as the individual matures and interacts with the environment.

According to Piaget, intellectual processes change during the early childhood years. The thinking of a four-year-old is qualitatively quite different from the thinking of an eight-year-old. The older child knows more and is able to do different, more complex things than the younger child. Although individual differences exist, Piaget believed that the thinking of all children tends to go through the same stages, and usually at about the same age.

Intellectual development, according to Piaget, falls into four clear stages, each defined by a characteristic way of functioning.

1. Sensorimotor stage   birth to 2 years
2. Preoperational stage
   (a) Preconceptual or symbolic   2 to 4 years
   (b) Intuitive or perceptual   4 to 7 years
3. Concrete Operations stage   7 to 12 years
4. Formal Operations stage   12 to 15 years

Children move gradually from one stage to the next. Each new stage is made possible by the learning of the previous stage (Piaget and Inhelder, 1969). Evidence shows that, as the new stage becomes part of the child's thinking, the child incorporates it into the solid foundation of the earlier stage. The following diagram illustrates how a child's thinking begins to move into the next stage before the child can be said to think in that stage — a gradual process of developing thinking skills.

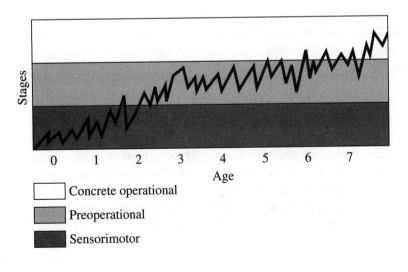

Concrete operational

Preoperational

Sensorimotor

SENSORIMOTOR STAGE The first stage in a child's mental development is influenced by what the child perceives. This perception matures gradually as the child experiences the environment by touching objects and interacting with people through his senses. Piaget called this the sensorimotor stage. As the preoperational stage begins, exploration continues in a sensorimotor way with the addition of language.

PREOPERATIONAL STAGE In the preoperational stage, the child begins to coordinate thinking as information and language expand, but in an inconsistent way. The child is still limited by what he or she actually sees or perceives, and lacks a real understanding of the rules governing the environment. The child finds it difficult to make consistent judgments and see logical relationships at this stage. When asked to tell the differences between two sets of objects or to determine if they are equivalent, a child will be influenced by the physical size or arrangement of the objects. The ability to see equivalence (to see that each group or set has equal numbers of objects) is basic to understanding mathematics. Thus, experiences must be provided that will help intuitive thinking to emerge.

The preoperational stage lasts from two to seven years of age, although some children may remain in this stage until eight or nine years of age. Much depends on the child's environment and learning experiences. Everyday play experiences at school and at home provide natural opportunities to use thinking skills in an informal social context.

Mathematical experiences for the child should present a minimum of perceptual difficulties (materials should be of a size easily handled and on a tray or clean desk for clear focus) so that the new learning will be relatively easy. Concrete materials must be made available for the child to manipulate, act on, arrange, and then classify. For example, we should use objects familiar to the child in daily living and play such as buttons, keys, small toy cars, marbles, rocks, chestnuts, and bottle caps.

CONCRETE OPERATIONAL STAGE The concrete operational stage, from seven to eleven or twelve years of age, is important because these are the years during which children are enrolled in elementary school. Although some children will enter this stage before they are seven, this age was set because 75 percent of Piaget's sample demonstrated logical thinking at seven years of age (Labinowicz, 1985). During this stage, the child begins to internalize actions with concrete objects. The child makes the operation or activity in thought. The thinking is no longer dominated by perceptual content. For example, the child can classify, place a series in order, and substitute one element for another by using mental schema; the child does not have to rely solely on manipulating the objects being considered.

Two basic principles are important to the study of mathematics and to a child's thinking: (1) conservation and (2) reversibility. The principle of conservation says that a set quantity of a substance does not change if the shape or appearance of the substance changes. For example, two sets of objects, such as:

$$\begin{matrix} O\ O \\ O\ O \end{matrix} \quad \text{and} \quad \begin{matrix} O\ O \\ O\ O \end{matrix}$$

can be arranged or the position changed:

$$O\ O\ O\ O \quad \text{and} \quad \begin{matrix} O\ O \\ O\ O \end{matrix}$$

and children at this level know they are still equivalent.

The principle of reversibility refers to a child's ability to mentally reverse a situation. In mathematics, for example,

$$O\ O \quad \text{and} \quad O\ O = \begin{matrix} O\ O \\ O \\ O\ O \end{matrix}$$

or 2 + 3 = 5, and

$$\begin{matrix} O\ O \\ O \end{matrix} \quad \text{and} \quad O\ O = \begin{matrix} O\ O \\ O \\ O\ O \end{matrix}$$

or 3 + 2 = 5. Children at this stage can reverse numbers mentally and know that the result is the same.

At the beginning of this learning and growth stage, the child still needs concrete objects to see, experiment with, and manipulate because the ability to remember is limited until conservation develops. Near the end of this stage, the child should be able to do simple problems without representation. The child is depending on his senses rather than relying on physical qualities.

FORMAL OR LOGICAL OPERATION STAGE The formal or logical operations stage begins during the upper elementary grades or junior high. The stage may be identified when a child is able to form concepts from abstract rather than from concrete experiences. In this stage the child is able to form and apply a variety of mathematical concepts.

Research has validated Piaget's theories of the stages of intellectual development (see, for example, Labinowicz, 1985). That is the stages of intellectual development always occur in the order described by Piaget, and a child cannot skip a stage. Intellectual development, then, is a progressive integration of structures beginning at birth and continuing throughout life.

FOSTERING THE GROWTH OF INTELLIGENCE

Guiding the growth of children's intelligence should be one of the major goals of early childhood education. Piaget's research provides a sound theoretical base for achieving this goal. He believed that individuals have to use their brain — and certain logical ways of thinking — to acquire new knowledge, and he developed the *equilibration model* to describe the process of acquiring knowledge and developing logical intelligence. The important factor in acquiring knowledge, he felt, is *self-activity,* and he described the nature of self-activity. "The pupil has to do" himself and for himself (Lavatelli, 1978, p. 36). The child must *act on* the materials herself in order to truly learn. Explanations by the teacher are not sufficient for learning to take place.

Piaget's conception of intelligence is embedded in a biological framework based on a tendency toward systemic equilibrium. When a disturbance occurs within one's body system, such as a rise in body temperature, numerous mechanisms, such as sweating, dilating of blood vessels, and increased heart beat, go to work immediately to restore the body to equilibrium. These are physical adaptations.

Piaget believed that similar adaptations occur in mental processes. The dynamics of the interaction between an individual and the environment tend to put the individual into a state of mental disequilibrium. When this state occurs, there is a basic drive to restore equilibrium, but these adjustments — unlike physical adaptations — are not automatic. The individual exercises control over these mental operations through a process labeled *equilibration.*

The process of equilibration, which operates continuously in all interactions between a developing individual and the environment, is what promotes change and adjustment — it is the motive force behind the "coming into being" of all developing structures (McNally, 1978, p. 10). Accommodation and assimilation come into balance and help the individual achieve equilibrium in preparation for a new disequilibrium. The balance achieved through accommodation and assimilation makes a person ready for further adaptation and modification.

Information comes into the brain through the senses. If it is understood as previously known information, it is *assimilated* in the brain. If the information is new, *accommodation* takes place. A child seeing green noodles on the plate for the first time must accommodate in order to make a new mental image after tasting the noodles. Regular colored noodles would be assimilated if the child had tasted them before. All new experiences require accommodation. Adults and older children have a good memory structure, so they assimilate information, recognizing it as known to them. Young children have a much less developed memory structure, so they require much more time and contact to remember, to assimilate. They often become bored with what is known well.

IMPLICATIONS OF PIAGET'S THEORIES FOR CHILDREN FOUR THROUGH EIGHT YEARS OF AGE

We have already discussed the importance of developing intellectual competence. Researchers agree that interventions promoting the development of intelligence are particularly important during the early childhood years. Piaget's writings provide a great deal of information and insight on how to help this development through self-activity.

Piaget believed that there is a parallel between the development of all logical thought in the child and understanding of the logic underlying mathematics. He believed that classification, ordering, and one-to-one correspondence were fundamental to a child's understanding of number. As children engage in learning activities in these areas, they assimilate new knowledge, change old ideas or some of their previous learning (reconstructing), and in so doing, improve their cognitive abilities. In this book, these logical processes (classification, space, numbers, and ordering) have been included in the sequence of learning activities for children at each age level. Let's look briefly at the way each develops in early childhood mathematics:

Classification: (Piaget, 1965) Simple sorting (not true classification): grouping objects according to a single property such as shape; more advanced (true) classification: finding the common property for a group of objects and then finding the same property in other objects in the group; classifying by more than one property at a time: discovering that an object can belong to several classes; using an all or some classification: for example, all have the same color but not the same shape; forming subsets of objects used.

Space and number: (Piaget and Inhelder, 1969) Establishing equality between two sets of objects on a one-to-one basis when the objects can be seen and manipulated; recognizing equality between sets of objects when they are not ordered or spaced equally; recognizing conservation of quantity when a liquid or objects are moved or placed in a different space; recognizing conservation of the whole when it is distributed over different sets such as 4 and 2 or 5 and 1; recognizing conservation of area when appearances change but nothing has been added or taken away.

Ordering: (Inhelder and Piaget, 1969) Ordering objects in a series according to one property; ordering things in two series when inversely related such as shortest to longest, lightest to heaviest; representing an order with the use of pictures or drawings; ordering a set of geometric shapes.

Most mathematics programs for early childhood education include classification, number, space, and ordering. However, many teachers are not aware of the thought processes involved in their development. In later chapters we suggest ways to select appropriate materials and guide children's activities as they learn these concepts.

Piaget used the "clinical interview" technique to test children on many tasks. Teachers can use this same method. In his book *Learning from Children* (1985), Ed Labinowicz has excellent suggestions for using this method.

The concept of *readiness* was also important to Piaget and has implications for modern instructional practices. Readiness depends on the child's fund of knowledge as well as skill and social-emotional level. Some concepts or skills must be learned before others; the more difficult concepts build upon simpler ones. The teacher must ensure that the proper foundation has been, or is being, laid as instruction is given.

To summarize the most important implications of Piaget's theories for teaching math to young children:

1. Intellectual development is a major goal and grows through assimilation and accommodation.
2. The child must act (mentally) on what is being assimilated.
3. The child needs to explore, manipulate concrete materials, use models, and respond to a variety of meaningful problem-solving situations. Both correct and incorrect responses are important — to build new concepts or to reconstruct before advancing to a new stage.
4. The teacher's role is to guide, stimulate, intervene when needed, and help children learn in their own unique way, with confidence and enjoyment.

MATHEMATICAL CONCEPTS AND THE DISCOVERY PROCESS

What is a "concept"? What are "math concepts"?

John Dewey, in his book *How We Think* (1933), has shown that "concepts enable one to generalize, to extend and carry over our understanding from one thing to another. Since concepts represent the whole class or set of things, they economize our intellectual efforts. The concept shows that a meaning has been clearly established and will remain the same in different contexts."

David Russell, in his excellent book, *Children's Thinking* (1956), summarizes the evidence he gathered on mathematical concept development:

> Mathematical concepts are closely related to the child's perception of number, space, time, weight, and related factors. In their earliest stages, accordingly, they are dependent upon many opportunities to manipulate and explore — an environment rich in blocks of different sizes and colors, toys that go, equipment that can be pulled, pushed, reconstructed, and

climbed. Such experiences seem to be necessary background for any verbalization of mathematical concepts and more exact use of them in appropriate conversational situations.

To illustrate, McNally (1978, p. 27) conducted an experiment on children's understanding of the concept of "alike." In the experiment he used structured materials for kindergarten from the TRIAD Mathematics Laboratory; these materials are used extensively in Australia and New Zealand.

McNally worked with three children, ages three, five, and six, and a group of colored flat attribute blocks of different sizes and shapes. He noted the following responses to the request "Hand me some blocks that are alike":

Three-year-old: The child handed him, in order, a blue circle, a blue triangle, and a red triangle. The child linked a blue circle to a blue triangle by color. Then the blue triangle to the red triangle by shape.

Five-year-old: The child handed him one red and one yellow triangle. When asked for more that "are alike," the child selected another set, red and yellow triangles. The experimenter placed the four triangles on the floor and asked the child to point to some more that were "alike." The child pointed to the red and yellow triangles again.

Six-year-old: The six-year-old handed him all the blue triangles in the pile, same color and same shape.

McNally concluded that, for the three-year-old, no true concept was formed; the five- and six-year-olds showed an understanding of the concept, but the six-year-old at a higher level than the five-year-old.

In concept development, the kind and quality of experiences provided for children are important. The following are some suggestions for guiding these experiences:

1. In the formative stage of concept development, activities should be simple and should involve the use of concrete objects and materials. Action experiences (self-activity) should be maximized.
2. As concepts are incorporated, complexity should be added.
3. Finally, the concept should be generalized and applied to other situations — situations that will make it richer and more meaningful, and that will enable the child to see that the concept can be extended to still other situations.

These steps are essentially the same as the "discovery process." When children explore materials in play without many adult rules or intervention, they do so more freely, and their thinking progresses in their own way and with more interest. Adults can ask appropriate questions carefully to stimulate and clarify concepts but not control the process entirely. Children progress through several stages in discovery: play, direction or purpose, and practice. Children should be able to approach the problem and accommodate the experiences in their own unique way and according to their stage of readiness.

TEACHING FOR UNDERSTANDING

Throughout this book we emphasize teaching with understanding, using hand-on-materials, involving children, and using a variety of teaching strategies. However, these suggestions simply point the way for teachers of early childhood years. Their understanding and love of children, patience, and creative teaching are the real, significant determiners of children's understanding.

Kathy Richardson, in a timely article, "Assessing Understanding" (1988), summarizes our views on this subject:

> If we are to give children appropriate kinds of experiences and aid their growth in mathematical thinking, we must accept the levels of understanding that are a natural part of young children's development and respect the complexity of the concept with which they are dealing. Once we accept and respect young children's thinking, we will also appreciate and even delight in it.

Teachers are the ones who must make the crucial decisions concerning the "just right" content and the "just right" sequence for mathematical learning. Only recently, however, have they been given just and respected treatment in curriculum planning.

Two important stumbling blocks have hindered creative teaching, valid appraisal of pupil achievement, and selection of appropriate content for mathematics curricula: (1) the composition of the decision-making teams; and (2) the use of standardized achievement tests as true measures of the teaching-learning process (Labinowicz, 1985).

The use of standardized achievement tests has prescribed and formalized mathematics curricula for years. According to many, "Nothing short of a moratorium on standardized achievement testing will free educators to listen to children and expand their perspective of teaching and learning" (Labinowicz, 1985, p. 396).

The meaningful approach to teaching mathematics received its original impetus from educators who saw the advantages of learning with understanding instead of learning by isolated drill. William A. Brownell (1947), an advocate of meaningful teaching, identified the four basic components of mathematics that children must understand: (1) basic number concepts, (2) fundamental operations, (3) important principles, relationships, and generalizations, and (4) the base ten number system.

Teaching for understanding requires considerable teacher preparation, guidance of learning activities, record keeping, and continuous evaluation of children's progress.

The following illustrates how a teacher can proceed using the teaching-for-understanding approach. This example shows the important steps of adding two two-digit numbers with **regrouping** ones to tens.

1. Use a problem situation: "If you have 25 jellybeans and a friend gives you 25 more, how many would you have?"
2. Use concrete materials. Here, use base ten blocks. Ask children to touch the materials as they answer. Have rows of the ten blocks for the tens column and single blocks for the ones column. One complete set should be displayed. Other sets should be available for children to use at their tables.
   "You had how many tens?" 10, 10
   "You had how many ones?" 5
   "How many tens were given?" 10, 10
   "How many ones were given?" 5
   "How many in all?" 10, 10, 10, 10, and 5, 5
3. Allow children to show ways to add. This is the semi-concrete picture stage.

Tens Ones		Tens Ones		Tens Ones
0 0 • • • • •	+	0 0 • • • • •	=	0 0 • • • • •
				0 0 • • • • •

10 + 10 + 10 + 10   and   5 + 5   =   50
20 + 5   and   20 + 5   =   50

4. Have children show and write the numbers:

$$\begin{array}{r} 25 \\ +25 \\ \hline 50 \end{array}$$

5. Allow children to create other examples. Provide work cards with problems designed for this level—for example: "You have 35¢ and you earn 25¢. How much do you now have?" _____ .

This next step is an extension of previous work, which involved problems such as 22 + 45 = and 20 + 30 = . Before reaching the point of adding two two-digit numbers and using regrouping, children should understand place values to show tens and ones, and should understand the concept of zero as a **placeholder**. They should be able to count by 5s and 10s to 50 or 100.

Piaget's Views on Understanding

Piaget has shown that to know (understand) a fact or skill a child must act upon the new information, modify or transform the new materials, and gain an understanding of the way the fact or skill is constructed. This process is called an *operation*. It is an internalized (mental) action by the child that modifies the new learning. Piaget (1969) describes an **operation** as having four fundamental characteristics:

1. It is an action that is internalized by the child, carried out in thinking as well as in some physical aspect (moving or touching).
2. It is an action that is *reversible:* For example, $1 + 1 = 2$ and $2 - 1 = 1$.
3. It involves *conservation:* $4 + 2, 5 + 1, 3 + 3$ are ways to make (name) the number 6.
4. It is part of a system of procedures, such as adding and subtracting.

Based on this process, it is important for teachers to guide new mathematical learning so that children make this learning part of their development (internalize it), recognize the reversibility or other ways to use the new data, show that it involves conservation, and see that it is part of a mathematical way of thinking.

Advantages of Teaching for Understanding

There are many advantages in teaching for understanding, including the following:

1. This approach increases the likelihood that mathematics will be used, retained, and enjoyed. In repeated studies of children's and teachers' attitudes toward arithmetic, Dutton (1951, 1964) found that favorable feelings clustered around success in math, good teaching, the ability to make math meaningful. Unfavorable feelings (65% of all statements) centered around lack of understanding, teaching that is disassociated from life, pages of word problems, and boring drill.
2. The approach encourages learning by problem solving instead of simply memorization. The use of instructional materials and problems relating to children's daily life provides motivation as well as meaningful approaches to teaching math with understanding.
3. Teaching for understanding provides a versatility of attack. After the concrete materials and the picture or semi-concrete stages, children are given the opportunity to explore new ways to work problems.
4. It allows for the strengthening of weak skills. Through self-activity the child becomes involved in finding and removing difficulties — in discovering how new learnings fit in with previous knowledge.
5. This approach provides a foundation for the transfer of information and skills. Children are guided to apply new learning and explore different examples.
6. It reduces the chance of absurd answers or solutions. This is an important part of problem solving: learning to estimate and to search for meaningful answers.

7. The approach builds confidence and willingness to face new problems. When math is understood, children are successful in their work and like mathematics (Dutton, 1964).

8. Finally, teaching for understanding increases respect for and an appreciation of the contributions of mathematics. When children understand, enjoy, and use math in daily life, they are interested in going on to more advanced work.

Contribution of Instructional Materials to Teaching for Understanding

Children are more interested in touching and manipulating materials than in listening to teachers explain. When children primarily control their exploration, they consider it play and are interested and they learn. Teachers can either obtain commercial instructional materials or create their own. A great variety of commercially produced manipulative materials, models, and mathematical devices are available, including tiles, unifix cubes, pattern blocks, attribute blocks, beads, play money, junk boxes, storage equipment, balance beams, scales, and base ten components.

Instructional materials are of two types: (1) discrete or separate (unrelated) materials and (2) structured materials (related to the structure of mathematics).

Discrete objects, such as containers of plastic beads, items found in junk boxes, or objects collected by children, can be used to teach several concepts:

- *Classification,* including simple sorting, all-some relations, class-inclusions
- *Space and number,* including one-to-one correspondence, conservation of quantity and conservation of a whole or a unit
- *Seriation,* including putting objects in order (shortest to longest), arranging objects in a series, and ordering sets of shapes.

Structured objects make a distinct contribution when used in the development of specific math concepts. For example, base ten blocks are used to help develop an understanding of place values to 100 or more, and to teach regrouping in addition and subtraction; the balance beam or scale is used to develop concepts of weight; a hundreds board is used to help develop sequences of numbers, ordinals, and patterns; and a wooden toy clock is used to teach time concepts.

Despite their contributions, however, instructional materials alone will not ensure pupil understanding of math concepts. Self-directed activities and teacher response to child readiness are indispensable as well. Children's thinking must be directed and guided toward the discovery of mathematical relationships and concepts. The use of a variety of materials, a multimodel approach (Dienes, 1964), is important, but so are teacher selection, guidance, and careful evaluation.

Suggestions for the appropriate use of instructional materials have been included in the following chapters and in Appendix B.

TECHNOLOGY FOR THE CLASSROOM

Among the latest instructional materials to enter the classroom are calculators and computers. We have included both in the mathematics program we recommend in this text for children four through eight years of age.

Calculators

In today's world, children must become *calculator literate*. They must understand how to use calculators in problem solving. Very young children (four years of age) can use calculators for exploratory activities. Then, as children gain an understanding of basic concepts and learn arithmetic operations, they can be taught useful calculator applications and skills. In Chapters 3–7, we describe age-appropriate ways in which the calculator can be used as a tool for learning mathematics.

Computers

More than any other tool, the computer has made inroads into daily life. In the classroom, it has become an integral part of instruction. Today, however, the emphasis has moved away from computers' providing drills on low-level skills toward their involving children in meaningful problem solving and concept development, and in making and using their own programs. Children, then, must learn how to use the computer — they must become *computer literate*.

To keep abreast of innovative programs in schools throughout the country, classrooms should be equipped with computers, projection devices, large-screen monitors, and telecommunication capabilities.

A discussion of computers and suggestions for selecting appropriate software are given in Chapter 9.

PROBLEM SOLVING

The National Council of Supervisors of Mathematics, in its 1988 position paper on essential mathematics for the 21st century, has emphasized problem solving as an important goal. Thus, problem solving should be integrated into the mathematics program for young children.

In this book, we describe a variety of problem-solving experiences. Through these experiences, children will learn to apply their mathematical knowledge and skills. We recommend the following five problem-solving approaches, and throughout the book we give suggestions for their use:

1. Use problem solving to explore the child's involvement with basic components of the environment.
2. Use problem solving to introduce new math concepts and to provide meaningful practice and applications for new learning.
3. Use mathematics concepts and skills to help children solve important problems in the classroom and to study other school subjects such as science and social studies.
4. Introduce creative, enjoyable problem-solving situations in the classroom (science center) such as those found in Measuring Bowser (the dog) (Willoughby et al., 1981).
5. Use the problem-solving situations presented in adopted textbooks to provide extensions and new applications, and to make adjustments for individual differences.

PRINCIPLES FOR GUIDING LEARNING ACTIVITIES

We have developed a number of principles to help guide teachers in the selection, organization, and presentation of mathematical learning activities for young children. These principles have grown out of discussions of the nature and structure of mathematics, child growth and development, and appropriate methods for presenting instruction based on the teaching-for-understanding method and concept development.

The principles are as follows:

1. The teacher should prepare an environment for children in which they can learn through active exploration and interaction with adults, other children, and hands-on materials.
2. The child must be considered an active participant in the selection, organization, and delivery of instruction. Children should select many of their own activities from a variety of learning experiences that the teacher prepares, including hands-on materials, games, puzzles, art, music, and dramatic play.
3. Instruction should be based on developing children's thinking and understanding. Provision must be made for individual differences within and among children.

4. To develop vocabulary, language, and self-esteem, opportunities should exist for active participation and involvement in learning activities centering around work with other children.

5. The mathematical content for learning activities should grow out of the components of the child's environment as well as from the organization and structure of mathematics.

6. Teachers should emphasize the development of mathematical concepts based on the structure of mathematics that children can discover, use, and apply to a variety of problems related to their life experiences.

7. Since problem solving is the goal of mathematics, basic work habits, techniques, and skills should be developed throughout each school day through a variety of learning activities.

8. Mathematics should make a significant contribution to children's thinking, to their use of specific terms, and to their success in other disciplines and activities.

9. Favorable attitudes toward mathematics should be fostered in order to promote children's enjoyment of and willingness to use mathematics, and to motivate them to continue with more advanced branches of the subject.

10. Evaluation of both successful teaching and successful learning should involve the use of appropriate, measurable objectives.

PURPOSES OF MATHEMATICS EDUCATION FOR CHILDREN FOUR THROUGH EIGHT YEARS OF AGE

Why is mathematics education important? It is important because it helps children acquire a good attitude toward, and understanding of, mathematics, as well as helping them acquire essential mathematics skills and furthering intellectual development. Let's examine each of these areas.

Attitude influences all aspects of mathematics instruction and learning and determines the amount of energy a child will put into the work. Attitude influences how often mathematics is used, the willingness to pursue advanced work in mathematics, and even the choice of prospective occupations. Teachers need to model positive attitudes, help children achieve success at their optimum level, and arrange a learning environment in which children can grow intellectually through self-activity and creative participation in a wide variety of meaningful activities.

Understanding each new aspect of mathematics learning and how it fits into the overall structure of mathematics is the most important part of the teaching-learning process. Ensuring children's understanding requires using appropriate and concrete instructional materials; guiding children's acquisition of new learning in ways that are appropriate to their unique developmental styles; and helping children show their understanding in a variety of ways. Since problem solving is the goal of mathematics, children need to experience a variety of problem-solving situations as they progress through the mathematics program.

Basic skills must be learned and used successfully as children progress through the mathematics program. Each fundamental math process involves skills that, if learned effectively, will help students compute more accurately and make the work easier. After children understand these basic skills, they can use a calculator to speed up calculation, ensure accuracy, and facilitate work on long problems. The teacher's role is to set the environment for self-activity, helping children identify and master the basic skills, and motivating them to identify their own progress and achievement.

Intellectual development depends on the cognitive structures available to an individual at any one time. These structures develop continually as the individual matures and interacts with the environment. Since their development falls into several clearly defined stages (Piaget), the teacher needs to identify the current stage and create an appropriate learning environment with appropriate concrete learning materials.

EVALUATION

Evaluation is the process used to determine the amount and quality of student understanding and achievement in mathematics based on clearly defined objectives. It is based on three elements: (1) progress is based on evaluation of objectives rather than on subject matter achievement; (2) a variety of techniques is used to measure student progress; and (3) emphasis is placed on the evaluation of a child's social growth and development. Evaluation should be an integral part of the teaching-learning process.

We are particularly interested in showing how evaluation is used to secure data on a child's understanding of mathematics, development of attitudes, acquisition of basic skills, and cognitive development. In the chapters that follow, we will show how teachers and students can cooperate to determine student progress in learning mathematics.[1]

SUMMARY

This chapter provides the foundation teachers need to determine what level of mathematics to teach young children. It also identifies the main principles of child growth and development involved in learning this material. In the chapter, we summarized the important theories of Piaget that help to identify the way intellectual development takes place and the relationship between intellectual structures and mathematical learning. In addition, we examined the major topics connected with teaching and learning mathematics, such as understanding, concept development, use of instructional materials, use of calculators and computers, problem solving, major goals, principles of learning, and evaluation.

ACTIVITIES FOR TEACHER INSIGHT

1. Piaget stressed the importance of self-activity in acquiring knowledge. Outline the way in which a teacher would apply this theory to the six- or seven-year-old group.
2. Take one mathematical concept that is part of a child's environment, such as measurement or time, and select a few materials to use in evaluating the child's understanding of the concept. Study the sequence involved in the concept as well as the age and maturity of the child.
3. Select a child (age and maturity known) and, using cubes or blocks, determine the child's understanding of one-to-one correspondence.
4. Recall your own experiences in learning mathematics during your early childhood years. Can you remember the point at which you were able to understand one or two concepts? What were your early attitudes or feelings toward math? When did you develop the computational skills used for one fundamental process, such as addition or subtraction?

NOTE

1. For a detailed presentation on evaluation, see Wilbur H. Dutton, *Evaluating Pupils' Understanding of Arithmetic* (Englewood Cliffs, NJ: Prentice Hall, 1964).

REFERENCES

BAROODY, A. J. (1987). *Children's mathematical thinking*. New York: Columbia University, Teachers College Press.

BROWNELL, W. A. (January 1947). The place of meaning in the teaching of arithmetic. *Elementary School Journal, 42*.

BRUNER, J. S. (1967). *Toward a theory of instruction*. Cambridge, MA: Belknap Press, Harvard University.

California State Department of Education. (1985). *Mathematics framework for California public schools K-12*. Sacramento, CA: Bureau of Publications.

California State Department of Education. (1987). *Mathematics—Model curriculum guide K-8*. Sacramento, CA: Bureau of Publications.

COPELAND, R. W. (1974). *How children learn mathematics: Teaching implications research*. New York: Macmillan.

DEWEY, J. (1933). *How we think* (p. 180). New York: D. C. Heath.

DIENES, Z. P. (1964). *Building up mathematics*. London, England: Hutchinson Educational Publishers.

DOCKRELL, W. B. (Ed.). (1970). *On intelligence: The Toronto symposium on intelligence*. London: Methuen Press.

DOPYERA-LAY, M., & DOPYERA, J. (1987). *Becoming a teacher of young children* (3rd ed.). New York: Random House.

DUTTON, W. H. (October 1951). Attitudes of prospective teachers toward arithmetic. *Elementary School Journal, 52,* 84–90.

DUTTON, W. H. (1964). *Evaluating pupils' understanding of arithmetic*. Englewood Cliffs, NJ: Prentice-Hall.

FURTH, H. G. (1969). *Piaget and knowledge*. Englewood Cliffs, NJ: Prentice-Hall.

HYMES, J. L. (1981). *Teaching the child under six*. Columbus, OH: Charles E. Merrill.

INHELDER, B., & PIAGET, J. (1969). *The early growth of logic in the child*. New York: Harper.

KAMII, C. (1985). *Young children reinvent arithmetic*. New York: Teachers College Press, Columbia University.

LABINOWICZ, E. (1985). *Learning from children*. Menlo Park, CA: Addison-Wesley.

LAVATELLI, C. S. (1978). *Piaget's theory applied to an early childhood curriculum*. Boston: Center for Media Development.

LOVELL, K. (1971). *The growth of understanding in mathematics: Kindergarten through grade three*. New York: Holt, Rinehart, and Winston.

MAXIM, G. W. (1985). *The very young* (2nd ed.). Belmont, CA: Wadsworth.

McNALLY, D. W. (1978). *Piaget, education, and teaching*. Cremorne, Sydney, Australia: Angus and Robertson Publishers.

National Association for the Education of Young Children. (1988). Developmentally appropriate practice in early childhood programs birth through age eight. Washington, DC: Author.

National Council of Supervisors of Mathematics. (1988). Essential mathematics for the 21st century (a position paper). Reston, VA: National Council of Teachers of Mathematics.

NELSON, D., & WORTH, J. (1983). *How to choose and create good problems for primary children*. Reston, VA: National Council of Teachers of Mathematics.

PETERSON, R. (1986). *The Piaget handbook for teachers and parents*. New York: Teachers College Press, Columbia University.

PIAGET, J. (1965). *The child's conception of number*. New York: W. W. Norton.

PIAGET, J., & INHELDER, B. (1969). *The psychology of the child*. New York: Basic Books.

RICHARDSON, K. (February 1988). Assessing understanding. *Arithmetic Teacher*.

ROSENBLOOM, P. C. (March 1962). Mathematics K-12. *Educational Leadership*.

RUSSELL, D. H. (1956). *Children's thinking*. New York: Ginn.

WILLOUGHBY, S. S. (1981). *How deep is the water?* La Salle, IL: Open Court Publishing.

CHAPTER 3

Mathematics for Four-Year-Old Children

Four-year-olds have their own ideas. They can plan and organize, and they show an interest in many things. They are mature enough and developmentally ready to learn and to explore many new, challenging activities at school. Because they are so ready to learn, some adults think that four-year-olds are ready for experiences that are "academically oriented" toward abstract mathematics. But what these children really need is adults who will stimulate them to learn and develop their own knowledge through experience with many activities. They learn mathematics best by becoming actively involved with hands-on materials that enable them to develop the mental structures that comprise this subject.

In the area of social and emotional development, four-year-olds spend some time testing limits in order to prove they are autonomous and therefore they work better in small groups of three or four children, where they don't feel overwhelmed. Often they withdraw from group play when more than two or three children join. They are easily discouraged if the task is too difficult. For these reasons, it is better to use materials they can explore individually; such materials allow them to construct ideas on their own while feeling no need to test limits. Several work areas with the same materials set up side by side allow children to work and share ideas simultaneously by watching each other and talking about their work.

Four-year-old children think mainly from an egocentric perspective. They are aware of themselves and willing to talk about their interests and experiences. The teacher must be able to listen and support this development of personal worth and individuality, and ask questions to stimulate thinking.

In both cognitive and affective development, four-year-old children believe what they see; they take things at face value. This limited skill level influences both their social interactions and their thinking in mathematics-related activities. They need help in proposing alternative solutions. It is important to help them test their ideas so they see for themselves why such ideas will or will not work. Dramatic play or social situations that arise during work with other activities often present problem-solving situations. When problems arise among the children, such as arguments over toys, teacher intervention can encourage growth in intellectual skills that carry over to mathematics. As the child's thought processes become more complex, intellectual problem-solving skills improve. Further details pertaining to physical, cognitive, and social emotional traits will be found in the appendix.

Readiness for school and concern over the unmet needs of children in their early years have become major issues in planning instruction for four- and five-year-old children. Language proficiency is the main component of school readiness. Descriptive terms, which a four-year-old learns through his or her use of exploring materials and equipment, provide the foundation for later mathematical experiences such as classifying, weighing, measuring, and estimating. Literature for young children often serves the dual function of leading to reading readiness and introducing mathematics in a social context within a story. Considerable attention, therefore, has been given to planning exploratory learning activities, language development, reading readiness, and appropriate materials to use with this age group.

LEARNING EXPERIENCES FOR THE FOUR-YEAR-OLD CHILD

The four-year-old child's world centers around the home, the outdoor space near the home, family, and neighborhood. The child is interested in what he can see, hear, smell, touch, and taste. Therefore, careful consideration must be given to the quality of experiences provided for children. Experiences children have with materials (space, shape, size, matching, measuring) and the words or symbols they learn while participating in these experiences lead to all-important growth in language and in thinking (Almy, Chittenden, & Miller, 1966).

The language used at home and at school is the foundation on which the total development of the child, including mathematical learning, is based. Language learning begins at home and contributes to the development of a child's social, emotional, and intellectual traits. Children need an expanded vocabulary so they can express ideas as thinking and problem solving take place. Where positive language learning occurs, adults are available for children to talk to, and to model correct and accurate word usage and pronunciation. Where it does not, language learning and development may be haphazard or even left to chance as children are allowed to waste long hours sitting in front of the television, or are often left alone with no one to talk to. Children, thus, enter preschool with varying backgrounds in language and mathematical experiences.

In the preschool classroom, mathematics instruction takes the form of manipulative experiences. It is done most effectively in a *social context*, not as instruction in abstract mathematical concepts. The teacher is the facilitator. Children explore by themselves, participate occasionally in small groups, or take part in large-group circle-time activities.

Four-year-olds use mathematics naturally as part of their play and exploration of what Piaget calls "social knowledge." The child "acts on" materials to learn. First in the home and then at school, math is an integral part of the child's experience. Most math learning for four-year-olds takes place in the context of play, as they participate in art, games, and cooking, do simple science exploration, and complete daily living tasks (Baker, Gardener, & Mahler, 1987). Children use mathematics without realizing it as they copy a block structure built by another child, put out plates on the playhouse table for members of a pretend family, adjust trike speed on path curves for centrifugal force, or comment on the number of children at the snack table. Playing simple table games like Lotto or dominoes involves mathematics. The minute the four-year-old feels the teacher change from using math in games or other social context to teaching it in a teaching situation, math has become abstract and the child's interest often disappears.

THINKING AND EXPLORATION LEVELS

After watching preschool children (three-, four-, and five-year-olds) explore materials in activities, we can posit four levels of learning in the preoperational stage.

Level 1   Focus on process of sensorimotor exploration of touching, watching, etc.

Level 2   Experimentation using one process at a time; beginning to combine processes

Level 3   Problem solving using processes; representation begins

Level 4   Systematic use of information gained in previous levels; planned representation

Since four-year-olds in one classroom may function at all four levels, activities and materials that allow and promote exploration at all four levels are the most helpful.

Sensorimotor exploration of materials and equipment to gather information begins in infancy and continues in preschool children, when permitted and encouraged by adults, as they play and explore in order to understand. To introduce new materials, the teacher should use a sensorimotor approach (the child touches to explore), as well as visual exploration as the teacher explains. Children respond automatically if materials are presented to invite exploration.

Thinking and exploration levels are shown in the following chart for three subjects: math, art, and science.

PREOPERATIONAL THINKING AND EXPLORATION LEVELS

Level	Science	Math	Art
Level 1 Focus on process and sensorimotor exploration	watches use of materials, smells, asks questions touches briefly, watches movements of animals and machines	puts train tracks together, says numbers, rote counting stacks blocks end to end uses colored rods as blocks	watches glue drip on paper, watches paint go on paper paints circles and lines touches collage materials, picture incidental
Level 2 Experimentation using one process at a time	tries combinations, compares two things sees what happens when pet rat eats, exercises, etc. tries pouring, measuring with water, cornmeal, etc.	aware of order of numbers to six uses numbers socially and experiments with patterns builds more and completes block structures	mixes paint to see colors made arranges materials in collage in random way makes more than one picture using process
Level 3 Problem-solving techniques using processes Combination of processes	uses techniques to solve problems to construct rat maze, pvc pipes in water play uses trial and error to test ideas	sees numbers used in environment: phone, house number, measures in cooking counts with one-to-one correspondence to six uses numbers in play sorts things by classifying	combines materials in planned collage paints representationally begins to write name and letters
Level 4 Systematic use of information gained in previous levels Planned representation	predicts outcome and repeats experiments makes comparisons measures with some accuracy	classifies in many ways repeats process alone and with precision (cooking) increases one-to-one counting to ten	expresses ideas about art verbally as well as doing the art activity dictates stories with pictures uses more art tools and materials

To illustrate how thinking and interest levels influence an activity, consider the Magic Potions activity in Chapter 10, in which children mix various household cooking ingredients and watch the reactions. For example, a child is fascinated by the fizz that comes when vinegar is mixed with baking soda. At level 1, the child is totally absorbed with just that reaction. At the second level, with teacher assistance, the child is interested in adding raisins to the mixture and watching to see what will happen, or in combining other substances besides vinegar and soda. At the third level, the child can use the reaction of vinegar and soda to blow up a balloon. (Four-year-olds need adult help to put the balloon on the bottle lip.) At the fourth level, the balloon size can be compared to the amounts of vinegar and soda used.

Four-year-old children are beginners. Life for them is complicated. According to James L. Hymes (1981), "They need success. Children ought to be free of cram sessions, tension-free as well as calamity-free and crisis-free." Children are excited by teacher enthusiasm when it is developmentally appropriate and part of a teacher–child relationship. They are very interested in the tasks of the grown-up world. Four-year-olds gradually revise their understanding of the world as they gain more information and thinking skills. They need adult help to do this. They learn best in groups of two to four children or in one-on-one exploration.

PLANNING AN ENVIRONMENT FOR EXPERIENCES WITH MATHEMATICS

Home and classroom are environments of loving care that are emotionally and physically safe to explore. As such, they provide opportunities and challenges for desirable child growth and development. Children's development is furthered by an enriched and diverse environment that includes opportunities for: exploring and using the physical surroundings; interacting socially with other children; and discovering the world in an individual, unique way. The teacher's role is to plan such a challenging environment, observe the children in order to identify the learning level each child exhibits, and intervene appropriately to ask questions that encourage reasoning. If a child ignores an intervention, the teacher waits for another opportunity or for more growth to occur (unless redirection or discipline is involved). Appropriate intervention is tricky: If done too soon, the child's own thinking and experience is interrupted or distorted; if done too late, the opportunity is lost. Young children all need some uninterrupted time to explore before teachers intervene. Effective intervention focuses on the child's interest not the teacher's idea alone.

PROBLEM SOLVING

Problem-solving behaviors begin very early (Tudge & Caruso, 1988) and the variety of techniques that children are taught is important. The more varied the methods or experiences, the greater the opportunity to learn. A teacher can interact briefly by showing an interest with questions, comments, or suggestions to "try this." The decision to intervene should be made carefully since the child's own exploration and problem solving or interaction with other children is as valuable as teacher intervention. Problem solving for four-year-olds becomes a grand adventure if presented as a game or if the teacher says, "We can solve this problem" when something occurs in the classroom. Children will model the teacher's approach to problem solving. If the teacher asks them to propose solutions, they begin to model this behavior.

When a problem arises, the teacher should involve the children in discovering solutions. For example, when two children struggle over the same carpet square to sit on, the teacher may ask, "What should we do?" One child's solution may be to put it up high and both children find a new one. Other examples of teacher questions include:

- "What can we do to stop the water?" as the hose makes a river. (See the Sand Box River activity in Chapter 10 classroom activities.)
- "Do we have enough snacks in the basket for our table? What can we do? What do we need?"

Activities such as Inventor's Corner, described in Chapter 10, have children construct something they need for play, such as traffic tickets, stop signs, "keep out" signs, and instrument panels for blocks made into a spaceship, by using available materials. The Magic Potions activity (Chapter 10) gives children a chance to see what happens when compounds are mixed (safely) and to predict outcomes. The teacher asks questions as the children experiment to encourage thinking.

Individual portion recipes (see Chapter 10) allow a child to see the entire process of making something and help develop problem-solving skills. Many precooking exploration activities such as measuring; using playdough; helping prepare snacks by cutting, grating, spreading, and so on must precede individual-portion cooking activities.

In these ways young children see themselves as capable of helping themselves, solving problems. Such self-perceptions not only contribute to mathematics readiness but bolster a child's self-esteem and self-image as a learner in school.

MATHEMATICS VOCABULARY AND LANGUAGE

There should be a continuous interplay between language and the handling, arranging, and sharing of items such as blocks. By saying, for example, "I need a square block," the teacher can help the four-year-old to show an understanding of the correct vocabulary and mathematical concept. Try to eliminate experiences that depend solely on language, however, and that do not allow the child to experiment or classify. Four-year-olds can talk while they play. Younger children or those with delayed language

Children describe the game card drawn and tell what they will do in their turn, which
helps them develop math language skills.

may not be able to manipulate objects and talk at the same time. Simple games can
provide math language experiences.

MATHEMATICS THROUGH CHILDREN'S LITERATURE

Reading and storytelling help to satisfy the basic needs of young children to relate to
others and contribute to language development, mathematics and science learning,
and success in school.

Teachers should establish a center where children can find picture books, listen to
stories, and share experiences centering around books. Create a place with comfort-
able chairs or a soft rug, and good light; it should be free of distractions such as room
traffic and outside noise. Never let the reading center be a place for punishment or
withhold stories during reading time as punishment.

Nursery Rhymes

Young children enjoy the variety, subject matter, and mood found in nursery rhymes. Although the content of some verses in Mother Goose books has been controversial (suggesting racial, ethnic, and sex bias), the teacher can carefully select verses that serve children's needs and tastes. Many Mother Goose verses introduce children to explorations in mathematics and science. These fall into several categories, including:

Fingerplays — "Pat-a-cake" (rhythms and patterns)

Counting — "One, two, buckle my shoe"

Days of the week — "Solomon Grundy, born on Monday"

Weather — "Rain, rain, go away"

Fingerplays serve several purposes. They help children move from individual to large-group activities. They also require children to use both language and muscle coordination parts of the brain simultaneously. As fingerplays are repeated, children increase memory skills and learn to make repeated rhythmic patterns. Finally, children enjoy the rhythmic chanting that is a part of most fingerplays and that sometimes tells a story. A rich resource of fingerplays and songs can be found in Brashears and Werlin (1981). These are appropriate for kindergarten as well.

Imaginative and Humorous Stories

Stories and poems that tickle the imagination of young children and make them laugh serve as good introductions to mathematics.

Picture books, such as *Rosie's Walk* (1968) and *Changes Changes* (1971) by Pat Hutchins, will delight the child who wants to read alone or look at pictures at the reading center. *Rosie's Walk* shows a sequence of cause and effect situations in pictures without words. *Changes Changes* tells a story with colored blocks and can be used to stimulate table block play.

Books that treat the troublesome "growing up times" with humor and imagination are also available. Leo Lionni's *Inch by Inch* (1987) describes the escapades of an inch worm who escapes becoming a robin's dinner. The book has a nature theme and is beautifully illustrated. Lionni's *Alexander and the Wind-up Mouse* (1969) is a fanciful story about a real mouse and Alexander, a toy mouse. Slightly more mature books include Wanda Gag's *Millions of Cats* (1938), which is a picture story so humorous and pleasant that the teacher will enjoy the story as much as the children. Each book has parts that involve mathematics.

Informational Books

A great variety of informational books has been written to introduce children to mathematics and science. Such books satisfy the young child's questions "Why?" "How?" "Where?"

Informational books fall into two general categories: (1) books that provide expert, scientific background material for children, and (2) books that present developmentally appropriate information for young children.

Jeanne Bendick is the author of science books for children. She presents science concepts in simple, interesting language along with humorous illustrations. An example of her best writing is *What Made You You?* (1971). It is a book for reading aloud to children and presents the interdependence of human, animal, and plant life.

The contributions of children's literature to mathematical learning has been carefully presented by Ann Harsch (1987). In this study, Harsch uses two books and their related concrete-level learning center activities to illustrate ways of dealing with prenumber skills. The two books are *Freight Trains* by Donald Crews and a picture book, *The Very Hungry Caterpillar,* by Eric Carle. Both help develop the concepts of classification, comparison, ordering, and one-to-one correspondence. The list of related books and references is excellent. See also Ballenger, Benham, and Hosticka (1984).

Teachers should make a collection of books that are accurate, carefully organized, up to date, and interesting to children, and that use mathematics or science in a meaningful way.

MATHEMATICS IN SOCIAL SITUATIONS

A beginning teacher should observe four-year-olds at play or during snack and focus on the use of math language and on situations where math is used. See if such situations as the following can be used to expand mathematics learning:

- dividing dishes in playhouse, setting the table
- "Mine is bigger" — "You're the littlest"
- sorting toys to use or share
- putting away unit blocks, matching shapes
- pouring sand, filling, carrying containers
- counting or passing cups, napkins, food
- helping to prepare snacks — cutting, pouring, measuring
- sequence of activity or game (Who does what? When?)

For example, a teacher may occasionally intervene in such play to ask questions that help a child solve a problem or that focus the child's interest. Of course, if done too often, this becomes "teaching" math not "using" math and the four-year-old child quickly loses interest (Harsch, 1987).

However, situations arise every day when math is necessary and its use appropriate.

- counting cups and napkins for each table or to put on a tray
- discussing how many crackers each child should take from the basket; counting how many children are at the table, how many empty spaces
- discussing who did not come to school today, who is missing from the group

ACTIVITIES CENTERING AROUND CHILD'S ENVIRONMENT

The suggestions for early mathematical experiences on pages 48 through 51, which are based on children's daily routines, explain and demonstrate the ideas and vocabulary children need before starting the abstract aspects of this subject. Too often young children are deprived of such experiences.

PRENUMBER EXPERIENCE

As children approach 4½ years of age, some will show readiness for prenumber experiences. At this point, children should have achieved a certain level of maturity and had certain kinds of experiences.

Four-year-old children need a variety of experiences before they are able to understand the abstract concept of number. We cannot see "number" — for example, we cannot see "three" (the symbol "3" is a shorthand form devised by humans). The *idea* of "3" is an abstraction for sets of 3 objects. A child can see 3 people, 3 animals, and 3 trees, and eventually will see the "threeness of three." Counting those at the snack table is a natural and concrete way for children to begin using numbers. Also, the Going Fishing game in Chapter 10 appeals to four-year-olds and involves counting. Use the abstract symbol, however, only when the child already grasps the idea, never as material from which a concept is taught (Kamii, 1982).

Activity	Math Concepts	Vocabulary
Food		
• setting the table	number and one-to-one correspondence, ordering sequence	too many, too few, too much, one more, one less, not enough, more than, less than, the same as
• mixing juice	sharing among others, measuring, estimating, counting	
• cooking snacks	measuring, mixing, cutting, spreading, grating	spoonful, bottleful
Dramatic play: hospital		
• arranging sick room, taking temperatures, bandaging, staff roles	time, measuring, testing, reporting, recording, bandage length, heart beat, temperature	
Dress up using playhouse		
• playing family roles	routines, sequence, role, imitation	tight, loose, right size, long, short, wide, narrow, too fast, too high, thin, thick, round
• being a community worker, firefighter, police officer	imitation, following rules	
Shapes		
• three dimensional	measurement, pictorial representation, telling stories	fat, thin, long, tall, smooth, rough, ragged, flat, round, curved, short, straight, bent, sharp, blunt, edge, side, face, corner
• using a "feeling" bag	classifying, describing	
• shapes around us	relationship to art, doors and windows, surfaces	
• construction with blocks or rods or unifix cubes	balance, position, one-to-one correspondence, ordering, ascending and descending order	
• tracing shapes	properties of: cube, cylinder, ball, cone, pyramid, square, disc, rectangle, circle, triangle; congruence, similarity, comparisons	

Activity	Math Concepts	Vocabulary
Water around us		
• washing ourselves and other things	time, space, plugs, pipes	
• plants and gardens, germination, growing, storing	schedules for watering, calendar, funnel, containers	
• cooking, freezing, melting, baking, boiling	temperature, evaporation, liquids to solids, mixtures, proportions, equal quantities, fractional parts, cause and effect	
• pets, bathing, drinking	size, shape, comparing food	
• rainy days, sleet, hail, pool	comparing, puddles, pools	
• streams, ponds, seashore, bridge, transporting, reservoirs	gases, liquids, float, sink	
Materials to use in science and art		
• sand	experiment, play, sort, order, use shape or space, covers as much as, weight, inner space, holds as much as	
• leaves, seeds, shells, nuts		
• paint	liquid, quart, gallon	
• clay and dough	shapes, heavy, light, gases, rises, firing, temperatures	
• wood	surface, measurement, classifying (kinds), growth rings, core, with the grain	
Travel, walking, riding, flying		
• walking around the block or neighborhood	departure times, arrival times, hours, days, weeks	
• riding to school, shopping, during vacations, going to work	linear measures, comparisons, ordering	
• flying on vacations, visits, trains	speed, fast, slow, miles per hour, money	

MATH ACTIVITIES INTEGRATED INTO OTHER CURRICULUM AREAS

Materials	Organization
Art	
geometric shape collage	Cut shapes from construction paper, place in middle of table, and allow children to choose freely.
three-dimensional wood collage	Place scraps from cabinet shop bins in the center of the table with base boards and glue bottles.
strips and circles collage	Cut different length and size strips and circles of construction paper to glue on base paper.
marble tracks	See Chapter 10.
mirror blots	See Chapter 10.
Table Toys — Manipulatives	
colored rods	Put out on table in dishes or on turntable and let children build with them as with unit blocks (in first grade they can be used to teach adding and subtraction).
button sorting	Put assorted buttons on a tray.
sand table (or water)	Use cups, containers for measuring and pouring; add plastic colored bears for sorting with strainers or hands
Science	
playdough	Make balls by palm rolling, sort sizes, cut with plastic knives.
cooking (science you eat) and individual portion recipes (see Chapter 10).	Prepare snacks involving counting napkins, cups, etc.; 1:1 for each child or for so many on a tray for the table.
	Cut bread, apples, bananas.
	Make:
	ants on a log: counting, raisins on peanut butter in celery (cutting sizes)
	mini pizza: sequence of putting toppings on muffin
	juice bags (see Chapter 10)

MATH ACTIVITIES INTEGRATED INTO OTHER CURRICULUM AREAS (*continued*)

Materials	Organization
Circle Time fingerplays (see Chapter 10)	count as part of song or rhyme; repeat patterns of movement; make shapes with bodies, arms
graphing in group	group children by: shoes, color hair, shirt color, etc. (more/less)
stories with math aspect	*Caps for Sale* (sequence): color hats, repeat motions, count monkeys
	The Very Hungry Caterpillar sequence (of food eaten), count
	Many stories include incidental counting and sequence questions
	Three Billy Goats Gruff: read book, then play-act the sequence

■   SORTING   Sorting sets of objects is a good way to begin learning about number. Children count more accurately when they move objects. The child may sort attributes such as color, friends, or shapes. She may group together three red balls, or three people or friends, or three shapes of objects, for example.

■   MATCHING AND ONE-TO-ONE CORRESPONDENCE   Children need to understand matching and one-to-one correspondence before they can understand "number." They go through a stage where they believe that row A, for example, has the same number of objects as row B. The children use visual clues to decide this, saying they "look the same" and take up the same space.

A. x x x x x
B. x x x x x x

Matching objects one to one is a visual way for children to see if one set has more or fewer objects than another, or the same number. Only when children can match easily will counting have any meaning since meaningful counting is matching objects against numbers. Children can learn rote counting but do not understand the meaning.

■ COMPARING Comparison is a concept children must understand before they can begin ordering. Children learn, for example, that 5 > 4 (five is greater than four) by comparing a set of 5 things with a set of 4 things. As soon as more than two objects are to be compared, the child will have to order according to a particular relationship, such as "is greater than," or in order to show sequence, such as an object is the third in the sequence. Graphing can also be used to show a comparison. And, more importantly, young children find it interesting, especially when it is directly related to them. For example, they can make a graph to show who is wearing a sweater or jacket, or to show who has on tie or buckle shoes. Graphing is discussed in Chapter 10. Baratta-Lorton, in her book *Mathematics Their Way* (1976), describes many graphing activities.

Once children understand these concepts, they can begin to grasp the concept of number — at first, saying the number, then reading the number, and finally, writing the number.

CALCULATOR AND COMPUTER INSTRUCTION AND SOFTWARE

Calculators

Until four-year-old children begin to understand the concept of number, calculators should be used only for play-acting adult roles. Children can use toy, "pretend" calculators in a pretend office, or while "shopping" or managing a checkout station in a pretend store. Although calculators involve numbers, children will use language to describe what they are doing with the calculator. They gradually learn the correct words to use (such as "Enter"), how to press the buttons or numbers, how to read the "display," and how to "clear" the calculator, and, finally, how to start over or try again. When children enter kindergarten, these experiences will help them to display and use numbers 1 through 10.

Computers

Four-year-olds can be introduced to computers at home or in the classroom.

At home, the software selected may or may not be developmentally appropriate. However, when a parent or a sibling provides an introduction and guidance, the four-year-old may use the computer meaningfully and effectively. Jennifer, for example, who is 4½ years of age, was introduced by her parents to two programs called First Letters and First Words on a Macintosh that had speech capability and a "turtle" with which to draw on the computer. She then spent several half-hour periods exploring and enjoying the computer, learning to recognize upper- and lowercase letters and playing Dinosaur Surprise, Card Circus, and Magic Letter Machine. She enjoyed the spoken reward messages placed in the program by her father to support her achievement after finishing a particular segment. When asked by her grandfather about the program, Jennifer said, "Come with me and I'll show you how it works." Her successful experiences with the computer led Jennifer to want to talk about and share them with someone else.

In the classroom, computer instruction must be given individually or in small groups. This will require the use of a teacher assistant to monitor a child's use of the program. Children like Jennifer, who are familiar with the computer, can help too. The computer is another important learning center in the classroom, but teachers must take care that it does not replace social, physical development, or creative activities.

Computer programs for the four-year-old child should be meaningful and age-appropriate. First Letters and Words are excellent. Facemaker and Fantastic Animals are also good programs. Linda Tsantis and others (1989) used these latter programs with 200 Headstart children and found that the children benefitted from the activities. We give more details of this experimental program in Chapter 10. Some software for the exploration of mathematical concepts and skills has also been developed for the four-year-old.

All software must match the developmental needs, abilities, and interests of the children using it. Before using beginning mathematics computer programs written for them, young children need to acquire computer keyboard skills. The language-oriented computer programs just described provide that skill.

DEVELOPING WORK HABITS

The four-year-old's attention span may be short — five to ten minutes for an activity or for one phase of an activity. Therefore, teachers should be prepared to make brief evaluations and find appropriate ways to continue the activity or terminate it. The development of work and play habits depends on the maturity of the child, the appeal of the activity, the child's previous experiences, and the role of the adult. Work habits, however, are highly correlated with learning, achievement in school, and success in mathematics.

Children who are able to persist at a task will learn more than those who give up as soon as the task becomes difficult. Children who pay attention, select tasks with some challenge, and work alone without unnecessary requests for help will also be high achievers. Acquiring these skills takes time and patient nurturing — valuing, watching, and questioning — by teachers.

Individual differences in work habits are easy to see in young children. These differences appear in interactions between the child and adults, and the child with specific activities. The interactions are influenced by the child's characteristics. For example, an adult may be attentive and nurturing to the dependent child. Or the adult may be attentive to children who reinforce the adult by responding with interest, attention, enjoyment, and compliance. Teachers need to be aware of how children's behavior influences their own and how children's behavior fosters or hinders the development of good work habits (Stipek, 1988).

Children's perceptions of their own competence and expectation of success affect their work habits. Children who expect to succeed will probably persist on a difficult task. They will try to complete a task without help. Children who fail usually try only tasks in which they think they can be successful. Teachers should encourage, not push. They should simplify the task so the child is challenged but can still succeed. For example, start a saw cut on soft wood (not hard wood) or ask the child to count four cups in each stack (rather than eight).

Independence and good work habits must be promoted. We can do this by providing intrinsically rewarding learning experiences, by encouraging children in order to extend learning, and by providing support for the development of good work habits.

SUGGESTIONS FOR EVALUATING CHILDREN'S UNDERSTANDING OF PRENUMBER CONCEPTS

As noted earlier, children must understand and be able to use prenumber concepts such as identifying, classifying, sorting, making a set of objects, one-to-one correspondence, and equivalent sets before they can apply an abstract number. They need to demonstrate the ability to perform each operation and to tell what they have done. The following evaluation procedures will enable the teacher to determine if the child understands the concept, as well as to show when additional time and experiences are needed. Playing games such as What Is Missing (see Chapter 10) helps teachers to check on the skill before making a formal evaluation.

We have given suggestions for several mathematical concepts and skills. Evaluate only one at any one sitting.

■ **IDENTIFYING ATTRIBUTES** Have a variety of objects on a tray or on a table for the child to touch or point to. Then say, "Show me":

> something blue
> something rough
> something round
> something wooden
> something to write with
> something heavy

■ **CLASSIFYING AN OBJECT BY ATTRIBUTE** Have 15 or 20 objects of different colors, shapes, sizes, textures, and so on, on a tray or table. Then say, "Show me":

> a rough block
> a round thing
> a blue bead
> a wooden box
> a heavy toy
> a red block

Next try two attributes, such as round and red. This may be too difficult for the less mature child.

■ **USING LANGUAGE TO CLASSIFY** Have a collection of five to ten objects. Pick one at a time and ask the child to tell something about it. Say "Tell me something about" (show the object and the child should respond with):

> It's plastic.
> It's heavy.
> It's a blue block.
> You can write with it.
> It's soft.

The child groups beads by color, making number sets in the cup.

Other responses should be encouraged, such as: "I have a blue block" or "This is a plastic toy." Encourage the child to think and respond. Give the child ample time to respond.

■ SORTING AND MAKING SETS Have a collection of familiar objects based on color and shape. Place the objects in front of the child and say, "Put these things in groups for me."

Have the child sort the objects and then justify the sorting. Pointing at a group, ask, "Why did you put these together?" To highlight a group, encircle it with string.

Point to a set of objects, such as a set of toys, and see if the child can say, "This is a set of. . . ." Have the child or a small group of children make a set and then describe it.

Say to a child or small group of children, "Make me a set of" and name a group of objects, such as buttons, toys, beads, and so on.

■ MATCHING SETS Match 5 spoons with 5 cups and 5 saucers.

SUMMARY

This chapter presents information for teachers on the physical, mental, social-emotional traits of four-year-old children. It also discusses preschool experiences for the four-year-old child, including: types of mathematical materials, how to create an environment for experiences with mathematics, language experiences, reading activities, and developing play centers that can be organized to promote children's mathematical learning as well as good work habits. Calculators and computers were introduced.

In the chapter, we raised the basic question teachers must frequently ask themselves: Is the new teaching and learning developmentally appropriate for the child? To answer this question, teachers must determine that the following four criteria are being met:

1. A match exists between what is being taught and what the child already knows.
2. The activity involved is interesting, and the child can do it with success and without frustration.
3. The activity is appropriate for the new information given.
4. The child has the requisite intellectual, physical, and social-emotional skills needed for success.

ACTIVITIES FOR TEACHER INSIGHT

1. Observe one child for several days (at school, in the home, on the playground, or at a combination of these). Record behavior you find appealing and behavior you find objectionable or uncertain. Then study the characteristics and traits found in Appendix A to see if you can find clues to how the child did certain things. What modifications would you suggest? What implications do you see for planning or modifying instruction in mathematics? How would you describe the child to another adult (Dopyera-Lay & Dopyera, 1987)?
2. Select one trait from each of the categories (physical, cognitive, and so on) listed in Appendix A for four-year-olds and describe how you would introduce a mathematics lesson or how you would plan a learning center to provide for children's exploration of that trait.
3. Visit a preschool in your neighborhood to study the way the classrooms are set up for four-year-olds. Draw a floor plan to show where learning centers are located and describe them.

4. Assemble appropriate attribute blocks and objects to use in determining the stage of development in understanding prenumber concepts of several children. After the evaluation, suggest the kinds of learning experiences you might use for each child.

REFERENCES

ALMY, M., CHITTENDEN, E., & MILLER, F. (1966). *Young children's thinking*. New York: Columbia University, Teachers College Press.

BAKER, K., GARDENER, P., & MAHLER, B. (1987). *Early childhood programs: Human relationships and learning*. New York: W. B. Saunders.

BALLENGER, M., BENHAM, N., & HOSTICKA, A. (1984). Children's counting books: Mathematical concept development. *Childhood Education, 61*(1), 30–35.

BARATTA-LORTON, M. (1976). *Mathematics their way*. Menlo Park, CA: Addison-Wesley.

BAYLESS, R. (1978). *Music: A way of life for the young child*. St. Louis, MO: C. V. Mosby.

BENDICK, J. (1971). *What made you you?* New York: McGraw-Hill.

BILLSTIEN, R., & HOLT, J.W. (March 1986). The turtle deserves a star. *Arithmetic Teacher*.

BRASHEARS, D., & WERLIN, S. (1981). *Circle time activities for young children*. Walnut Creek, CA: Starlite Printing.

CARLE, ERIC. (1978). *The very hungry caterpillar*. New York: Philomel Books.

CLITHERS, D. (June 1987). Learning LOGO "instantly." *Arithmetic Teacher*, pp. 12–15.

CREWS, D. (1978). *Freight train*. New York: Greenwillow.

DE LA MARE, W. (1947). *Rhymes and verses: Collected poems for children*. New York: Holt.

DOPYERA-LAY, M., & DOPYERA, J. (1987). *Becoming a teacher of young children*. New York: Random House.

DUTTON, A. (1988). Child development laboratory syllabus. Modesto Junior College, Modesto, California.

ELKIND, D. (1987). *Miseducation: Preschoolers at risk*. New York: Alfred A. Knopf.

FREEMAN, M. (1969). *Finding out about shapes*. New York: McGraw-Hill.

GAG, W. (1938). *Millions of cats*. New York: Coward-McGann.

HARSH, A. (September 1987). Teach mathematics with children's literature. *Young Children, 42*, 24–29.

HUTCHINS, PAT. (1970). *Rosie's walk*. New York: Scholastic.

———. (1971). *Changes, changes*. New York: Aladdin Books.

HYMES, J. L., JR. (1981). *Teaching the child under six*. Columbus, OH: Charles E. Merrill.

KAMII, C. (1982). *Number in preschool and kindergarten: Educational implications of Piaget's theory*. Washington, DC: National Association for Education of Young Children.

KOHN, B. (1964). *Everything has a shape*. Englewood Cliffs, NJ: Prentice-Hall.

LIONNI, LEO. (1974). *Alexander wind-up mouse*. New York: Borzoi Books.

McCLOSKY, R. (1941). *Make way for ducklings*. New York: Viking Press.

NELSON, J. N., KILLIAN, J., & BYRD, D. (1988). A computer in preschool: What happens? *Day Care and Early Education,* summer edition.

RADEBAUGH, M. R. (1981). Using children's literature to teach mathematics. *The Reading Teacher, 4*(5), 902–906.

STIPEK, D. (May 1988). Work habits begin in preschool. *Young Children, 43,* 25–31.

SUTHERLAND, Z., & ARBUTHNOT, M. (1986). *Children and books.* Glenview, IL: Scott-Foresman.

TSANTIS, LINDA, WRIGHT, J., & THOUVENELLE, S. (January-February 1989). Computers and preschoolers. *Children Today,* pp. 21–23.

TUDGE, J., & CARUSO, D. (November 1988). Cooperative problem solving in the classroom: Enhancing young children's cognitive development. *Young Children, 44,* 46–52.

ZAFFO, G. (1959). *The giant nursery book of things that go.* New York: Doubleday.

CHAPTER 4

Mathematics for Five-Year-Old Children

Five-year-old children are at an impressionable period in their growth and development. They are ready to do things. For these children, teachers must create an environment that builds confidence, self-assurance, and a positive attitude toward self and school.

Five-year-olds have a growing interest in the functional aspects of oral and written language, such as using new words, trying to write their names, and reading signs or labels. They respond to environments that include many opportunities to discover words designating work or play areas because the context in which the words are presented is meaningful.

These children are ready to work or play in small groups, as long as they are interested in the activity. They may seek time to be alone or to have parallel play. They like to play with children their own age. Because of their physical development, they enjoy outdoor play and using large muscles to manipulate toys, equipment, and materials.

In cognitive development, most of these children are still in the preoperational stage (Piaget). They rely on intuitive thinking and are gradually correcting and refining intuitive impressions by extending, differentiating, and combining information. We are concerned with the development of logical thinking as it relates to mathematical ideas and to children's conception of number. In this chapter we discuss cognitive behavior pertaining to: identification, classification, and ordering according to certain properties; equivalence and inequivalence; and the operations of combining and separating based on certain principles.

MATHEMATICS PROGRAM FOR FIVE-YEAR-OLD CHILDREN

In Chapter 3, we discussed developmentally appropriate prenumber experiences for four-year-old children. Those learning activities provide a natural lead-in to mathematics work for five-year-olds. However, because there are many kinds of preschools and because not all children have access to these schools, the mathematics program for the five-year-old must encompass those same prenumber experiences discussed for four-year-olds. At this level, then, instruction involves both review and reteaching.

In kindergarten, the educational program focuses on the nature and needs of children five and six years of age. Schools handle the age and developmental differences of these children in a variety of ways. Some schools have half-day programs to allow for two groupings of children. Other schools have a K, 1, 2 ungraded primary that enables them to design a developmental curriculum around the specific needs of individual children.

SCOPE AND SEQUENCE CHART

As we have noted, teachers must identify children's development levels to ensure that learning activities are appropriate for their stage of development. To help teachers, we have created a chart that outlines the *scope* (content and structure) and the *sequence* for mathematics instruction for each age group.

The following scope and sequence chart outlines a mathematics program for five-year-olds. It offers suggestions for sequences or activities for the whole class and for small groups, and names activities that are used throughout the day, during the month, or for special events.

THE IMPORTANCE OF LANGUAGE TO THINKING AND LEARNING MATHEMATICS

The language a five-year-old uses provides clues to the child's thought processes. The child achieves the ability to reason, which is part of operational thinking in mathematics, by manipulating objects in the physical world. Also verbal expression becomes clearer as thinking becomes more logical. When presented with concrete objects such as cubes, disks, or counters, the child's language will indicate his or her level of understanding. The preoperational child, for example, while comparing two quantities, will respond "There is a lot" or "There is a little." Children at the concrete

SCOPE AND SEQUENCE CHART FOR MATHEMATICS: FIVE-YEAR-OLDS

Scope	Time	Sequence			
Math components		Whole-class introduction	Small-group activity	Daily	Events/ seasons
Free explorations, materials, and work stations	2–3 wks.	x	x	x	
Counting, rhythms, writing numerals, sequencing, ordering, form	4 wks.	x	x	x	
Sorting and classifying, observing, predicting	4 wks.	x	x	x	
Environmental components, comparing attributes, measuring, weighing, shapes, time, graphing	3–4 mos.	x	x	x	x
Number, and math concepts, unit and "oneness," one-to-one correspondence, ordinals, more than, less than, cardinal numbers	3 mos.	x	x	x	
Using numerals 1 through 10, applications to games, recording, graphing, combining, separating, conserving	5 mos.	x	x	x	x
Problem solving, making problems, estimating, making predictions	throughout year	x	x	x	x
Calculator and computer explorations and use of programs	as ready	x			

operational level will use words to show the relation between two quantities, by saying how many "more" or "less" or by indicating "the same amount." To speak about two properties in one sentence, such as "The rod is long and red," requires considerable understanding as well as experience in using language to express the mathematical thinking.

Language difficulties occur when the child has not had enough experience with a mathematical concept, is not mature enough for the work being attempted, or has not learned the words to describe the mental operations being attempted. Preoperational children use their own personal language and aren't aware of "socially shared meanings" (McNally, 1978; Burk, Snider, & Symonds, 1988). Consider some of these language patterns that a child might use:

- Short unfinished sentences: "The rod is . . ."
- Repetition of conjunctions while the child is thinking or grasping for words: "So, so, so, or and, and, and . . ."
- Incomplete ideas: "The block I had is . . . is . . . is . . ."
- Limited adjectives or adverbs to describe an operation
- Interruptions in thought: "You see, and, and . . ."
- Terms used inconsistently in different situations

HELPING THE YOUNG CHILD WITH LANGUAGE

In relation to learning new mathematical concepts, the main goal of language development is to communicate ideas clearly. Children need rich and varied experiences in order to express and describe mathematical ideas.

The following suggestions should help teachers guide children in language development:

- Maximize two-way conversation. Think about who's talking, take turns, listen.
- Give friendly help; don't be critical or embarrassing.
- Provide a good model in a natural situation and relate the language used to the mathematics concepts being developed.
- Match the modeled form with the child's stage of development. Make tasks fun and desirable.
- Give clear directives involving one idea: "Give me a red ball." Then, as the child matures and can hold more than one idea in mind at one time, say "Now show me a large, long rod."
- Help the child with plurals (show several), prepositions (in, on, over), disjoint sets ("This is not red"), modifiers (more, less, larger).

Common difficulties that teachers have in helping children with language development include:

1. Their own poor logical organization of thinking: not being clear on what is asked or commanded, or speaking before thinking through the idea or command.
2. Confusing the child with a negative response. Be direct and positive. Use language such as, "Let's try again," "What do you think now?" "Tell me more," "I see another way." Avoid expressions such as, "No, that's wrong!"
3. Saying too much and confusing the child. Be direct. "Look at the first block. Now put the block where it belongs."
4. Trying to accomplish too much. Have a terminal point: "Before we stop, let's try two more times. Then we can clean up."

Mathematics Vocabulary

The following vocabulary and concepts are important for all children four through eight years of age. These terms will be used over and over as the teacher interacts with children in meaningful mathematical activities. With hands-on materials, children can explore the meaning of a math concept and can learn the vocabulary needed to describe it.

in a region, inside the boundary, outside, gateway, open curve, closed curve, same shape as

covers, covers as much as, covers more than, covers less than, covers the least, surface

long, short, longer than, shorter than, not as long as, not as short as, the same length as, longest, shortest

big, large, small, little, bigger than, smaller than, larger than, middle or medium size, smallest, biggest, different size

full, empty, holds more than, holds less than, holds as much as, the same amount

light, heavy, lighter than, heavier than, the same weight as

first, second, third, . . . fifth, next to, last place

bottom, top, middle, left, right, in line, front, lowest, underneath

yesterday, last week, tomorrow, noon, morning, evening, now, a long time, a short time, a longer time

penny, nickel, dime, quarter, half-dollar, dollar, dollar bill

tall, taller, tallest

square, rectangle, triangle, circle, line, path

colors—red, yellow, blue, green (and others as needed)

ORGANIZING THE CLASSROOM FOR MATH

The first section of the math scope and sequence chart for five-year-olds shows that time must be spent to help children learn about materials and work stations. Before school opens, the teacher must plan and organize the classroom so that appropriate materials and supplies are ready for use in the daily program. Practical work stations must be established for math and other subjects, and consideration must be given to how they will be used: Has sufficient space been alloted for work? Has provision been made for cleaning up? For storage of materials? There should be ample space (such as a large rug) for whole-class activity; small group or individual play areas; and stations for painting, reading, and computer use; and a dress-up or play center.

To help beginning teachers organize their classroom for instruction, some school systems pair a new teacher with an experienced teacher in an adjoining room whose class is of comparable age. The experienced teacher, together with the principal and supporting supervising staff, can help the new teacher make a strong, satisfying beginning to the school year. [Two excellent references for classroom organization are *Mathematics Their Way* by Mary Baratta-Lorton (1976) and *Box It or Bag It Mathematics* by Donna Burk and others (1988).]

Free Exploration of Materials

Allow time during the first two weeks of school for free exploration of materials and work stations. One way to do this is to divide the class into two groups. One will have free play with math materials such as pattern blocks; the other will be directed to work stations where clay, drawing, and picture books are available. The teacher will ask for volunteers to work at the various stations, which may be designated by a color or a name. Establish a way to indicate that all activity should stop and that everyone should wait for teacher direction or assistance—for example, ring chimes, flash a light, or stand in a certain spot and request that "all eyes should be here." After about 20 minutes of an activity, switch so that the other half of the class can explore the new materials.

Children will need instruction on how to find a work station (picture, name, color) and how to work in an area. Instruction should be brief but clear; it should be reviewed or evaluated each day during these first weeks, and followed regularly. Following are some instructions you may want to use:

When at a work or play station:

1. See how things are arranged.
2. Leave the work station the way you found it.
3. Put your waste things in the basket. Clean up.

A work station on the rug allows children to explore math materials.

Using math materials:
1. Find space to play (at arm's length from other children) or room to sit.
2. When you make something, you alone can "mess it up" or knock it down.
3. No one must throw or roll any material.
4. Materials cost money, and we use them with other children. *Never take them out of the room.*
5. There are containers for each kind of math material. Use them when you put things away.

Review the rules periodically. To focus children's interest on a particular problem, such as "messing up" another child's pattern or structure, have two children role-play a situation using prearranged structures made with unifix blocks. Have one child knock a structure down and the other child quickly retaliate. Then get children's suggestions on how to solve the problem. Ask questions or simply listen. To start a discussion, you may ask: "How do you feel when this happens to you?" "Why did someone do it?" "What can be done so this will not happen?" Children's suggestions may be to stay in your area, help others, ask for permission, leave enough room for work, use only the blocks you start out with, have enough space or use the cardboard for making a pattern or structure.

To introduce a second set of math materials, such as wooden cubes, divide the class into three groups so that children will rotate among the new material and other choices. The two sets of math materials should be spaced far enough apart to allow for free exploration. Groups should rotate every 15 to 20 minutes.

At the close of the work periods, discuss things that you observed. Have children make suggestions for improvement. Introduce one or two easy rhythmic clapping exercises: clap, clap, clap, clap, clap, clap / pause / clap, clap, clap / pause / CLAP!

COUNTING

A major goal for five-year-olds is to be able to count, read, and write numerals to 10, as well as understand sequence, ordinals to fourth or fifth, and one-to-one correspondence, by the close of the school year. Five-year-olds are introduced to counting by adults at home and at preschool. They may not, however, understand sequence, order, or one-to-one correspondence. These concepts are learned through the use of hands-on materials and in easy steps.

A variety of games and practical problem situations should be used to help each child achieve the skills involved in counting. For example, to give children initial experiences in oral counting, teachers can use activities such as the following: Have three or four children stand or sit when counted, play clapping games, bounce a ball to count the bounces, swing a pendulum to count the forward or backward swings, and sing counting songs.

Then write the numeral on the chalkboard or on an easel as children do a variety of activities, such as

- Have children stand as one child counts one, two, three. The teacher writes 3.
- Children take steps, counting one, two, three, four as they step. The teacher writes 4.
- Children step on large numerals one, two, three, four, spaced out on a number line for easy steps. The teacher writes 4.

Other activities include asking questions such as, "What numeral comes after the 3 or 4?" "What is the second numeral? The last?"

Activities to teach the ordinals through 1st, 2nd, 3rd, and 4th include having three children stand in a line facing a chalk mark on the floor and asking, "Who is first? Who is second? Who is last? Who will be first to sit down? second? third? last?" At an appropriate time, introduce the names first, second, third, and 1st, 2nd, 3rd.

WRITING NUMERALS

Several approaches may be taken to help five-year-olds learn to write the numerals 1 to 10. Mary Baratta-Lorton (1976) suggests teaching the writing of numerals as an art lesson, not as a math lesson, and to do so long before children need to use them. Constance Kamii (1985), reporting on studies conducted in Geneva, Switzerland, states that even without formal instruction many kindergarten children are able to write numerals when asked to represent graphically objects such as pencils or toy cars. In experimental work with four- and five-year-old children, Wilbur Dutton (1963) found that children learned to write numerals easily in play when hands-on materials such as colored rods are used. In this study, children were asked to identify and write the number of rods used in a game or lesson. The children practiced writing the new numeral with the help of cards showing the numeral, the beginning sequence for the numerals, and dot-to-dot templates. These children talked about the last numeral learned, the numeral before the last, and counted in reverse, a difficult concept.

A variety of procedures and materials is used to teach children to write numerals. Most teachers agree that clear, simple models are needed for children to follow. The most popular materials include:

dot-to-dot with starting points	sandpaper or rough surface for start	templates to trace

Some teachers provide opportunities for children to explore numeral forms with the use of: people numbers, playdough, fingerpaint, yarn, easel painting, clay, pipe cleaners, and rope (Burk, Snider, & Simonds, 1988).

In learning to write numerals, children's eye-hand coordination must be developed, and the slant of the paper used for writing numerals must be adjusted to the individual child. Left-handed children need to have the paper slanted to their left so they can use the writing instrument easily and, at the same time, see what they are writing. Many teachers are discovering the importance of using easy-flowing pens and regular pencils with soft lead. The scope and sequence chart shows numerals being used in a variety of settings throughout the school day.

CLASSIFYING THINGS AROUND US

Five-year-olds, who are in the preoperational stage of the thinking process, are thinking about their world. They are trying to sort out, describe, and understand what they see. Celia Lavatelli (1973, p. 44) describes this developmental stage.

We know that the child is developing notions of space and number, and how the two are related. We know that the child is beginning to order things and events, to arrange them in a series from small to large, short to tall, first to last or light to heavy. *We know what the important cognitive developments are* for most children, and we can plan a curriculum centered on classification, space, number, and seriation.

During this stage, children learn about similarities and differences of objects and events in their environment. Some classifying consists of two parts, such as tall and short. Classifying helps children think about things in their environment in terms of particular properties. Soon they discover that further classifying is necessary — that subsets are needed.

Tall and short can also be part of a continuum, such as one that includes *taller* and *tallest* or *shorter* and *shortest*. The properties of the environment tend toward a continuum. Some properties, however, do not form a continuum; for example, a square is either square or not square. Other elements may be excluded from classification because they do not possess a certain property. Difference or similarity may be expressed by using *same* or *equivalent* for sets with an equal number of units, and *inequivalent* for sets with an unequal number of units.

The following is an introductory lesson for teaching children to classify and sort objects found in their classroom or environment.

AIM

Children use hands-on "junk" materials to show different ways to sort and classify objects. The teacher introduces the activity with a problem: "I have a box of things collected here at school and they are all mixed up. How could you find a way to keep them or to put them into other containers?"

MATERIALS

A box containing plastic beads (of five colors) and some other materials, such as a box of "junk" materials collected at school or brought by children, such as bottle caps, crayons, pencils, paper clips, buttons

Paper plates, lids, or plastic boxes (to use when children decide what they want to put in them)

ACTIVITY

1. Children are on the rug or at a math center; materials are in a box by the teacher.
2. Have several children volunteer, one at a time, to look in the box, take an object out, and describe it. Ask: "What do you have?" Child: "A white button, a string of beads, a crayon, and so on."
3. Empty the box of "junk" on the floor: "How can we find ways to separate these things?"
4. Children suggest, "Put them in boxes, bags, lids, paper plates, and so on."
5. Have children, one at a time, select an object to place in a container. Direct children so that all containers have an object in them.

6. Children continue to select and place objects. Begin to ask questions — "Why did you put your object on the plate?" *Accept all answers without comment* in order to get clues to children's thinking through their use of language.
7. The lesson can close with children telling what they see on the paper plates or in the containers used. Take one plate at a time and get several responses from different children. Children might classify objects by such properties as color, size, shape, or by similarity: all buttons, all paper clips, and so on.
8. Class puts the "junk" in the storage boxes and collects the containers.

The next lesson could be a small-group lesson for part of the class or for the entire class seated at tables if the teacher has enough "junk" and containers for this type of lesson. Children work in pairs to repeat the activity.

For the group lesson, children will decide for themselves how to sort objects. Have more junk than boxes for each table to ensure a "left over" problem. The teacher can move around and ask questions: "Why are these here?" "Have you tried putting things together?"

At the close of the lesson, have a group sharing time. Children can describe their groupings of objects and begin to use classification vocabulary, such as *same color,*

Children describe objects grouped by color or size.

same size, wooden objects, all beads, they are all plastic, small, large; they may also describe the need to combine objects. The teacher asks, "Did you have things left over?" "What could you do with them?"

Sequencing Classification Activities

Five-year-olds learn the classification process step by step, including

1. Simple sorting by a single property (as shown in the previous lesson)
2. Finding a common property of a group of objects
3. Finding the same property in other groups of objects
4. Using more than one property at a time, such as color or shape
5. Using all-some classification, such as having the same color but not the same shape
6. Classifying and forming subsets of objects, such as: short and long / shorter, shortest / longer, longest

As children progress through the school year, gain background experiences, and mature, they will begin to use number to answer, "How many in a group?" "How much larger or smaller?" and to combine groups and name the new groups. And as they begin to use number to classify objects and groups, they begin to learn to order objects in a series. Ordering was involved when we suggested subgroupings such as long, longer, longest.

COMPONENTS OF CHILDREN'S ENVIRONMENT

We have stressed throughout the importance of building a mathematics program based on the components of children's environment (which is important if children are to see the relevance of mathematical ideas to everyday living) and on the organization and structure of mathematics. The content (scope) of the mathematics program is defined by the synthesis of these elements. The methods and levels (sequence) of presentation are defined in terms of the child (developmental appropriateness).

The following chart shows the main components of children's environment, the concepts involved, and the vocabulary used. The scope and sequence chart suggests three to four weeks for an examination of these components. Opportunities to teach and use all of them will arise every day. For example, time can be a part of activities throughout the day, and color will be used in art, in identifying groups, and in the use of materials. A discussion of the components follows.

COMPONENTS OF CHILDREN'S ENVIRONMENT

Concepts and Vocabulary	Concepts and Vocabulary
Classifying	*Position*
• sorting by properties	• inside
• finding a common property	• outside
• finding the same property	• on the line
• all-same classification	• between
• forming subsets	• around
Time	*Covering property*
• sequences of time	• covers as much
• ordering time	• covers less
• clock time	• covers least
• school time	*Color*
• intervals of time	• white
• shortest and longest	• red
Length	• blue
• shortest and longest	• yellow
• units — nonstandard, standard	• green
• things to measure with	• black
Size	*Money*
• biggest, smallest, same	• one cent, 1¢
Shape	• five cents, 5¢
• square	• one dime, 10¢
• triangle	• one dollar bill
• circle	*Patterns*
• cube or block	• matching
Mass — weight	• repeating
• heavy	• completing, making
• light	*Geometric shapes*
• same weight	• boundary
Capacity	• curve (open, closed)
• holds as much	• outside
• holds more	• inside
• holds less	*Logical thinking*
Thickness	• single attribute
• thicker than	• color and shape
• thinner than	• size and shape
• depth	• size and color
	• part-whole relationships

Time

Long before the five-year-old has developed an adequate vocabulary to describe time and other aspects of the environment, the child knows about smooth and rough, hardness and softness, quietness, and movement. The child's world is taking on meaning as well as shape.

Children are surrounded with sequences of **time,** which are part of the total environment. Some of these sequences include: night follows day, the moon rises and progresses toward fullness, the stars are arranged in shapes and clusters, birds hatch from eggs in approximately three weeks, fruit ripens at certain times, and — for children living near an ocean — the tides rise and fall to bring many changes in nature.

Now, as the five-year-olds come to school, bringing their already rich experiences with time sequences, they are faced with new situations pertaining to their day and ordered by an adult who uses "clock time." Duration of time (how time passes) is a difficult concept that is beyond the comprehension of young children. Time is not usually understood completely until ages eight or nine. Five-year-olds cannot "read the clock face." They learn this skill when they begin to read and to use numbers to tell "how many" or "how much." When one asks a five-year-old, "What time is it?" the child usually responds in terms of what is happening right then or what is important to the child. He or she may say "It's time for lunch," "It's TV time" ("Sesame Street"), or "It's time to go home." Other words may preface these responses such as, *almost time, nearly, just before,* or *about.*

The six-year-old who understands one whole and one-half may be able to use "clock time" broken into parts of an hour. The eight-year-old will be able to use "clock time" involving minutes. At school, the child's concept of time is extended and enriched by two new time sequences relating to the environment: (1) time for specific school activities such as resting, play, or lunch, and (2) amount of time in relation to an event. The child's understanding of the amount of time used, as well as the ability to record time should develop gradually and meaningfully. Such beginning activities as the following can be used: clapping hands (how many claps) while the teacher is ringing a bell and stopping when the minute is up; using a three-minute sand timer; and setting a wind-up timer to play a game such as musical chairs — circulating until the timer dings.

Here are some other activities involving time:

1. Use circle time for sharing. Have children select an object or an event to tell about. After each child's report ask: "When did this happen? What time was that?"
2. Encourage the use of time words. Ask "What will you do tonight?" "What will you do Sunday?" Use words such as *yesterday, last night, weekend, tomorrow.*

3. Use the sequence of the child's day, such as, "What do we do when the bell rings?" "When will we have lunch?" Use words such as *daytime, nighttime, storytime, morning, afternoon.*

Spread these activities over several days and use the vocabulary informally with many activities throughout the year.

Length

Length is determined by a single dimension. This makes direct comparisons easy. Introductory experiences with length require that children compare or classify objects as long or short. Other lessons help children discover objects that are neither long nor short. Their concept of length may be extended by providing a criterion length (middle-sized, as long as, or different from). Children's judgment of length depends on their ability to conserve. This is especially true when flexible, nonstandard units are used to make comparisons — for example, when a string is used to measure children's height.

Standard units, such as a regular ruler or metric ruler, are usually introduced in first grade along with simple fractions such as one whole, one-half, and one-fourth. The need for standard units could be illustrated by recording children's heights on a piece of paper attached to the wall.

The following is an introductory lesson in measurement.

AIM

Children use sticks to show long and short and use the correct vocabulary.

MATERIALS

Box containing many sticks, some long and others clearly short
String to make a circle or "boundary" for sticks or boxes

ACTIVITY

1. Seat children on the floor, grouped in front of two circles made with string or marked with chalk. Place the box containing the sticks between the circles and arrange it so that the children cannot see the contents:

long sticks   box for sticks   short sticks

---

2. Ask several children (one at a time) to come and look in the box. Each returns to a seat without telling the others what he or she has seen. After five or six children have done this, ask, "What did you see?" "How could we find ways to tell how long they are?"
3. Choose one child to take a stick from the box, place it in one of the circles, and sit by that circle. For example, if the stick is long, the child puts it into the circle on the right and sits by that circle. If the stick is short, the child places it in the circle on the left and sits by that. After several children have participated (with teacher assistance), ask other children to make selections (without teacher assistance). Continue until the children see the basis for classification. If children have suggested boxes, rather than circles, use them.
4. Then ask, "Where are the short sticks? Where are the long sticks? Who can give me a short stick?" Point to sticks in a circle and ask, "Why is this stick here?" If a child has put a stick in the wrong circle, ask, "Does this stick belong here? Where shall we put this stick?"

For another lesson, use sticks classified as neither long nor short. Add another circle or place these sticks between the two circles.

Size

Introduce children to the concept of **size** through objects that are big or small. Attribute blocks can be used for this work (but only size should be considered). Then move to an intermediate classification of neither big nor small (middle-sized). When children are ready, introduce a criterion size such as bigger, smaller, biggest, and smallest.

Shape

Children should be able to identify, select, classify, and name the **shapes**: square, rectangle, diamond, triangle, and circle. This knowledge is important in preparing them for work in spatial relations such as open and closed curves. Shape is one of the properties of attribute blocks used in work in logic. No attempt should be made to use formal logic terms.

AIM

Children select an attribute block and name its shape.

MATERIALS

Box with attribute blocks
Display cards for shape

Four circles drawn on the floor or identified with string or hoops.

ACTIVITY

1. Have several children, one at a time, look into the box and return to group without telling the others what they saw.
2. Ask some of these children to tell what they saw.
3. Choose a child to take a block from the box, place it in a circle, and then sit by that circle. Choose another child to repeat the procedure.
4. After a small group has participated and all circles have appropriate shapes in them, allow the other children to select blocks and ask them where the blocks should be placed.
5. Introduce names by asking, "Where are all the circles? Triangles?"
6. Distribute blocks so that each child in a group or class has one. Then ask the child to name the block held.
7. A variation on this activity is a game called "Pass the Block." Each child in a group or class is given a block. Then the teacher or a child says "Begin." Children continue to pass blocks around the circle until the signal to stop is given. One child is asked to name the block he or she is now holding. For each round, different children start the game, signal stop, and name the block. This last child then becomes the new leader.

Mass

Mass is not an observable property. Thus, children have to discover relationships by handling and estimating or by using a balance scale. Later in the year, when children are reading and writing numbers, a weighing scale with standard units of weight can be used.

Use a balance scale to let children discover heavier than, lighter than, or the same as. Young children relate size and weight. So use a variety of objects and shapes to show that size does not necessarily indicate heavy.

A game will help children estimate the relative weight of objects. A child holds an object in each hand and tries to determine which is heavier or lighter. Then the child puts the objects on a balance scale to check the estimated responses. Teach the correct vocabulary (heavy, light, heavier, lighter, the same weight).

Capacity

Capacity involves making judgments based on several properties of the container, such as size, height, width. Young children have difficulty with conservation and equivalence when different shaped containers are used to hold the same amount of water or sand. A child may make an assessment of the amount based on a single criterion — for example, the height or width of a container.

The child can learn about capacity by using a variety of containers to discover how much, holds more, and holds less. A distinction must be made between what a container holds or is holding and what the container will hold when full.

With sand, the child needs to discover that a full container means leveling off at the top with a ruler or piece of wood.

Thickness

Thickness is an attribute by itself. To overcome the association of size with thickness, the child needs to have many opportunities to see and feel objects that are thick and thin. Books can be used to demonstrate thick, thin, and multiple attributes: a thin and green book, a thick and red book, and so on.

Pair off the children so they can make comparisons and develop the vocabulary, such as "Find a thin block," "Find a thick block." Then have the children confer with each other to check answers so that more thinking occurs.

Give books to a group of five or six children to pass around. When a leader says "Stop," each child describes the book he or she is holding. Then the children compare books: "My book is as thick as yours" or "My book is thicker than yours."

Position Property

Position words are needed to express relationships and are used in almost every lesson: *space* — inside, outside, on the line, between, around; describing *patterns* — next to, under, over, behind, to the left or right, above, below, first, second, in between.

The Covering Property — Area

Young children are introduced to the concepts of **surface** and **area** through experiences with the covering property of objects. A variety of hands-on materials should be used to help children understand the concept that objects have a covering property.

Two kinds of relationships can be discovered: equivalence (covers as much as) and inequivalence (covers more, most, less, least). These relationships can be illustrated for the child by covering one object with another, and by covering the surface of a large object with smaller objects. These smaller objects used for covering, which may be blocks, cubes, or the like, serve as nonstandard units.

A lesson plan on the covering property follows.

AIM

Children cover objects and use appropriate terms: *covers, covers as much as, covers more (than)* and *covers less (than)*.

MATERIALS

Flat objects such as lids, paper, counters, books, bottle tops, cards, half sheets of newspaper spread on the floor or on child's desk, crayons and pencil

ACTIVITY

1. Each child selects one object to put on the newspaper, outlines the object (traces around it), and shades the outline. The child then takes another object to place near or over the space colored on the paper and says, "This covers more space (or less space)."
2. Children working in pairs or in a group can show each other their work. One child points to or tells which object covers more and then marks the object with an X to show his or her choice.
3. Steps 1 and 2 may be repeated using other objects.

Color

Although it is not a mathematical property, color is used to help develop logical thinking and number concepts. For example, when pattern blocks are used, the color may name a distinct property for each block. Shape and color may be used to classify the "not-properties" in beginning logical thinking, such as "is not red" and "not a circle." Colors are used in many ways to identify groups, work stations, patterns, materials, and pictures.

Money

When a child can recognize a one-cent coin, coins can be sorted by names, such as 5 cents, 10 cents. Then operations can be undertaken on the basis of one-to-one correspondence to check equivalence.

Since U.S. currency is based on a decimal system, there will be many uses for pennies and nickels as the child learns to sequence numbers to 10 and comes to understand the zero as "not any," "none," and later (first grade for most) as a placeholder in base ten.

Children can learn about money and the responsibility it entails through home and school activities such as the following:

- Being given an allowance for school lunch, Sunday school, buying at a neighborhood store
- Having a savings account at school or at home for future purchases, trips, projects
- Receiving money for work done at home or for friends or neighbors
- Saving money for the family by such activities as turning out the lights, taking care of clothing, not wasting food, thinking of necessities first
- Shopping for food, including making a shopping list, choosing brands, comparing prices, saving money with coupons, and taking advantage of store specials

Children learn the important concepts and vocabulary of money, as well as simple problem-solving techniques relating to it through discussion and participation in a wide variety of activities.

Patterns

The existence of a pattern allows children to do some informal analysis and synthesis. In a **pattern,** certain properties are repeated. Thus, children can analyze by looking for parts that make up the unit and synthesize by putting the parts together to form a unit.

To confirm that a pattern exists, the child must look ahead to see the next unit and look back to a previously defined unit to check for similarity. Children need to make a variety of patterns such as those shown in the following lesson.

AIM

Children understand the concept of a pattern and tell how the pattern is repeated.

MATERIALS

Pattern blocks or beads on a string to show the beginning of a pattern

ACTIVITY

1. Child begins a new pattern by adding other blocks or beads.
2. Child continues the pattern or removes the beads to make another pattern.
3. Provide strips of paper so children can draw or stamp the patterns they make.

OTHER LESSONS

Children learn to discover patterns: matching, completing, and repeating patterns, and creating new ones. Make patterns with fruit or vegetables cut into halves, colored rods, or unifix blocks (diagonal, straight line, around); perform rhythm patterns that involve snapping and clapping.

Children use colored rods as a tiny block set to form patterns.

Geometric Shapes

Young children are introduced to geometry through many interrelated, exploratory activities. Children are taught to identify and compare the properties of closed curves, boundaries, the concepts of inside and outside, open curves, and gateways (entrances).

AIM

Make a closed curve (with a fence or corral) and use appropriate vocabulary to tell where an object is in relation to the closed curve (region, boundary, outside, inside).

MATERIALS

Toothpicks
Small sticks
Cars
Toy animals

ACTIVITY

1. Children build a fence or corral out of rods or sticks. There is no opening in the boundary.
2. Children put animals or objects *inside* the boundary. Some animals may be outside the boundary.
3. Children tell what is "inside" and "outside" and use the words *boundary* and *region*.
4. Intervene at appropriate times to guide and to ask: "What would happen if one stick were taken out?" "Where is the bear or horse?" "Can this animal be outside the region?" "Can you place an animal on the boundary?"
5. A follow-up activity for the lesson or for the next day could be to have a child choose a starting point and, with a crayon, trace the boundary of a region drawn on a piece of paper. The child does not lift the crayon until he or she returns to the starting point. The child then colors the region.

    Other regions can be added by using a different color for each one. These concepts are easily related to gardens: The boundaries are retaining walls or borders, the areas encompassed, and seasonal arrangements of flowers or plants with different colors.

Logic

Logical thinking is introduced through structured materials such as attribute blocks. With such materials, the teacher can talk about logical relationships such as: classification by a single attribute; classification by conjoint (joined or united) attributes; and the part-whole relationship.

Attribute blocks may be described by shape, color, size, and thickness. Experiences with them include such activities as identifying, classifying, searching for similarities and differences, and expressing attributes as not-properties — that is, as not having the properties.

AIM

Children identify two conjoint attributes through the use of attribute dice and make sets of elements with two conjoint attributes.

MATERIALS
Attribute dice (color)
Attribute dice (shape)
Set of closed curves for each child

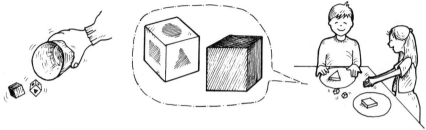

ACTIVITY
1. Children sit in groups at tables or desks with a set of attribute blocks. Each child rolls both dice and chooses a block with the color and shape shown on the top of the dice.
2. The child names the attribute and places the block in one of the closed curves. At each turn, the child adds new members to the set.
3. Children tell the teacher what the set contains, such as "My set has a round, blue block." Children tell each other what their set contains.

A variety of games can be played to practice using correct language as well as to identify elements in a set.

AIM
Children identify attribute blocks by using not-attributes and necessary vocabulary.

MATERIALS
Attribute blocks
Display board such as a flannel board, magnetic board, or a chart arranged on the chalkboard

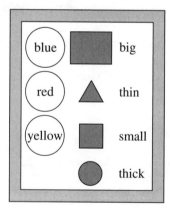

ACTIVITY

1. Have a child stand in front of the class. Ask the others to describe the child: tall, with brown eyes, and so on. Do this with several children.
2. Have the class use not-attributes to describe the child: not short, not a boy, and so on.
3. Play "I Spy." Say, "I spy something that is not on the floor." Children then respond, "Is it on the desk?" Answer, "No, it is not on the desk." Continue until the block is named or the object is found.
4. Using a display board similar to that shown, have the children respond to questions about an attribute block while you make an X on attributes not possessed by the block in order to emphasize "not." When the board is complete, the block being studied is revealed to the class — for example, "The block we were identifying is red, square, small, and thick." Then children can make statements such as "The block is not blue, not round, and so on."
5. Another variation is to have children close their eyes. One child is picked, who then selects a block to hide. You call on pupils to guess which block: "Is it yellow?" The child responds by using the not-attributes: "It is not yellow."

   Or have a child leave the room while the class selects a block and places it where the child returning cannot see it. The child asks questions of the class: "Is it a circle?" The class answers, "No, it is not a circle." Shapes and other attributes can be added.

MATHEMATICAL IDEAS AND CONCEPTS

Left on their own, young children will not learn much about the structure of mathematics or the potential the subject has for helping them solve problems or improve their ability to think. By using the components of children's environment, however, teachers can help them see the relevance of mathematical ideas to their everyday living.

Mathematical ideas and concepts are developed in the mind of the learner. Young children depend on first-hand experiences. These provide the incentive for learning as well as serve as the vehicle through which mathematical content is discovered. This relationship between children and their environment generates the content for mathematical ideas.

The major mathematical concepts and ideas recommended for five-year-olds and discussed in the following sections are: understanding the unit; working with sets and subsets (groups and subgroups); one-to-one correspondence, including equivalence and inequivalence; comparing sets; and properties of numbers — cardinal, ordinal.

The topics are appropriate for five-year-olds: They are manageable and, by the close of the school year, most children should understand them.

Constance Kamii supports our approach to mathematical learning in two publications. In *Young Children Reinvent Arithmetic* (1985), she builds a program for first-grade children based entirely on "situations in daily living" and on group games that provide opportunities for children to think. Kamii and Connie K. Williams (1988) suggest three ways to encourage children's thinking: (1) use situations meaningful to the child, (2) provide time and opportunities for children to make decisions, and (3) let them exchange viewpoints with their peers. "We must replace worksheets with an environment that offers ample opportunity for children to think as they manipulate objects" (Kamii, 1988). Textbooks and worksheets for children should be resources that teachers will use at appropriate times during any unit of work, but the main teaching tool should be objects in the environment.

The Unit: The Property of "Oneness"

Prenumber experiences with hands-on materials usually center on the properties of size, shape, color, or similar aspects. In counting objects, however, a child will not be concerned with these properties. Nor will the child necessarily understand that the objects being counted are being regarded as separate units.

When we consider an object as a unit in itself, we are including the properties of the object. A child may think of an apple or a pencil without thinking of all the properties of the apple or the pencil.

This is the abstract property of number — a property that defines elements on the basis of quantity rather than quality.

The property of "oneness" is shown in the following lesson.

AIM

The child makes a set of three objects and uses the numeral 3 and the word *three* to tell how many elements are in the set.

MATERIALS

Three cards, 3″ × 5″, with three pictures on each — for example, ball, glove, bat; apple, orange, banana; shoe, boot, slipper

Three cards, 5″ × 7″, with the numeral 3

Three cards, 5″ × 7″, with the word *three*

Three blank cards, 5″ × 7″, on which to place sets of objects

Box of junk materials

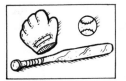

ACTIVITY

1. Ask three girls to stand. Ask, "Who can name this set or group?" (set of three girls)

2. Make groups of other objects such as 3 books, 3 chairs, 3 objects from the junk box. Children identify the set and name the number of elements. Write 3 on the chalkboard or on the easel along with the word *three*.

3. Ask three children to come to the front, one at a time. The teacher may have them hold hands or stand close together. Have children count as each comes up: "One, two, three" children. Write 3 and *three* again.

4. Have a volunteer place three objects from the junk box on a blank 5″ × 7″ card. Then place a card with numeral 3 and a card with word *three* next to the set of three objects. Repeat this with two other volunteers using the other two blank cards. Identify the sets.

5. Distribute hands-on materials in work areas, and have all children explore making groups of three.

6. Other lessons should include making sets of three and then writing the numeral 3 to tell how many. The concepts of one more than two, more, and less should be developed and understood.

Using Sets and Subsets

A **set** is a collection of things such as objects, ideas, colors, and so on. The units that make up the set are called **members,** or **elements**. A set with no members is called an **empty set**. When a set is organized with several distinct groupings of elements or is split up into such groups, these are called **subsets**. For example, in a set of six red balls (three large and three small), the three small red balls are a subset of the set of red balls. Braces may be used to designate sets such as $\begin{smallmatrix} 0 & 0 & 0 \\ & 0 & 0 \end{smallmatrix}$. For hands-on experiences, however, we need a variety of containers or boundaries in which to hold or distinguish sets — for example, cups, one's hands, a plastic bowl to cover a set, a piece of cardboard with a number (for example, 5) written on it to "hold" a set of five objects chosen by a child, or children's milk cartons with the top cut off. Other boundaries can be made with plastic hoops, or pieces of string, or can be shapes made with chalk or crayon. The boundary helps to give a set an appearance of being together.

ONE-TO-ONE CORRESPONDENCE To discover or show the relationship between the quantity of elements in two or more sets, we "pair off" the elements in each of the sets. This is called **one-to-one correspondence**. Elements may be paired off in any order. In the figure showing set A and set B, there is one-to-one correspondence between the two sets. The sets are equivalent.

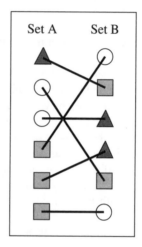

In the two sets shown in the following figure, there is only partial one-to-one correspondence. The two sets are inequivalent.

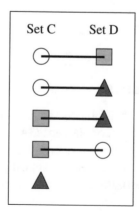

COMPARING SETS Children learn to compare sets by discovering that there is more or less in one set than the other, or that two sets are equal. Two sets are equal when they have the same number of elements and each element of one set is identical with an element of the other set. In making comparisons, we use the idea of a unit or oneness. Each element has exactly the same value quantitatively as each other element. In the process of making comparisons, the child soon discovers how to combine elements and how to separate elements. This process is shown in the following lesson.

AIM

Children use hands-on (junk) materials to make a set of four objects. They show their understanding of four, more than, and less than.

MATERIALS

Wooden pattern blocks (10 or 12)
Three blank cards 5″ × 7″
Three flashcards with the numeral 3 on each
Three flashcards with the word *three* on each

ACTIVITY

1. Show a set of three properties using pattern blocks. Children name the set. Then write 3 and *three* on the chalkboard and show the flashcards with 3 and *three*.
2. Have three children volunteer, one at a time, to make sets of one, two, and three objects.

one   two   three

3. Arrange the sets in order.
4. State, "We are now going to make a set with one more member than the last set." Children help you make a set of four. The new set is added to the sets with 1, 2, 3 members. Children compare and use more than, less than.
5. Children volunteer to make different sets of four and use flashcards to show the numeral 4 and four elements.
6. If desired, have children work at a variety of work stations in pairs and/or groups. If the first part of the lesson is fairly long, perhaps have a follow-up lesson later during the day. At work stations, children help each other while you observe, make suggestions, and ask questions: "What do you think?" "What do you have on the card?" "Show me how you made your set." Children may compare reference cards and pictures of four objects to their set.

7. Display a chart such as the one shown in the following figure. Ask the children to count objects in each set.

To give children experience in finding whether sets match and comparing sets by pairing, several practical activities can be organized using nuts and bolts, milk cartons and straws, and jars with screw tops. Use one set of materials for a lesson. Questions used to stimulate the matching and comparing might be: "Who thinks there are enough nuts for the set of bolts?" "Are there enough straws for the set of milk cartons?" "How can you find out if there are enough (nuts, lids, straws) for each set?"

Ordinal and Cardinal Numbers

In the previous section, we showed the use of number in making sets and recording the number of elements in the set. This process, based on counting, provides us with opportunities to develop the use of ordinal and cardinal numbers. For example, in the last section, we compared sets of four to show that 4 is one more than the last number (3) and that 3 is one less than 4. The cardinal number 4 was used to tell how many were in the set. When a child thinks four, this should include the number's reference to one in two, two in three, and three in the number four. This thinking, according to Piaget, is the synthesis of two kinds of relationships: (1) order and (2) the hierarchically inclusive (1, 2, 3, 4) four. If a child does not understand this, he or she might think that the last element used to make a set of four means 4.

Ordering does not show quantity. Ordinal numbers are used to show part of a sequence, a position, or a way to arrange objects and people. When children build sets, they learn the ordinal and cardinal properties of numbers. The five-year-old will be able to make practical use of the ordinals from 1 through 5.

USING NUMBERS 1 THROUGH 10

Instruction up to this point should have provided five-year-olds with the skills and concepts necessary for using numbers in the many enjoyable activities and games centering around their environment and problem-solving situations. In this chapter, we discuss this use of numbers. In addition, we continue using numbers to make sets in order to discover new concepts and skills, extending this activity through sets of 10.

Instruction at this time should be structured around: concept development, improving skills, providing for individual growth in math, and applying math and problem solving to a great variety of special occasions and seasonal events. A suggested weekly program to provide for these learning activities is shown next.

Time	M	T	W	TH	F
20–30 minutes Whole class	Concepts Problem solving	Concepts Problem solving	Concepts Problem solving	Special events Environmental problems	Special events School events Special days
20–30 minutes	Group and individual work stations	Group and individual work stations	Group and individual work stations	Whole class and groups	Whole class and groups

For full-day kindergartens, there can be two short periods for math three days a week and longer periods two days each week. The longer, unbroken periods are for special events, parties, cooking, and surprise math events. Friday can be a special, fun day where math is used in surprise events and activities. Half-day kindergartens should have the same enriched program as the full-day kindergartens. However, the number of learning experiences will have to be fewer. Either program should help children learn to read, write, and use numbers 1 through 10 as part of meaningful daily activities.

PROBLEM SOLVING

Five-year-olds need many opportunities to discuss ideas, make observations, organize their thoughts, and, with hands-on materials, use trial-and-error procedures to discover solutions to practical, everyday problems.

Most word problems, which involve one-step and several-step actions, can be solved with three basic procedures: combining, separating, and comparing.

Five-year-olds can use these procedures to solve a number of problems.

Combining
1. Children wearing something blue stand, are counted, and the number is recorded.
2. Children wearing red stand, are counted, and their number is recorded.
How many in both groups or sets?

Separating
Place a set of four unifix cubes on a table.
1. Ask a child to take two cubes away.
2. How many cubes are left?

Comparing
Ask all the girls in the class to stand.
1. Count and record the number.
2. Count the boys seated. Record the number.
Are there more girls than boys? Fewer? The same?

These three procedures can be applied to many problems growing out of daily activities and environmental topics.

A multiple approach should be used to help children learn to solve math problems. Five situations that can be used in problem solving were presented in Chapter 2. The following are suggestions for using those five situations with five-year-old children.

1. Use the child's environment.
   Each topic, such as time, provides many situations in which meaningful problem solving can be applied — in this case, for example, using a timer (sand or wind-up type) to see how long it takes to clean up, getting ready for lunch, and so on. Compare these times with times recorded on other days: Did the activities take more, less, or the same amount of time?
2. Introduce daily math lessons.
   The class has worked on pattern making with manipulatives on previous occasions. Teacher: "Yesterday we made patterns with beads and laces." (Shows one of the patterns.) "How was the pattern made? How is the next pattern [shows another string of beads] made? How is this pattern different? What could you do to repeat one of these patterns?" (Child shows a strategy.) "What could you do to make a different pattern?"
3. Use daily class activities.
   "John said there is one piece missing in the puzzle he used today. What can we do to find it? What can we do if we don't find it? What can we do so that this will not happen again?"

4. Use teacher intervention to provide new, creative problems.

   "Mrs. Jones believes they have an extra hamster that could be given to the school. Could we have a hamster in our classroom? What would we need to get? What would happen to the hamster on weekends? On holidays? On very cold nights?

5. Use textbooks.

   One modern textbook series lists these problem-solving applications: Plan what to do; guess and check; use logical reasoning; use a picture; make a list; find a pattern; and use story problems and situations made up by children.

CALCULATORS

Kindergarten children should have many opportunities to engage in free play and exploration with calculators.They need to learn the importance of calculators and to discover ways to use them as they learn how to read, write, and use numbers 1 through 10.

Suggested uses and skills include:

1. Learning to display numbers 1 through 9 and clearing the display after each entry
2. Increasing numbers such as 5 or 6 by adding one to each previous number.
3. Subtracting by taking away one number from a previous number.
4. Beginning to enter two-digit numbers — first 10, and then 10 and one more, and so on.

COMPUTERS

Computer software for teaching math to young children is being developed at a rapid rate. Besides the programs developed by numerous commercial companies, school districts throughout the United States are developing experimental programs involving the use of computers and calculators. The National Diffusion Network (NDN) has been funded by the U.S. Department of Education to help schools improve their education programs through the adoption of already developed, rigorously evaluated, exemplary education programs. NDN has two related resource projects that give schools assistance with the development of innovative educational programs, including the use of computers. These are the State Facilitators (SFs) and Developer Demonstrators (DDs).

Because of the rapid growth in preparing and using computer software, some criteria are needed to help teachers and curriculum developers select software that is developmentally appropriate for children. In Chapter 9 we discuss the importance of selecting computer software that meets the needs of children and that emphasizes problem solving and enriches children's mathematical learning. The following three developmentally appropriate software programs have been selected on the basis of these criteria:

1. *Draw Kindercomp* by D. Davis. Spinnaker Software, 1983. Ages 3–8. Includes six program options: Draw, Scribble, Names, Sequences, Letters, and Math.
2. *Panda Workout: How to Weigh an Elephant,* Educational Technologies, 1985. Ages 4–8. Helps children experiment and discover their own creativity and problem-solving skills.
3. *Facemaker* by D. Davis. Spinnaker Software, 1986. Ages 4–12. Children build a face using mouth, eyes, ears, nose, and hair options that allow them to explore, discover, and use their creativity and problem-solving skills.

Although software programs contain instructions, lesson plans, procedural advice, and suggestions for evaluation, teachers will still need in-service education and preparation in order to use them.

Computers are being installed as learning centers in many kindergarten classrooms so that small groups of children can use them. The teacher must play an active role in their use, encouraging, questioning, prompting, modeling, and mediating children's interaction with them.

EVALUATION

Evaluation procedures have been incorporated into each sample lesson plan in this chapter. These procedures include: using a practical, measurable goal for the lesson or activity; allowing individuals opportunities to demonstrate or show their understanding with concrete materials; providing activities that summarize and allow the group or class to show understanding of the concept being explored; and selecting and assigning appropriate follow-up activities. Five prenumber assessment items given at the close of Chapter 3 may be used with five-year-olds.

The child's role in evaluation should include: self-correcting activities with concrete materials that allow the child to show his or her understanding of each new skill or concept; the use of pictures or semiconcrete materials that demonstrate the child's progress in moving toward the abstract; and the child's ability to write and use the abstract form or operation and to tell others what has been done.

The child's attitude is important. Each learning activity, especially those in problem-solving situations, should be a time of self-appraisal, where the child seeks understanding, corrects answers, and explores other ways to find answers and solutions. The child must also find ways to record progress, including sharing and demonstrating understanding with parents. Learning mathematics should be enjoyable!

The teacher must establish a practical recording system, one that is manageable and appropriate for each unique teaching style. Suggestions for developing recording systems and assessment techniques are given in Chapter 8.

SUMMARY

Five-year-olds, while ready and eager to do things, are mainly in the preoperational stage of cognitive development. They rely on intuitive thinking and are extending, differentiating, and combining their action images, and correcting their intuitive impressions of reality.

In this chapter, we developed a scope and sequence chart to show the main mathematical concepts and skills for a mathematics program for this age level.

We gave suggestions for helping young children with language development connected with mathematical learning, and presented a math vocabulary list. The beginning math program for five-year-olds includes suggestions for free exploration of materials, counting, and learning to write numerals from 1 through 10.

The components of children's environment are identified and sample lesson plans given to show the relevance of mathematics to their everyday living. It is the relationship between children and their environment that generates the content for mathematical ideas. Mathematical ideas and concepts are developed in the mind of the young learner. The main mathematical ideas and concepts recommended for five-year-olds include: understanding the unit; working with sets and subsets; one-to-one correspondence, including equivalence and inequivalence; and properties of numbers, such as cardinal and ordinal.

The chapter closes with a discussion of computer programs appropriate for five-year-olds and suggestions for using meaningful assessment and evaluation techniques.

ACTIVITIES FOR TEACHER INSIGHT

1. Language influences the child's thinking and behavior. Show how this statement is important to mathematical learning for five-year-old children.
2. Emphasis has been placed on children learning mathematical concepts by

using hands-on materials. What are some implications of this approach to the development of critical thinking and attitudes toward mathematics?

3. Select a modern textbook prepared for use in kindergarten or first grade. Study the examples and illustrations used to introduce one topic, such as measurement or time. Compare these with the list of components of children's environment given in this chapter. Do the examples and illustrations agree with the list? How appropriate are the examples used?

4. Given two children — one who demonstrates one-to-one correspondence and one who does not — list some important considerations for presenting a new math concept, such as ordinal numbers, to each child.

REFERENCES

ALMY, M., CHITTENDEN, E., & MILLER, P. (1986). *Young children's thinking*. New York: Teachers College Press, Columbia University.

BARATTA-LORTON, M. (1976). *Mathematics their way*. Menlo Park, CA: Addison-Wesley.

BAROODY, A. J. (1987). *Children's mathematical thinking*. New York: Teachers College Press, Columbia University.

BURK, D., SNIDER, A., & SYMONDS, P. (1988). *Box it or bag it mathematics*. Salem, OR: Math Learning Center.

CHURCHILL, E. M. (1961). *Counting and measuring*. Toronto: University of Toronto Press.

DUTTON, W. H. (1963). Growth in number readiness in kindergarten children. *Arithmetic Teacher, 10*.

GREGG, E. M., & KNOTTS, J. D. (1980). *Growing wisdom, growing wonder: Helping your child learn from birth through five years*. New York: Macmillan.

HITZ, R. (1987). Creative problem solving through music activities. *Young Children, 42*(2), 12–17.

HYMES, J. L. (1981). *Teaching the child under six*. Columbus, OH: Charles E. Merrill.

IBARRA, C. G., & LINDVALL, C. M. (1982). Factors associated with the ability of kindergarten children to solve simple arithmetic story problems. *Journal of Educational Research, 75*, 145–155.

KAMII, C. (1982). *Number in preschool and kindergarten: Educational implications of Piaget's theory*. Washington, DC: National Association for the Education of Young Children.

KAMII, C. (1985). *Young children reinvent arithmetic*. New York: Teachers College Press, Columbia University.

KAMII, C., & DE VRIES, R. (1980). *Group games in early education*. Washington, DC: National Association for the Education of Young Children.

KAMII, C., & WILLIAMS, C. K. (1988). How children learn by handling objects. *Young Children, 42*(1), 23–26.

KRAUSE, E. F. (1987). *Mathematics for elementary teachers: A balanced approach*. Lexington, MA: D. C. Heath.

LABINOWICZ, E. (1985). *Learning from children*. Menlo Park, CA: Addison-Wesley.

LAVATELLI, C. (1973). *Piaget's theory applied to an early childhood curriculum*. Boston: American Science and Engineering.

McNALLY, D. W. (1978). *Piaget, education, and teaching*. Cremorne, Australia: Angus and Robertson Publishers.

STENMARK, J. K., THOMPSON, E., & COSSEY, R. (1986). *Family math*. Berkeley: University of California Press.

CHAPTER 5

Mathematics for Six-Year-Old Children

Most six-year-olds are eager to go to school. They want to learn to read, write, and count. They love rhymes, singing, games, and playing with other children at recess time. They are active—at times noisy and boisterous. Losing a baby tooth is an important event, symbolic of the fact that they are "growing up" and facing new demands and expectations by adults. In spite of many new tasks, including learning letter forms and numerals; longer work periods; and the need to follow directions, they like their teachers. They especially like teachers who are kind and fair, who give appropriate praise and approval, and who accept them as they are.

In cognitive development, these children begin the year in the preoperational stage, relying on preconceptual or intuitive thinking and gradually moving toward the concrete operational stage. Their attention span has increased so they can work individually and in small groups for 20- or 30-minute blocks of time. They demonstrate considerable verbal ability. They are becoming interested in games and rules that help them learn about mathematical concepts and problem solving.

At the beginning of the school year, the teacher must first identify the developmental level of each child and then diagnose the level at which each child is functioning in mathematics. There will be pronounced differences between children who have been in kindergarten and those who have not, even though what was learned in kindergarten may seem to have been forgotten (in this case, the child usually recalls the information after a brief review).

MATHEMATICS PROGRAM FOR SIX-YEAR-OLDS

Until now, most of the six-year-old child's mathematics learning has been informal, centering on the child's environment at home and at school. We want to maintain this approach, which has meaning for the child and which is based on the use of hands-on materials, direct experiences, and discovery. At the same time, however, we must now go beyond this natural, informal approach to introduce our notation system, which is made up of numerals and place value. This system, in turn, is part of a larger symbolic, abstract, arbitrary association system. We must bring the two systems together: (1) the child's way of learning in a meaningful everyday living and daily use context that makes sense and (2) a number system that is an abstract symbolic system requiring new techniques for understanding and for practical applications. We must approach this last task by understanding and respecting the difficulties of math concepts and finding ways to clarify these concepts so the child is the one who builds an understanding of each new aspect.

To help them plan their daily and weekly developmental programs, teachers can use the scope and sequence chart and the chart showing components of children's environment presented in this chapter.

The scope and sequence chart summarizes the mathematics program for six-year-olds. The major topics introduced into the program for five-year-olds have been extended and appropriate review is provided. We have not repeated the instructional steps used in helping children learn to write numerals 1 through 10. However, teachers must provide time and learning opportunities for those children who are just beginning to write numerals and classify objects according to several characteristics.

Six-year-olds require many opportunities to apply new math concepts. Writing numerals on strips of paper gives practice in sequence.

Scope		Sequence			
Math components	Time (Days)	Whole-class activity	Small-group activity	Special events	Seasonal
Free exploration, language, vocabulary	7	x	x		
Use of materials and work areas	7	x	x		
Writing numerals 1–10: • sequence and form • hand–eye coordination	17	x	x		
Counting: • sequence • identifying quantity • one-to-one correspondence • 2s, 5s, 10s to 90	14	x	x	x	x
Classifying properties: • similarities, differences • sorting	10	x	x		
Utilizing components of environment: time, length, size, shape, covering, money, etc.	20	x	x	x	x
Number—concept, symbolic: • number lines • putting together: addends up to 4 addends up to 6 addend doubles 2 + 2 up to 10 + 10	26	x	x	x	x
Taking apart: • 1–5, 6–10, 11–18 • two-digits without regrouping	26	x	x	x	x

SCOPE AND SEQUENCE CHART FOR MATHEMATICS: SIX-YEAR-OLDS (*continued*)

Scope		Sequence			
Math components	Time (Days)	Whole-class activity	Small-group activity	Special events	Seasonal
Place values	18	x	x		
Pattern extensions	8	x	x	x	
Fractions: $\frac{1}{2}, \frac{1}{4}$, equal parts	10	x	x	x	
Calculators		x	x	x	
Computers: readiness and instruction			x	x	

The time allotments for each learning task are suggestive. For this age group, more time should be spent on the experiential aspects of the programs — teachers should provide many opportunities for applying mathematical concepts. Through these experiences, children will build their own understanding of each new mathematical concept or skill. Special activities involving mathematics, such as cooking, building models, treasure hunts, and so on, should be planned for part of each week throughout the school year.

In a later section we discuss in detail the components of children's environment that follow from the scope and sequence chart and thus are relevant to mathematics learning.

LANGUAGE DEVELOPMENT

In Chapter 4, we discussed the importance of developing young children's vocabulary — both the general vocabulary, so they can communicate their ideas, and a specialized mathematics vocabulary. We also gave suggestions for guiding children's language development.

In this chapter we emphasize the importance of learning activities that contribute to cognitive development as well as to language development. We believe that optimal development in these areas occurs when (1) the level of cognitive development enables the child to learn new concepts involving specialized vocabulary; (2) the child is intrinsically motivated and is able to regulate the new learning; (3) opportunities exist for a variety of interactions with other children, and (4) the child participates actively with hands-on materials, which helps to develop real meaning.

In terms of the mathematics vocabulary, teachers must carefully monitor the child's understanding and use of operational (mathematical) words. Operational words are formal mathematical terms for which no alternatives exist. The child must understand their meaning precisely in order to use them. With general vocabulary words, the child can make substitutions and use variations. Cawley (1985) has shown that unless the words are both appropriate to the context and meaningful to the child, problem solution becomes difficult, even impossible. Thus, teachers must carefully differentiate between closely related or visually or auditorily similar words.

Another topic important to mathematical learning and language is whether children understand more than they can express verbally. Piaget (1977) answers this question by stating that

> at the more elementary levels, pupils will be far more capable of "doing" and "understanding in actions" than of expressing themselves verbally. . . . "Awareness" occurs long after action. (pp. 731f.)

Children of this age can often show a solution or idea rather than explain it verbally.

We suggest that teachers must spend a great deal of time helping children to use simple, accurate terms when talking about mathematical experiences. Of course, any response that children give must be accepted, but teachers can provide numerous opportunities for children to refine their language as they deepen their understanding of mathematical concepts.

CLASSROOM ORGANIZATION

Classroom Space and Materials

Primary-level teachers will want to organize the classroom in their own unique, creative way. Much depends on the size of the room, materials and equipment available, and the kind of math program outlined in the school's curriculum guide. However, certain basic areas are found in most classrooms. Foremost is an open area that is used for discussion, demonstration, and whole-class activities. This area may be defined by a rug, a circle shown by tape or paint, or by chairs around the rug or circle.

Math materials are organized in containers on open shelves so that children can help themselves.

Other areas in the classroom must be partitioned off or otherwise defined to provide work and play areas for a variety of learning activities. These include: storage space for the general math materials used for the unit being taught; an art center with easels, clay, and so on; a reading center with books, an easy chair, or rug; a small-group center with tables for a math or reading group; chairs and tables for individual seatwork; a dress-up and play center or block-building area with props; a computer center if the school provides one; storage space for special games; and ample bulletin boards and display areas. A secure supply cabinet with ample shelving and containers for pencils, crayons, felt pens and markers, scissors, paste, and paper is also needed.

Teachers will have to decide, before instruction begins, on how the room will be arranged. Some teachers like to have all work centers labeled by name and color; pictures displayed that are appropriate for the first instructional period; and charts ready for beginning such activities as keeping a daily calendar and keeping track of the weather, attendance, and birthdays. Other teachers prefer to have children help plan and organize many of these activities. For the beginning teacher, learning centers and special events areas should be well defined and, before school begins, plans should be made for their use. See Chapter 10 for suggestions on managing class activities and lesson plans.

Components of Children's Environment

Components of the environment for six-year-olds are the same as for five-year-olds, but their coverage goes beyond that for the younger group. The following chart summarizes the new material.

The chart will help teachers prepare weekly and yearly plans for activities to use with mathematics concepts, problem solving, and special events and seasons. In the following sections, we develop sample lesson plans for properties of size (length, width, height), time, money, patterns, and area. A discussion of part-whole relationships leads into a discussion of number work and the basic operations of addition and subtraction of whole numbers.

LENGTH, WIDTH, HEIGHT AS PROPERTIES OF SIZE Several lessons are needed to help children identify and understand criteria for classifying objects according to size. The first step is to review lessons given in kindergarten involving big and small. Then help children discover other relationships between these, such as bigger and smaller. As in other lessons involving classifying, the child should have opportunities to feel, manipulate, compare, and then "think" about an object without actually seeing it.

The next stage in developing the concept of size is to help children discover relationships among the attributes of length, width, and height. These three attributes are developed together because they are closely related. In a lesson designed to identify

COMPONENTS OF CHILDREN'S ENVIRONMENT

Concepts and vocabulary	Concepts and vocabulary

Length
- ruler, yardstick
- standard units
- comparing, shortest, longest

Time
- making clock faces
- telling time to hour, half
- hour, using time with
- activities, kinds of clocks
- birthdays, calendar, seasons

Money
- coins: 1¢, 5¢, 10¢, 25¢, 50¢
- bills and notes: $1.00, $5,00, $10.00
- buying, selling without regrouping
- savings, school lunch, admissions

Patterns
- figure patterns
- number patterns: row, column, diagonal

Covering property (area)
- using variety of shapes to cover surfaces: rugs, carpets, wallpaper, pictures

Color
- identification and use with attribute blocks
- comparing groups and materials

Logical thinking skills
- identify nonattributes and attributes
- use of more than one attribute
- part-whole relationships
- similarities and differences

Geometric shapes
- finding shapes in classroom, playground
- shapes in patterns, two dimensions
- boundaries for garden
- perimeter (around) patterns and shapes with geoboard

Mass and weight
- balance beam
- scales
- heavy, light, heavier, lighter

Capacity
- liquids
- sand
- containers
- comparisons
- quart, pint, gallon
- units to use

the shapes of several attribute blocks and to develop the words needed to describe these blocks, children will be examining the relationships among the attributes. For example, a child compares two blocks to see if they have the same width. Then the child observes the length of the two blocks. Finally, by standing the blocks on end, the child gains some understanding of height.

The child learns how to "think" about attribute blocks and to use words to communicate their ideas about them. Words such as *big, bigger, small, smaller, wider, taller, square,* or *rectangle* will be used meaningfully and accurately. The child's concept of size will grow to a new, meaningful level, and the child will be ready for more advanced work with the concept, applying it to objects in the environment or in mathematical work for seven-year-olds.

The following sample lesson provides opportunities for children to gain an understanding of size.

AIM

Children touch objects and use the correct language to describe the attributes of a set of two objects.

MATERIALS

Pair of long and short rectangles with different widths
Pencils and crayons of different sizes
Pair of long and short fraction tiles or rods
1-foot ruler and yardstick

ACTIVITY

1. Children are seated on a rug or arranged in a circle on the floor.
2. Place materials in pairs so that their attributes, such as long and short pencil or pencil and crayon, can be compared.

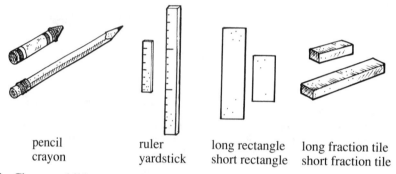

| pencil | ruler | long rectangle | long fraction tile |
| crayon | yardstick | short rectangle | short fraction tile |

3. Choose a child to come and touch each object of a set to identify one attribute. For example, the child touches the pencil and crayon and says, "This is a long pencil, and this is a short crayon." The child then chooses someone from the group to take a turn. This child identifies another set; shows an understanding of shape, long, and short; and uses complete sentences to describe the objects.
4. Other children use long and short to describe the sets of objects.
5. You may wish to plan three lessons to develop the concept of size—one on each attribute. Or, the third lesson could be used to combine all three attributes to describe the size of an object. Adjust the activity to the children's level of development and understanding.

In each lesson, invite the children to help a child who needs assistance with words or comparisons.

Follow-up lessons could include using picture cards showing pairs of objects or ditto sheets with line drawings of pairs of objects. Have children describe them, and have them connect two single objects on a page by drawing a line, and then compare them. Children can work in small groups or in pairs to compare and describe the length, width, and height of the set chosen. The teacher can observe and check a child's understanding of the concepts by asking the child to tell the attributes of the pairs chosen.

Special days, such as birthdays, provide excellent opportunities to use the properties of length and height—for example, to measure and record children's height, foot length, arm length, or hand span.

TIME   Most six-year-olds will have been enrolled in kindergarten and therefore exposed to the concept of "telling school time." They will also have grown in their understanding of certain time sequences around them: TV time, story time, bedtime, and seasons of the year—the time to plant flowers or to harvest crops. Extensions and applications of time are built on this meaningful background.

Children need to explore ways to determine time and to use intervals of time to regulate activities and events. Several lessons will be needed to extend children's background for understanding "clock time."

One lesson might be centered around how people measured (told) time before there were clocks. Use picture books and illustrations to help children recognize that these early earth dwellers used the sun, moon, and the behavior of birds and animals to determine time and seasons. Show that celebrations and dances centered around seasonal changes, and that these early people devised special equipment to tell "seasonal time" and "day time." For example, the Indians of the Southwest (mesa and cliff dwellers) made holes in special adobe buildings, and when sunlight coming through the holes touched a certain spot, they knew that the season for planting had arrived and that this was the time for "planting dances."

Other experiences involving "time before clocks" might include "water time." Demonstrate, for example, a device used in earlier times where water dripped into a container that would, after a determined interval of time, tip to spill out the water. These are examples that six-year-olds can enjoy and understand.

After exploring natural time, teachers might take several lessons to develop the concept of artificial time and study the uses of mechanical devices.

AIM

Children discover how to make a clock face and to write numbers from 1 to 12 on a clock face.

MATERIALS

Pieces of white cotton string 36″ long
1 clock face with movable hands
1-foot ruler
Yardstick

ACTIVITY

1. Use a ruler to measure the length of a child's foot.
2. Then place a yardstick on the floor to explore the (linear) length of several "foot lengths."
3. Examine the face of a clock. "Could we measure the path (distance) that the hands take to move around the face starting at 12 and making one complete turn?" Use the sample clock to demonstrate the movement of the minute hand.
4. Make a circle with one piece of 36″ string. Then take a second piece of string and fold it in half. Mark the two ends with red (or a color that will be easily seen). Now fold the string one more time and mark the new folds.
5. Make a circle of the second string and place it on top of the first string. The red marks will show the fourths (quarter hour). Mark the clock face with the 12, 3, 6, 9.
6. Place a third string (marked at the ends and folded as in step 4) lengthwise on a piece of paper (like a number line) and write, at quarter intervals, the numbers 12, 3, 6, 9. These quarter marks help the children place numerals on the clock face easily and accurately. Without such help, they tend to bunch numbers into many irregular patterns.
7. Have children name the numbers as you write them on a clock face shown on an easel or chalkboard; start at 12:00 and move "clockwise."
8. As a follow-up activity, you might give children ditto sheets and have them fill in the missing numbers on a clock face that already shows the numbers 12, 3, 6, and 9.

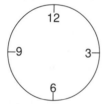 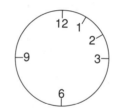 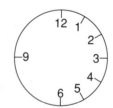

Additional lessons, such as the following, can be presented when children are ready for the new work:

1. Use several clocks — windup, battery driven, electric with a cord, digital.
2. Help children discover how the clock is "powered" to move the long and short hands. Beat a small drum to show the length of time for one minute. Have a clock with a sweephand to show seconds and one minute.
3. The lesson can stop at this point. As follow-up work, have children place or color long and short hands on clocks to show "on the hour" for different times.
4. When children are ready, tell time "to the hour" for a few important occasions such as the time to come to school, lunch time, or the time to go home.

Drawing clock faces and writing numbers on a clock face to show the exact points is too difficult for most children, as is dividing a circle into halves, quarters, and twelfths. It is a poor use of children's time. So use prepared ditto sheets for each lesson, with the key points for that lesson already established.

MONEY Money is important to six-year-old children. Children have many opportunities to learn about money at home and through experiences shopping, but basic concepts are learned at school. Because money is so appealing to children, they enjoy participating in learning activities about it.

Some of the concepts children should learn are the following:

- Money is used to buy many things.
- Objects or materials may be sold for money.
- Money has a place-value system that is related to our number system.
- Money is made of coins and paper (notes or certificates) that have specific values.
- The purchaser must use appropriate change when buying.
- Making change involves putting together and taking apart.
- Estimating is involved in buying, making change, selling, and reading and writing "money names" and "numbers."

The sequence in which these money concepts are presented should follow the child's development and progress in learning number concepts. When the six-year-old child can read and write numerals to 10 and understands how to put ten together and to take ten apart, money can be introduced using 1¢, 5¢, and 10¢ coins.

Children should understand the coins and bills used in the United States. This brief outline lesson shows how some of the important skills and concepts may be introduced.

- COINS

AIM
Children use coins, number lines, and place-value holders to show their understanding of U.S. coins.

MATERIALS
Several number lines prepared in advance on a large chart (which is reusable)
Piggy bank
Box of coins with 20 nickels, 10 dimes, 4 quarters, 2 half-dollars, and 1 silver dollar
Money rack (to put money in rolls)
Money chart or card

ACTIVITY
1. Bring a full piggy bank or begin by asking children about their savings banks. "How do you get the money out? How do you count the money?"

2. Identify the coins and begin the process of counting by placing coins on a money card that shows a penny, nickel, quarter, and half-dollar. Each child names a coin and places it on the card.

3. Money racks are used to hold coins so they may be counted and put into paper wrappers provided by banks—a roll of pennies is 50 pennies (50¢), a roll of nickels is 40 nickels ($2.00).

4. Count by 1s, 5s, and 10s. Relate this to the coins—1¢ + 1¢ + 1¢ + 1¢ + 1¢ = one nickel. Use number lines to show coin values and groups of coins.

5. Follow-up work to reinforce the lesson could include the use of money charts showing coins ranging from one penny to one dollar. Children, each with a money chart, work in pairs or in small groups to play money and place coins in appropriate columns. When children are ready to make change, they use a money chart that shows the coin, such as one quarter, followed by " = ? ? ?" Children use pennies, nickels, or combinations of coins to make one quarter.

■ PAPER MONEY

AIM

Children demonstrate their understanding of paper money $1.00 to $10.00 with the use of bills.

MATERIALS (in U.S. currency — bills)

10 one dollar bills
2 five dollar bills
1 ten dollar bill

ACTIVITY

1. Review the work of previous lessons—counting by 5¢ and 10¢ to $1.00.
2. Help children see the need for paper money. "When you go shopping for groceries, would you take a bag full of pennies, nickels, and other coins?"
3. Build $5.00 with one dollar bills. Then make a $10.00 bill with 10 ones.
4. Make exchanges such as two $5.00 bills for one $10.00 bill.

Lesson plans showing how coins and bills are combined and using money for buying school supplies or for selling articles at a yard sale are found in Chapter 10.

The sequence in which skills and concepts are presented to children should follow other work being done at that learning level. For example, experiences with money involving regrouping in addition and in subtraction should be reserved for eight-year-old children.

PATTERNS   Pattern work is an important part of teaching mathematics. It needs to be included in the program so children can expand their understanding of similarities and differences. Repetition in a pattern occurs to show distinctive features.

Children must examine each unit in a pattern to discover similarities and differences. They learn to analyze patterns by looking at what comes before and after each unit.

At each learning level, children need to discover ways to use patterns in mathematics and in everyday activities. The six-year-old child should be introduced to patterns: rhythmic clapping, unifix cube patterns with alternating colors, the pattern of beads in a necklace, patterns used in clothing, and patterns used to decorate and surround a figure or space.

Patterns made with blocks, beads, and similar objects help children recognize a cardinal number quickly. Activities should center around work with a number name or number symbol. Patterns can be used, for example, to illustrate square numbers, odd and even numbers, and natural numbers in configurations of three, five, and so on, or numbers in domino configurations.

■ SQUARE NUMBERS   Square numbers are numbers equal to the sum of preceding consecutive odd integers, such as $4 = 1 + 3, 9 = 1 + 3 + 5, 16 = 1 + 3 + 5 + 7$, and so on.

```
 1      4       9        16          25            36
 •     • •    • • •    • • • •    • • • • •    • • • • • •
       • •    • • •    • • • •    • • • • •    • • • • • •
             • • •    • • • •    • • • • •    • • • • • •
                      • • • •    • • • • •    • • • • • •
                                 • • • • •    • • • • • •
                                              • • • • • •
```

■ ODD AND EVEN NUMBERS   Which have a "leg"?

```
 1      2      3      4      5      6      7      8      9     10
 •     • •    • •    • •    • •    • •    • •    • •    • •    • •
              •     • •    • •    • •    • •    • •    • •    • •
                     •     • •    • •    • •    • •    • •    • •
                                   •     • •    • •    • •    • •
                                                •     • •    • •
```

■ NATURAL NUMBERS IN CONFIGURATIONS OF THREE

```
 1     2      3       4        5        6       7       8       9      10
 •    • •    • • •   • • •    • • •    • • •   • • •   • • •   • • •   • • •
             •       • •     • • •    • • •   • • •   • • •   • • •   • • •
                              •       • •     • • •   • • •   • • •   • • •
                                                       • •    • • •   • • •
                                                                       •
```

■ NATURAL NUMBERS IN DOMINO CONFIGURATIONS

1	2	3	4	5	6	7	8	9	10

Learning about patterns helps children develop their skills in counting, comparing, sorting, and using a variety of materials. We particularly like pattern blocks, unifix cubes, pegboards, and multilinks for helping children explore and make a wide variety of patterns.

Children can create a pattern with alternating colors in the form of a train using unifix cubes. They can count the number of "cars" for the whole train or for different colored parts. The train can be broken into groups of three, four, or five. It can be made with the cars two or three cubes wide. Such projects enable children to examine patterns up and down, across or sideways, and diagonally.

Some teachers have children use crayons or felt-tipped pens to make and color different patterns, but we feel that the use of hands-on materials has distinct advantages over this type of activity. With commercially prepared, three-dimensional materials, patterns can be made quickly and arranged without encountering such problems as keeping colors within the boundaries, using a wrong color and not being able to erase it, and taking too much time.

AREA Beginning work with area centers around establishing the concept of "surface." A child learns through a variety of activities that there are many kinds of surface: the floor, wall, play areas, roads, table tops, and so on.

The child also discovers that there are different ways to cover a surface, such as covering one object with another — for example, placing a large piece of paper over a smaller one — and covering a large surface with smaller objects — for example, using 12″ × 12″ tiles to cover a floor or the top of work areas in the kitchen.

Accurate, appropriate vocabulary and language should be used, including *covers, covers as much as, covers more, covers less, surface, covers most, covers least.*

Discovering that surfaces may be measured and the quantity of required covering material determined begins with establishing nonstandard measures. Children can experiment with unifix cubes (covering spaces on a page, within a closed curve, or on chart paper) to discover different patterns.

Children can make estimates and approximations to determine the number of units needed to cover a surface. When they do this by tracing a block or cube, they need to understand that the boundary line is only approximately accurate and that it is outside the surface covered.

The following lessons will help children learn the vocabulary and develop an understanding of the covering property and how it is used to make comparisons such as covers the most and covers least, and covers less than.

AIM

Children demonstrate their understanding of the covering property by using a variety of objects to show covers as much (as), covers more (than), and covers less (than).

MATERIALS

Newsprint or newspaper spread on the floor
2 crayons of different colors
Assortment of flat objects such as square, triangle, circle, books, and pieces of cardboard

ACTIVITY

1. Demonstrate tracing around an object (square). Then color the inside of the closed area.
2. Place another, larger object (cardboard) over the shaded area and use a different colored crayon to outline its shape; show the area covered.
3. Children tell which object covers more than, and identify the surface that is less than (underneath part).
4. Have two children choose objects and repeat the process, using correct vocabulary to describe the space covered by each object.
5. Children select two other children to continue the lesson. "Which object covers more? Which object made this surface? Which object covers less?"
6. Follow-up work could include continuing the work in small groups and having children demonstrate their understanding of the covering property and correct vocabulary.

AIM

Children order an assortment of flat objects from largest to smallest and demonstrate their understanding of covers more than, covers less than, covers the same as.

MATERIALS

Large hand towel (largest)
Paper towel
2 pieces of 8½" × 11" paper (same as)
Handkerchief
3 pieces of cardboard of varying sizes

ACTIVITY

1. Demonstrate that one object is larger than another by first comparing them side by side and then by placing the smaller object on top of the larger object. Call attention to the "more than" parts of the larger object.
2. Invite one child to find two objects and compare them, using complete sentences to say, "This is smaller than or this is larger than."
3. Ask, "Can we arrange the objects from largest to smallest?" Help one child at a time to place an object in a row, in the proper sequence. Help them arrange the two pieces that are the same as.
4. As a follow-up, give each child a ditto page of five different-sized rectangles. Have the child number them in order from 1 (for largest) to 5 (for smallest). If time is available, have the child cover the shapes on the ditto page by tracing a rectangle or other shape and write L for larger and S for smaller.

PART-WHOLE RELATIONSHIPS The concept of the part-whole relationship is basic to the four fundamental operations of addition, subtraction, multiplication, and division. At this point, we are ready to extend the concept of number for the six-year-old child. We do this by identifying the link between part-whole relationships and number.

First of all, recall that conservation, as a mental operation, is basic to all rational thinking, including mathematical thinking. The ability to conserve is linked to the child's development and to the mathematical concepts he or she is learning. When children can conserve, they understand that a certain quantity is invariant or unchanged in amount, even though its appearance changes or its elements are rearranged. The amount of sand or liquid remains the same when poured from one container to another. Likewise, discrete materials (counters) may be spread out, clustered, and rearranged, but the initial quantity remains the same — constant.

When children begin to learn about number and the structure of the number system, this concept of constancy enables them to understand that what they see may change, but the basic, underlying situation does not. They must be able to think about an initial situation, keep it in mind (internalize it), and then judge a new situation in relation to what has been internalized.

Two mental operations are involved: conservation and reversibility. For example, a situation may involve five elements in a set. The quantity of elements remains constant even when renamed as $4 + 1 = 5, 1 + 4 = 5, 3 + 2 = 5, 2 + 3 = 5$, and $5 + 0 = 5$. The child can mentally move forward and backward, keeping in mind the "fiveness" of five. This process involving conservation and reversibility has been identified as *operational facility*.

The foundations for logical thinking have developed and the child understands relationships in a psychological way, not just the characteristics and shape of objects.

This is the stage of operational facility, which enables the child to do logical thinking. At this point, the child is ready to do mathematical thinking — an integral part of logical thinking.

NUMBER: DISCOVERING RELATIONSHIPS AMONG DIFFERENT QUANTITIES – ADDITION AND SUBTRACTION

During the first part of the school year, six-year-olds have learned to count, read, and write numerals 1 through 10. They have had many opportunities to explore a variety of hands-on materials and to work in groups and by themselves. Experiences with environmental components have helped them to measure, weigh, compare, estimate, and discover ways to use number to identify elements in a group. These experiences have led them to understand part-whole relationships. Now we begin to focus on helping children discover relationships among different quantities, by combining (addition) and separating (subtraction).

ROADBLOCKS TO LEARNING

Addition is easy and natural for most six-year-olds, and they produce correct answers in a variety of ways, especially when instruction focuses on their ways of thinking. However, in the past we have hindered children trying to combine numbers in their own natural, childlike way. Let us look at how we have done this. What are some of the "roadblocks" that have been thrown up to meaningful thinking about addition?

Some of the difficulties children encounter in addition center around adults' conceptions of the way children should learn and use basic addition (and subtraction) facts. In the past, for example, we have assumed that, from the beginning, children should use pencils to record or show relationships. Instead, we need to center instruction and children's activities on the development of "thinking" — on the mental processes that children use. Pencils should be used only when children need to record answers they have already discovered and internalized.

Learning the basic one hundred addition and subtraction facts has also caused many difficulties for young children. Although drill procedures have been discouraged, they still persist, along with the use of flash cards and an abundance of worksheets. Their use encourages children to work in a thoughtless, mechanical way. In such situations, instruction has focused on the production of written answers. Teachers have invented ways to practice these one hundred facts and have then corrected the worksheets. In these classrooms, children view the teacher as the one who makes the important decisions as well as the one who determines what is right and wrong.

In other classrooms recently, due in part to the influence of the New Math, teachers have emphasized the use of equation forms involving new symbols and variables that may conflict with the way the child thinks and talks.

In both of the preceding situations, adults' conceptions of how children learn have been more important than how children actually learn. This must change. Instead, we need to use the information we already have concerning the way a child produces an answer and base our instruction on that, with the help of hands-on materials. For example, we can encourage a child to use hands-on materials to show how an answer was achieved. Thus, the child may put out four cubes or markers, show the answer with fingers, or count on from a known number — first 4, then 5, 6, 7. By encouraging these strategies, we are allowing the child to internalize the procedures used to get the answer. We are helping the child develop a unique, individual, mental structuring he can use to find answers.

Another roadblock centers around the use of appropriate word problems. Some teachers introduce word problems as applications of basic facts after the facts have been learned. However, word problems should be introduced at the same time that children are learning addition facts. There are several reasons for this. First, children need to construct mathematical concepts out of their own reality. Word problems, based on daily life, help them do that. In this book we use word problems extensively in connection with the components of children's environment. Second, research (Kamii and Williamson, 1988, p. 92) has shown that first-graders can easily solve verbal problems without formal instruction. In fact, in this book, we suggest that word problems be used to introduce new mathematical concepts and operations.

A final problem involves the sequence in which addition facts are presented. In the past this has been determined by arbitrary arrangements, such as addition sums through 6, sums through 10, and extensions to include sums through 18 (9 + 9). However, research shows that this sequence should be based on the magnitude of the addends that children are developmentally able to understand and learn.

We begin our presentation of the addition process for six-year-olds by following a practical, developmentally appropriate sequence for introducing addition facts (Kamii and Williamson, 1988, p. 73). This sequence includes:

1. Adding addends to 4
2. Adding addends to 6, using 5 as an intermediate higher-order unit rather than 6
3. Adding doubles, 2 + 2, 3 + 3, to 10 + 10
4. Set partitioning of 10 and of sums already known

ADDITION WITH WHOLE NUMBERS

Adding Addends to 4

When children learned to count and write numerals 1 through 10 in kindergarten, they started with whole-class activities using a variety of hands-on materials and numeral models. For follow-up activities, children worked in pairs and in small groups to experiment with making groups or sets such as 4. At the next stage, they made sets and recorded the number using number cards. In first grade, these activities must be reviewed and extended to include work in the concept stage. In this stage, children learn to combine elements into a set, separate these elements, and discover new relationships between sets.

To begin work in the concrete operational, or concept stage, the children must learn to partition a set, such as 4, into different combinations and orally describe what they do for each combination. Children can work in pairs to play a variety of games, such as covering part of a set or hiding part of a set. Then one child must tell what part is hidden, what part is shown, and how much the two parts make together. At an appropriate time, the written number symbols are related to each combination, such as 3 and 2 make 5 or 2 and 3 make 5. Children change roles so that one child makes a combination and the other child responds and records.

A variation of this hide, or cover, activity is to place five disks (each disk has one painted side and one unpainted side) in a carton. One child shakes the carton and rolls out the five disks. The other child describes the combination shown and records the number of disks with painted side up and the number with unpainted side up, such as 2 painted and 3 unpainted make 5 disks.

Next, extend this activity by having one child cover part of a whole set and the other child record using conventional notation — for example,

$$\begin{array}{r} 2 \\ + \; 3 \\ \hline 5 \end{array} \quad \text{or} \quad \begin{array}{r} 3 \\ + \; 2 \\ \hline 5 \end{array}$$

For a weekly plan, three or four days may be taken with concept development of this type. Then on the fourth day textbooks and appropriate duplicated materials could be used. The fifth day could be special activities, such as making a calendar, working with clocks, or measuring children's growth in height.

The use of color, pictures, and manipulatives along with pages of written (symbolic) work is commendable. However, teachers must provide careful guidance for each textbook assignment, taking care not to include activities that are inappropriate for the class or for an individual. For example, pictures may be colorful and pleasing to the child but they do not constitute semiconcrete number. Number is an idea that, when understood, may be imposed on an object by a child. When a child has constructed the idea of "five," for example, we can expect him or her to produce a variety of symbols, including pictures.

To illustrate the need for teacher guidance, we want to describe a page from a 1988 first-grade textbook. Pictures on the page show two children with several colored blocks placed by a written number combination. A child reading the page is expected to see the relationship between these blocks and the number combinations.

On this same page, without the blocks, we found these combinations:

$$\begin{array}{ccc} 2 & 0 & 0 \\ +\,0 & +\,1 & +\,0 \end{array}$$

Zero has a very special place in our base ten numeration system. We pointed this out in Chapter 1 in connection with the structure of our numeration system. Gradually and meaningfully, we need to help children write and use 10. Later the child can understand that zero means no one is shown in the ones place and one ten is shown in the tens place. At this level, however, how will the child add nothing to 2, 1 to nothing, and nothing to nothing? There were 130 pages with similar activities and repetitions of zero combinations. Place value was finally started in combinations with the use of money to write 10¢.

The use of zero in worksheets at this level probably stems from the unrealistic, outmoded belief that children should learn the 100 basic addition and subtraction facts from tables and charts.

Adding Addends to 6 Using 5 as an Intermediate Higher-Order Unit

In addition, we may consider the group of numbers 1 through 5 as easy numbers and the numbers 6 through 10 as more difficult numbers to work with. If we consider 5 as an intermediate higher-order unit in this group, we can help children make new constructions out of what is already known. For example, although a child could count by ones to find the sum of 4 + 2, it would be easier to have him start with 5 and think the sum without counting beginning at 1. It is important here to get the child *to think* (to combine mentally) and to produce new knowledge in relation to what is already known. We want to encourage children to develop strategies that are meaningful and that help them discover relationships between and among new addition combinations. This type of mathematical thinking depends on conservation — the ability to focus on and to discern quantity even in the presence of distractions, such as moving forward and backward on a number line or using different combinations to name the number 5.

Adding Combinations of Doubles and Set Partitioning

Another strategy that can be helpful in addition is to have the children think in terms of doubles, such as 2 + 2, 3 + 3, up to 10 + 10. This is another example of mental regrouping and of building new concepts based on what children already know. In a combination such as 6 + 5, for instance, instead of counting to find the answer, the child could think, "Two 5s are 10 (5 + 5) and one more makes 11." When children are in the second grade, they will be able to use doubles to pick up or combine tens in adding three or four numbers in a column.

Separating an addition combination into parts (set partitioning) involves **compensation** — that is, an increase in one addend necessitates a corresponding decrease in another. This principle was used in the example 6 + 5 above. Set partitioning enables children to use a variety of self-discovered techniques in addition work and problem solving. With set partitioning, children can easily add combinations such as 8 + 6, 9 + 6, and 5 + 9 by first adding to 10: (8 + 2) + 4 = 14, (9 + 1) + 5 = 15, and 4 + (9 + 1) = 14. Some techniques will be explored in the third grade, particularly with multiplication: $15 \times 5 = (10 \times 5) + (5 \times 5) = 50 + 25 = 75$. Children will discover how to use number lines, to move forward to add and backward to separate or subtract. We want to eliminate mindless techniques and practices such as memorizing number facts without understanding them, writing answers to combinations they already know and that are repeated many times, and using arbitrary rules without thinking. Children learn to use a variety of ways to name the same number of an addend or sum. This process of set partitioning is basic to understanding place value, which we use in our base ten numeration system.

Beginning Place Values: Adding Two-digit Numbers Without Regrouping

Adding two-digit numbers should begin when children have demonstrated a sound understanding of part-whole relationships applied to groups of objects up to ten. They must also understand one-to-one correspondence and seriation in counting and writing numbers. Teachers can introduce adding a one-digit number to a two-digit number with the use of counting by 2s, 3s, 5s, and 10s — for example, 2, 4, 6, 8, 10, 12 [(10 + 2) = 12]; or 5, 10, 15 [(10 + 5) = 15]. By using 10s, teachers can introduce children to adding two two-digit numbers — 10 + 10 = 20, 15 + 10 = 25, and so on.

Teachers can also use hands-on materials such as play money or base ten blocks to help children discover the addition process in a meaningful way. For example, to help children understand how to combine tens, the teacher might ask, "If you have one dime (10¢) and you find another dime (10¢), how much money would you have?"

If a child says, "Two dimes," ask for another way to tell how much money the child has — 20 pennies or 20 cents, or two dimes make 20 cents.

Daily experiences in the classroom should provide many opportunities to extend children's understanding of and use of two-digit numbers. For example, such numbers can be illustrated by amount of lunch money for one or two days, number of school days in two months, attendance (boys and girls), cost of buying things at the store or cost of objects labeled and priced at the math center, and estimating number of objects in different groups (two bags of jellybeans).

Place value is introduced by helping children understand the use of zero to record not any and no ones, and later as a placeholder in larger numbers such as 105, to show no tens. Teachers should be able to introduce place value with examples like

$$
\begin{array}{r}
21 \\
+\ 34 \\
\hline
\end{array}
$$

The numerals are placed in the order shown so that ones and tens can be added. Children can explore the process with play money, by first showing two dimes and one cent added to three dimes and four cents, then grouping them, and finally writing the numerals.

Barratta-Lorton (1976) advocates using other bases as an important introduction to base ten place value. However, we highly recommend deferring this work until upper grades.

In the following section, we begin our discussion of subtraction. Keep in mind, however, that although, in this chapter, we present addition and subtraction separately, we do so only for convenience and organization. The two processes go together.

SUBTRACTION WITH WHOLE NUMBERS

Problems found in real-life situations should be used to help children focus on the subtraction process. The emphasis should be on getting children to think in their own way and use strategies of their choice. As in other areas, the teacher's role is to guide children in making the transition from these informal, childlike techniques to the oral language and written symbols that form the structure of the subtraction process.

Teachers can employ a number of strategies. For example, they can have children play games to make combinations of a number, such as 4. The teacher or child can use a hand or a bowl to cover sets of cubes. The other children have to think the number of cubes seen and then tell the number aloud. Then sets may be partitioned into two groups and one group covered. Children have to think first of the total number of cubes covered and in sight. This process is addition. Then they use the same process to think of the total number of cubes, take away the number uncovered, and tell the number covered. This is subtraction.

Children can also make up story problems to show their understanding of subtraction. For example, four birds were sitting on the electric wire outside our window. Three flew away. How many were left? Five children were playing in the sandbox. Two children went to wash their hands. How many children were left?

For follow-up work, children can be organized into small groups to play a memory (thinking the amount) game in subtraction.

AIM

Children learn to show and tell the number left when asked to remove or cover a certain number of markers.

MATERIALS

Number cards with numerals -1 to -8
Cards for children to count and display eight markers on

ACTIVITY

1. Each child counts out eight markers on a work card or work space.
2. One child, holding the set of cards -1 through -8, selects a card and displays the number, such as -3, and then covers the card.
3. Children remove three markers or objects and tell the number left.
4. The child showing the cards points to a child in the group and asks, "What did you do? How many do you now have?"
5. Children are encouraged to check each other's display and answers.
6. The pack of cards is passed to the next child and the activity repeated. More or fewer than eight markers may be used.

Children use their own language, gradually learning to use words such as *take away, minus* ($-$), *plus* ($+$), *the same amount,* and *equal* ($=$). Equation forms and so-called number sentences are best left for grades two and three, preferably grade three.

Some textbook writers have advocated the use of number families such as the family of eight—that is, all the numbers that can be subtracted from 8 beginning with 1. Some teachers might even impose this type of pattern or table on children rather than let them develop their own patterns. We believe such number families are inappropriate for many children.

Subtraction with Two-Digit Numbers

To teach subtraction involving two-digit numbers, teachers should use story problems, hands-on materials, money, and base ten blocks. First subtract a one-digit number from a two-digit number. Use story problems to make the work interesting. For example, the teacher could relate the following: There are 15 books on the shelf at the library center. Four children each take a book to read. How many books are left on the shelf? Or, Jim has 18¢ and spends 5¢ for a piece of bubble gum. How much money does he now have? Children can respond aloud and the teacher can record the amounts remaining.

The steps taken to show the subtraction can be demonstrated with multilink blocks.

AIM

The teacher uses multilink blocks to show subtraction of a one-digit number from a two-digit number, and the class responds orally and makes suggestions.

MATERIALS

Small table to display multilink blocks
Box of multilink blocks

ACTIVITIES

1. Present a story problem such as, "If we have 15 multilink blocks and we give 4 blocks to someone in this class, how many blocks will be left?"
2. Children may respond quickly with "Four."
3. Then say, "Some children think 4 blocks will be left. Let's see if this is the correct number of blocks."
4. With verbal help from the children, take one multilink block at a time and join them together to make a group of 10 (you may wish to make a total group of 15, and then take away 4 before using the place value involved in this lesson).
5. Place the group of 10 on the table top: "Now how many blocks are on the table?" Children say, "Ten, a group of ten."
6. Ask child to complete the set of 15 by placing 5 more multilink blocks on the table. Then ask, "How many do we have on the table?" Child says, "Fifteen." You may ask, "How do you know that?" The child then shows and tells.
7. Ask, "How many were we going to give to someone?" Children respond with "Four."
8. Children tell how many are left and then make up word problems to fit examples such as 18 − 6, 16 − 6, and so on.

Follow-up work may be given at another period during the day or the next day after a short class review of the steps needed for the work. Children could work in pairs or in small groups to play games involving putting beans into a counting dish and then taking some away, according to the number shown on a worksheet, such as 15 beans take away 5. How many beans are left? One child can count out or subtract and the other child can record, thus showing the tens and ones used in the lesson.

As we showed in the addition section, several lessons and follow-up work may be necessary before children can record abstract numbers. In this final stage, children will need hands-on materials to check answers and help make the transition to abstract numbers.

Subtracting One Two-Digit Number from Another

Teaching subtraction of one two-digit number from another will probably come near the middle of the school year for most children, much later for others. At this point, children should have learned to count to almost 100, and reviewing these larger numbers, as well as counting by 10s, will help children with the subtraction process.

Use money to introduce the operation since it provides immediate interest and connects with children's experiences. The following is a sample lesson plan.

AIM

Children use hands-on materials (play money) to show the value of two-digit numbers (40¢, 50¢), to subtract smaller two-digit numbers from larger ones, and to justify their answers.

MATERIALS

Sets of plastic money — 1¢, 5¢, 10¢
Display area (table or mat) where children can see
Objects to buy, with prices attached, such as a pen for 35¢, a pencil for 10¢, crayons for 45¢

ACTIVITY

1. Ask, "If you have 45¢ and you buy a pen for 35¢, how much money will you have left?"
2. Children help to show the money we have, 45¢: 10¢ + 10¢ + 10¢ + 10¢ + 1¢ + 1¢ + 1¢ + 1¢ + 1¢ = 45¢. Then ask, "How much money do we have? How did we make the 45¢?"
3. Place the pen on the table and ask, "How much does the pen cost?" (35¢)
4. Next ask, "Will someone show us how much money we will have left if we buy the pen for 35¢?"
5. A child takes away three dimes and the five pennies, and says, "I took away 35¢ and there is 10¢ or one dime left."
6. Ask the rest of the group, "Do all of you agree? Could you do this problem another way?" Children may use three dimes and one nickel instead of the five pennies. Using 25¢, 10¢, and 10¢ is too difficult for this age level because it would involve regrouping or making exchanges with the 25¢.
7. Several more story problems, using the objects labeled and priced, should follow. If necessary, help the children make up the word problems.
8. The follow-up lesson, with pairs or groups of children, should follow on the second day. A brief review should precede this work. Children will play buying and selling with objects labeled and priced or with duplicated sheets showing the objects and the prices. Children's roles will change: first buyer and then seller. Both children should agree that the sale and exchange of money is correct.

If worksheets and textbooks are used, teachers should be sure to include hands-on materials and a few word problems as well — for example, "You have 50¢. You buy . . . for 30¢." The subtraction examples should be varied and should extend gradually but *without any regrouping*. As with addition of two-digit numbers, place values for ones and tens can be continued and the teacher can make reference to what is being subtracted, such as tens or ones.

PROBLEM SOLVING

Six-year-old children have developed cognitively and have learned many new mathematical concepts. This combination enables them to learn and apply a variety of problem-solving techniques. The approach to solving problems with a variety of strategies must be continued and expanded. With the development of concepts for adding and subtracting two-digit numbers, children will be able to solve word problems involving combining, separating, and comparing. In addition, learning to read, to write, and to record short sentences and stories enables six-year-olds to use a variety of materials, practice sheets, and textbooks for problem-solving activities.

Reviewing our multiple approach to problem-solving work, we have included these new extensions:

1. New environmental activities include beginning to tell time to the hour and half-hour; measuring with nonstandard and standard units, with rulers marked in inches and centimeters; using shapes to define space and to cover surfaces; buying and selling using money; and starting class projects such as making a calendar, recording weather, and measuring children's height.

2. Daily math lessons include word problems appropriate for each new math concept and encouraging children to tell and demonstrate the problem-solving strategies used.

3. New problem-solving activities are identified, and solutions found in connection with class routines, such as "How many lunches will we order if three children go home?"; sharing ideas in group work and play; and using a greater variety of materials and equipment.

4. Opportunities for teacher intervention are increased due to the maturity of the children and their cognitive development. Birthday charts could be introduced and ways to record birthdays could be explored. Special holidays such as Dr. Martin Luther King's birthday provide many opportunities for problem solving, that is both mathematical and social in nature.

CALCULATORS

Children should begin to use the hand-held calculator as they progress through the mathematics program for five-year-olds. As six-year-olds, their skills should extend to include the following:

1. Showing numbers on the calculator as they are learned and sequenced, such as 10. Then responding to a request to show a number that is before 10, after 10, and so on.
2. Displaying two- and three-digit numbers such as 10, 20, 50, 100.
3. Counting by 2s, 3s, 5s by continuing to press a number, such as 2, 2, 2.
4. Working in reverse by starting with a number such as 10 and taking away 2s.

COMPUTERS

The software suggested for use with kindergarten children in Chapter 4 is appropriate for use with children four through eight years of age.

Selecting appropriate, developmental software is a responsibility shared by teachers and other personnel connected with the improvement of instruction and curriculum development. Each school district must select software to support its own math program. The following is some of the software that is available and desirable.

In Chapter 4 we referred to the National Diffusion Network (NDN). One NDN program developed and used in the South San Francisco Unified School District is *Astra's Magic Math*. This is a beginning, multisensory program that teaches math skills through sequentially developed, self-contained units designed to combine manipulation, writing, and language activities. The work is motivated by the use of Astra, a friendly character from outer space. There are 22 units, such as shapes; one-to-one matching; patterning spatial relationships; counting and writing by 1s, 2s, 5s, 10s; ordinals; and number sequencing.

Two typical programs are *1st* and *2nd Math* and *All about Time*.

1st Math: Main Menu and *2nd Math: Car Race* by Elmer Larsen, 1986. IBM PC and PC Jr. Requires IBM color-graphic card. The program is for four- and five-year-olds and has delightful characters and colorful animated programs that provide practice on early number concepts and basic operations. *Car Race* is used for practicing basic facts and has a birthday puzzle that can be personalized through a "parent option."

All about Time, 1986. Apple II, Family 64K. For very young children below grade two. Gives practice using both regular and digital clock faces. Follows a girl through an average day and relates time to a day's activities.

EVALUATION

In this book, we stress evaluation as an integral part of the teaching-learning process. Evaluation requires the consistent use of a variety of techniques and instruments. In this chapter, we used these evaluation procedures:

1. Word problems to introduce new concepts and to stimulate children's thinking. Children demonstrate their understanding of a new concept by making up their own appropriate word problems.
2. Hands-on materials to evaluate the child's thinking, understanding, and application of new math concepts. With the use of multilink blocks or base ten blocks, the teacher can make displays and ask probing evaluation questions. Or the teacher can ask the child to make the displays, perform the operations, and tell what was done. The child can then make up appropriate word problems to show an understanding as well as an application of a concept.
3. Questions. Labinowicz has made important suggestions pertaining to "asking the right questions" or "rewording questions" in terms of children's language and experiences with mathematics. He has classified questions (1985, p. 222) according to the purpose they serve in the instructional process: to gain direct information, to focus, to determine appropriateness, and to broaden the area of study (open-ended questions).
4. Paper and pencil test items to evaluate an individual's or a small group's understanding of math concepts. Numerous examples of these will be found in the chapter on evaluation.

SUMMARY

In this chapter, we outlined developmentally appropriate mathematical content and activities for six-year-old children. These outlines center around the content drawn from the structure of mathematics and from experiences relating to children's environment. The outlines are built on the math program for five-year-olds and simply extend each major topic and math concept.

The main number work for six-year-olds centers around beginning work in putting together (addition) and taking apart (subtraction), with extensions to include two-digit numbers without regrouping. We identified major roadblocks to desirable mathematical learning, such as drill, workbooks, premature use of equation forms, and reliance on adult patterns of thinking about how children learn rather than trying to elicit children's own thinking. This last enables children to construct their own meaningful math concepts and problem-solving techniques.

We presented components of children's environment, including size, time, money, patterns, and area.

We also presented lesson plans and suggestions for classroom management, along with daily and weekly developmental programs that define the essential, relevant components of the concepts to be taught, the order in which these occur, and the relationships among them.

Finally, we made suggestions for extending problem-solving strategies, evaluating math concepts, and extending the use of calculators and computers.

ACTIVITIES FOR TEACHER INSIGHT

1. The language children use to describe a mathematical operation, such as subtracting a one-digit number from a two-digit number without any regrouping, gives clues to the way they think, the strategies they use, and some information about the operation. Using multilink blocks, base ten blocks, or money, interview one or more six-year-olds to learn their vocabulary, strategies for solving a word problem, and thought processes. Then suggest the next steps the children should take in order to extend or improve in one of the operations.

2. Visit a first-grade classroom and study the way the room is arranged for whole-class instruction, small-group activities, and storage of mathematical materials and supplies. If possible, plan time to talk to the teacher about the organization used. Make a list of things you would need help on before beginning a first day of school in your classroom.

3. At the symbolic level of number, children learn to record abstractly with a numeral or numerals. List the steps you would take to prepare a six-year-old to use abstract symbols in an example such as $14 + 5$. How could you find out if the child was ready for this type of recording?

4. Problem solving is a main objective for mathematical learning. Write one or two math word problems which involve problem-solving strategies that are developmentally appropriate for six-year-old children. Justify your examples.

REFERENCES

Activity Resources. (1987). *Educational material — "I do — I understand."* Hayward, CA: Activity Resources Company.

BARATTA-LORTON, M. (1976). *Mathematics their way.* Menlo Park, CA: Addison-Wesley.

BURK, D., SNIDER, A., & SYMONDS, P. (1988). *Box it or bag it mathematics. Teacher resource book K-1.* Salem, OR: Math Learning Center.

California State Department of Education. (1985). *Mathematics framework.* Sacramento, CA: The Department Publishers.

CAWLEY, J. F. (Ed.). (1985). *Cognitive strategies and mathematics for the learning disabled.* Rockville, MD: Aspen Systems Corporation.

CREWS, D. (1978). *Freight train.* New York: Greenwillow.

DAY, B. (1983). *Early childhood education: Creative learning activities.* New York: Macmillan.

HENNINGER, M. (1987). Learning mathematics through play. *Childhood Education, 63*(3), 167–171.

KAMII, C. (1985). *Young children reinvent arithmetic.* New York: Teachers College Press, Columbia University.

KAMII, C., & DEVRIES, R. (1980). *Group games in early education.* Washington, DC: National Association for Education of Young Children.

KAMII, C., & WILLIAMSON, C. K. (1988). How children learn by handling objects. *Young Children, 42*(1), 23–26.

LABINOWICZ, E. (1985). *Learning from children.* Menlo Park, CA: Addison-Wesley.

LAVATELLI, C. S. (1978). *Piaget's theory applied to an early childhood curriculum.* Boston, MA: Center for Media Development.

McCRACKEN, J. B. (1987). *More than 1, 2, 3: The real basics of mathematics.* Washington, DC: National Association for Education of Young Children.

National Science Teachers Association. (September 1987). Outstanding science trade books for children. *Young Children, 42.*

O'HARA, E. (October 1975). Piaget: The six-year-old and modern math. *Today's Education,* pp. 32–36.

PETERSON, R. (1986). *Handbook for teachers and parents.* New York: Teachers College Press, Columbia University.

PIAGET, J. (1973). *To understand is to invent.* New York: Grossman.

PIAGET, J. (1977). Comments on mathematics education. In H. Gruber & J. Voneck (Eds.), *The essential Piaget.* New York: Basic Books.

SCHICKEDANZ, J. A. (1988). *Strategies for teaching young children.* Englewood Cliffs, NJ: Prentice-Hall.

SUYDAM, M., & REYS, R. (Eds.). (1978). *Developing computational skills.* Reston, VA: National Council of Teachers of Mathematics.

ZIEMER, M. (September 1987). Science and the early childhood curriculum: One thing leads to another. *Young Children, 42.*

CHAPTER 6

Mathematics for Seven-Year-Old Children

At each learning level, teachers must have information about each child's developmental pattern and the child's unique background of experiences, which influence his or her readiness for learning in school. We believe that for every child there is an optimum stage of development for learning mathematics — a time when the child will learn more readily than at any other time.

The main characteristics of seven-year-olds are (1) their hand and eye coordination and their ability to use large and small muscles have improved; (2) their attention span has increased and thinking is not dominated by perceptual content; (3) reading skills have developed rapidly and they can use simple picture dictionaries to discover the meaning of new words as well as how to spell many words; (4) they are becoming more independent and seek friends outside the home; and (5) they seek to make things correct and to avoid mistakes. Teachers need to adjust work periods to the seven-year-old's attention span and abilities. They must also provide many opportunities for self-expression in oral and written work, music, art, and dramatic play.

The seven-year-old child is ready for a wide variety of new learning activities. However, it is crucial that teachers carefully guide these learning activities, since concrete operational thinking is still new to the child. The work completed in first grade must be reviewed and, when necessary, revised and enriched. The development of the mathematics vocabulary and the use of language to express mathematical ideas continue to be important.

MATHEMATICS PROGRAM FOR SEVEN-YEAR-OLDS

The scope and sequence chart in this section helps to identify the mathematical program for seven-year-olds. Each major mathematical strand has been extended to show new work and to provide continuity in the program. The components of chil-

SCOPE AND SEQUENCE CHART FOR MATHEMATICS: SEVEN-YEAR-OLDS

	Scope	Sequence			
Math components	**Time (Days)**	**Whole-class activity**	**Small-group activity**	**Daily**	**Special events**
Numeration: • reading and writing numerals • place value, ones, tens, hundreds	21	X	X	X	X
Subtraction of whole numbers: • from 10 • from 18 • two-digit • three-digit	40	X	X	X	X
Addition of whole numbers: • sums through 10 • sums through 18 • two-digit • three-digit • introduce column addition • three digits high	40	X	X	X	X
Environmental components (shown in another chart)		X	X		X
Fractions: • one-half • one-fourth • one-third	8	X	X	X	X
Multiplication: • multiples of 2, 3, 4, 5 • factors in multiplying 2, 3, 4, 5 • use of zero and order property	12	X	X	X	
Problem solving: • develop new strategies • picture, list, make patterns • find data, make word problems	14	X	X	X	X
Calculators and computers: extension and use		X	X		

dren's environment are merely noted on this chart; a detailed summary of these components is given in another chart later in the chapter.

The time allotted for each major strand is suggestive. Approximately two-thirds of the school year should be devoted to mathematical components and one-third to the environmental components. Of necessity, there will be much overlapping of the two areas. Special activities that apply and extend concepts acquired during the week can be planned for Thursdays or Fridays. The environmental components will provide many opportunities for interesting and meaningful follow-up activities.

EXTENSIONS AND CLARIFICATION OF MATHEMATICS LANGUAGE

We have stressed the importance of language development for each learning level in this book. For seven-year-old children, the development of mathematics language must be further extended and clarified. The learning activities related to the components of their environment must be enlarged upon and new concepts developed as they advance in school. When children can use the mathematics vocabulary and symbols simply and accurately, they will better understand both the environmental components and the new concepts.

The teacher has two important tasks with respect to this process of language extension: (1) examining, and rebuilding when necessary, for clarity and accuracy the child's existing mathematics language; and (2) providing guidance and modeling for new vocabulary and communication of mathematical ideas.

Teachers must give careful consideration to the preparation and presentation of mathematical materials to ensure that they are at the correct language level for seven-year-old children. Materials must be readable, express ideas accurately, introduce new terms clearly, and communicate ideas simply and straightforwardly.

COMPONENTS OF CHILDREN'S ENVIRONMENT

The environmental components shown in the chart reflect the cognitive development of seven-year-olds, which enables them to explore such components in greater depth and at a greater level of mathematical difficulty. Coverage of the components continues and extends mathematical concepts and skills presented during the previous year.

In the following sections, we discuss the more important aspects of children's environment in greater detail, showing extensions and new applications, and suggesting ways to combine them with the mathematical strands.

COMPONENTS OF CHILDREN'S ENVIRONMENT

Scope	Sequence			
Components of children's environment	**Whole-class activity**	**Small-group activity**	**Daily**	**Special events**
Measurement • length, width, height • units of measuring • centimeter, meter, kilometer, perimeter • weight	X	X		X
Time • hours, quarter hour, past hour, to hour • time intervals • calendar	X	X	X	X
Money • 1¢, 5¢, 10¢, 25¢, 50¢, $1.00 • paper bills 1, 5, 10 • making simple change • adding and subtracting • buying and selling	X	X		X
Patterns • new rhythms • number patterns • similarities, differences • practical uses	X	X		X
Geometric aspects • area: surface, square units, closed curves, lines, space, plane figures • congruent figures • symmetry	X	X		X
Logical thinking • problem solving • cause and effect of changing numbers • explain answers	X	X	X	X

Size

To begin a discussion of size, teachers should review and extend the three attributes used to help six-year-olds gain some understanding of size: length, width, height. The vocabulary used to classify different objects also needs to be reviewed. These include: *bigger, smaller; more, less; longer, shorter*.

Begin by comparing pairs of objects: pen, pencil (length); table top, door (width); two children's feet (length); two dolls or two children (height); two books (width). Follow this instruction with pairs of objects, using the symbols greater than ($>$) and less than ($<$).

Seven-year-olds should now be ready to learn about measurement. Teachers can introduce the use of the 12″ ruler, yardstick, and tape measure by measuring the children's hand span, arm length, and foot length. Measurement will be by feet, inches, and half inches.

Then children can measure each other's height. Two children can measure a third, with one holding a tape measure on the floor and the other stretching the tape to touch a ruler placed on top of the third child's head. The teacher can record the child's height (in feet and inches) on a chart prepared for the class. Ditto sheets enable children to record their current height and growth over several months. The teacher has to determine how many lessons to devote to measuring children's height during the year — possibly every two months.

After measuring the height of several children, the group or class can use 1-foot rulers to measure and compare the length of a set of objects, line drawings, or rectangular shapes. The teacher can make a set of 3″ × 5″ or 5″ × 7″ work cards out of posterboard paper in two or three colors and write assignments on each card. Color indicates the level of difficulty. Then, at the mathematics center, the children, individually or in groups, can complete the activity. An assignment for an advanced level might be on a red card and could read:

Use a measuring tape to record your answers on the paper next to the card *RED 1 Measuring*.
1. How high is your table?
2. How long is your table?
3. How wide is your table?
4. How tall is one of your friends?
5. How wide is the classroom front door?
NOW, PLEASE PUT THIS CARD IN THE RED SET, 1.

Teachers should introduce metric measurement using the centimeter as the unit of measurement. Begin with a series of lessons using a ruler marked off in centimeters to measure objects in the classroom. The measurements should be approximate — millimeters should not be used and the two systems of measurement should not be compared. Answers, for example, might indicate that the pencil is about _____ centimeters long, the eraser is about _____ centimeters long, and the desktop is about _____ centimeters long. Follow-up work should have the children measuring lines and shapes to the exact number of centimeters. The teacher can premeasure lines, shapes, and objects so that children can measure successfully.

Weight

As the children go beyond using the words *heavier* and *lighter* to using standard units of measure, weight measurement becomes more accurate. Calibrated scales should be introduced to provide greater accuracy. Pounds and ounces as well as kilograms are introduced as new vocabulary. A variety of objects can be weighed and compared. Teachers should select objects whose weight is in even numbers or in simple fractional parts. When weighing objects, children of this age become confused by fractions and confused when ounces must be changed to pounds.

When addition and subtraction skills are more developed — at the end of the year — more complex weights can be used in planned activities.

Time

Review the lessons on time prepared for six-year-olds. Then, after children understand that the clock face is divided into half-hour and quarter-hour segments, present a series of lessons on telling time to the hour, the half hour, and the quarter hour. The large Judy Clock, with movable hands and visible, functioning gears, is excellent for demonstration and for pupil participation in telling time intervals.

For follow-up activities, teachers can use individual $3\frac{1}{2}'' \times 3\frac{1}{2}''$ cardboard dials, or they can buy rubber stamps of circles about $2''$ in diameter to use as clock faces. Both can be used to mark and teach divisions as small as five minutes. Also, duplicated clock faces help children concentrate on learning to tell time rather than on trying to place the numerals at exact points on the clock face.

The concepts of "past the hour" and "to the hour" have to be presented gradually, after children have mastered telling time to the hour and half hour. The reading and writing of time words should also be introduced gradually.

five to   five past   half past

Time can be discussed in connection with particular events, such as different class activities, lunch, and going home. Introduce the concept of length of time (for a particular event or activity) along with time schedules. Ask children to "watch the time," be "ready for clean-up," put materials away and be "ready for lunch"; or talk about the time taken to clear the room or school for a fire drill.

At home, children will be exposed to electric digital-display clocks. These popular clocks are found on radios, microwave ovens, VCR equipment, and the dashboards of recent cars. On these clocks, the hour and the minutes past the hour are both identified in numerals. For example, 8:50 is read as 8 hours and 50 minutes.

Although many seven-year-olds will not be able to understand this type of clock, or what it means to tell time to the minute, teachers should introduce it to them. If possible, have a digital-display clock in the classroom, and use it along with the regular circular-faced clock after children understand telling time to the hour and half hour. Compare the clocks on the hour or half hour, and explain that both show the same time. For example,

8 o'clock   8 o'clock and 10:30   10:30

Extend the discussion to quarter hours—quarter past or before the hour—if children understand one-fourth.

Large intervals of time such as weeks, months, seasons, holidays, and school years provide learning opportunities that are meaningful and enjoyable for children. Teachers can use their creativity to devise ways to help children anticipate and participate in important events centering on some aspect of time. For example, one teacher has a chart with pegs, and on it she hangs cards with the names of the days of the week as they occur; this helps children learn the order of the days of the week. Days of the

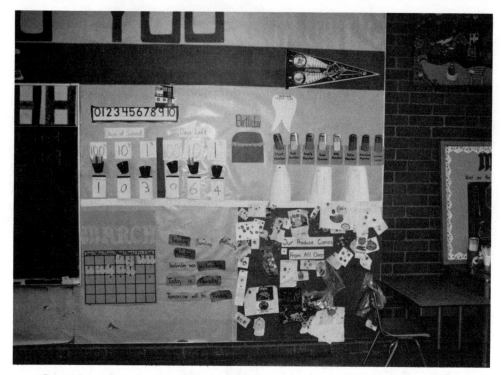

Straws in pockets show number of school days, visually demonstrating the difficult concept of place value.

month can be handled in the same way to help children learn numerical sequence. A chart can also be made to show weather conditions and, for older children, graphs can show the number of days of cloudy, sunny, or wet weather.

Another teacher has children wash and save milk straws, which they use to record days of the school year. The straws are stored in containers labeled to show days 1 to 9, bundles of 10s to show periods of ten days, and bundles of ten 10s to show 100 days. The teacher develops interesting story problems at appropriate intervals, such as "How many more days of school?" "How many days until Christmas?" Children build bundles of tens and hundreds and show how the total number is written, using correct place values.

Money

Seven-year-old children are ready to use money to make purchases at the market or at the school store. They have developed addition and subtraction skills and understand the use of place value in showing cents, such as 25¢ is the same as $.25.

Some schools have a bank in which children can keep reserves for lunches and supplies, as well as protect money brought to school. Numerous lessons can be developed around savings accounts, lunch money, and buying at the school store.

The emphasis at this learning level should be on simple buying and making money exchanges without regrouping. For example, using charts or displays that show a variety of articles priced from 5¢ to 25¢ children can decide what they can purchase with 25¢ or 50¢.

Work cards can be prepared for individual and group practice.

Money Card I. At the store	USE LINED PAPER FOR YOUR ANSWERS
25¢ 10¢ 50¢	What can you buy for 50¢?
5¢ 25¢	What can you buy for $1.00?
50¢ 10¢ 15¢	Can you buy three things for 30¢?
10¢ 10¢ 10¢	What can you buy for 25¢?

PUT THIS CARD BACK IN THE MONEY BOX.

Money Card II	USE LINED PAPER FOR YOUR ANSWERS
50¢ 25¢ 10¢	With the coins shown on the left, how many ways can you make:
10¢ 10¢ 25¢	
50¢ 25¢ 5¢ 10¢	1. 50¢ 2. 25¢
10¢ 5¢ 5¢ 25¢	3. 20¢ 4. 35¢
10¢ 5¢ 10¢ 5¢	5. 75¢ 6. $1.00

PUT THIS CARD BACK IN THE MONEY BOX.

Story problems and activities involving buying at the market or school store can be placed on the work cards.

At this level, children can be introduced to bank notes, and do some computation with notes that are multiples of ten, such as $10.00, $20.00, $50.00, and $100.00. Reading and writing these values should be within their understanding of place value. Teachers can introduce the decimal point to show the separation of dollars and cents without going into the place value of decimal fractions. In the same way, they can present putting together and taking apart without regrouping. The following are some examples.

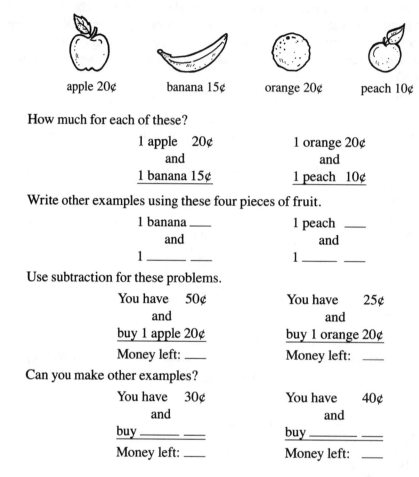

apple 20¢   banana 15¢   orange 20¢   peach 10¢

How much for each of these?

1 apple	20¢		1 orange	20¢
and			and	
1 banana	15¢		1 peach	10¢

Write other examples using these four pieces of fruit.

1 banana ___		1 peach ___
and		and
1 ___ ___		1 ___ ___

Use subtraction for these problems.

You have	50¢		You have	25¢
and			and	
buy 1 apple	20¢		buy 1 orange	20¢
Money left: ___			Money left: ___	

Can you make other examples?

You have	30¢		You have	40¢
and			and	
buy ___ ___			buy ___ ___	
Money left: ___			Money left: ___	

Patterns

For seven-year-olds, work with patterns involves searching for new ways to use patterns in their everyday activities. Begin by reviewing patterns the children discovered during their last year in school; then extend these by adding new elements. For example, with a known fingerplay pattern of snap, clap; snap, clap; snap, snap, clap, clap, ask "What are the elements (parts)? How are they different?" Next ask, "How can the pattern be repeated and then extended?" To repeat, the child may do snap, clap; snap, clap; snap, snap, clap, clap; and then go back to snap, clap, and so on. To extend the pattern, the child can do several rhythms following the last snap, snap, clap, clap—for example, snap, snap, snap, clap, snap, snap, snap, clap, then two quick snap, snaps to stop. See Baratta-Lorton (1976, pp. 35f.) for ideas for dot, block, bead, and border patterns.

Concrete materials are also good for showing patterns. For example, a child can build a shape with ten blocks:

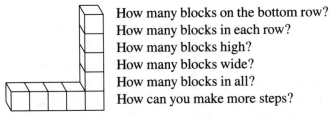

How many blocks on the bottom row?
How many blocks in each row?
How many blocks high?
How many blocks wide?
How many blocks in all?
How can you make more steps?

The number patterns first used with six-year-olds are still useful for this age group. Show and discuss with the children, for example, the hundred square:

$$
\begin{array}{l}
1, 2, 3, 4, 5, 6, 7, 8, 9, 10 \\
11, 12 \ldots \ldots \ldots 20 \\
\vdots \qquad\qquad\qquad \vdots \\
91 \ldots \ldots \ldots 100
\end{array}
$$

The missing number square and odd and even squares:

1_____ , 3_____

11_____ , 13_____ , _____

21_____ , _____ , _____ 28

Continue to look for similarities, differences, repetitions, and practical uses of patterns with the children.

Area

Review the concepts of surface, texture, and covering a surface and extend these by relating them to patterns and measuring units. Establish a *standard unit* that is identified by size (for example, 2″ × 2″ square blocks) rather than by formal unit of measurement (inches, feet). Seven-year-olds can understand such units since they are familiar with the use of blocks or counters to cover a defined surface as well as to show a particular pattern. Children can count the number of squares needed to cover a surface. They can also tell how many rows it takes to do so and the number of squares in each row.

To show children how standard units are used to cover large areas such as floors, tables, or work areas in the kitchen, use pieces of linoleum, rug, and wallpaper. Cut these into 6″, 12″, and 36″ squares.

Continue working on accurate vocabulary and language. Help children see that the unit used to cover a surface, such as colored tile squares, usually has a pattern and that units may be rearranged into larger, different patterns.

Logic

Following the sequence of work relating to logic in the last two chapters we can begin to see the importance of properties such as shape, color, size, and thickness that enable a child to classify, identify, explore similarities and differences, and see part-whole relationships. These are important aspects of deductive reasoning and logical thinking.

For logical thinking to take place, children must be able to derive information from an object, a group of objects, or some problem in the environment and then transform that information. The following example is appropriate for seven-year-olds:

1. Have the children identify one property — size, color, shape, and so on — of an object such as a cube. Then have them match or make groups of cubes based on more than one property.

2. Have them think of two properties and look for objects with those properties to make a group or set. For example, they can think *wooden and red*. Then they can find blocks with these two properties and group them together. The children can then say, "We have a group of blocks that are all wooden and red."

3. Vary the criterion for grouping. For example, one child selects boys wearing something red. The next child might group others in the class by color of hair and eyes.

4. Begin with a whole group of blocks, cubes, or other objects, and have the children make subgroups or subclasses. For example, have them group all that are red, all that are square. Their ability to do this is important to their understanding the whole-part relationship, which is needed in addition and subtraction.

By accepting a variety of "ways to think" and by asking children to explain why they think or believe a certain way, the teacher is encouraging deductive reasoning and logical thinking, as well as helping children make important progress in mathematical learning.

NUMBER

The number work for seven-year-olds is built on the foundation established during the previous year. The work is extended according to the children's development pattern.

Each strand related to children's environment and the essentials of modern mathematics is included.

For each area of number work at this level, teachers should provide hands-on materials, integrate problem solving, and encourage pupil self-activity in order to ensure children's understanding of each new concept and skill. Piaget (1964, pp. 8f.) summarizes this approach:

> To know an object, to know an event is not simply to look at it and make a mental copy, or image of it. To know is to modify, to transform the object, and to understand how the object is constructed. An operation is thus the essence of knowledge; it is an interiorized action which modifies the object of knowledge.

Numeration

At this level, we continue and extend the work of reading and writing numerals by introducing place value and having the children apply the concept in order to increase numeral size. For seven-year-olds, the work is confined primarily to two- and three-digit numbers.

Children can easily build numbers up to 100 based on their knowledge of place value by using concrete materials (base ten components and one hundred number tiles). For reference and for continued work in this area, teachers should acquire place-value charts and base ten blocks.

To help children understand place value, teachers can follow these steps:

1. Use the concrete. Show the
   number 111 using base ten blocks.

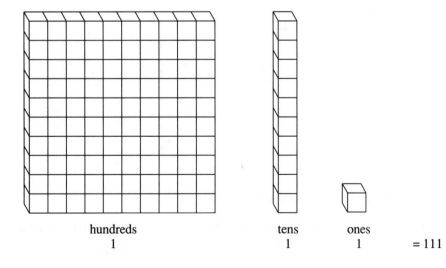

| hundreds | tens | ones | |
| 1 | 1 | 1 | = 111 |

2. Show the same number by drawing
   pictures of squares.

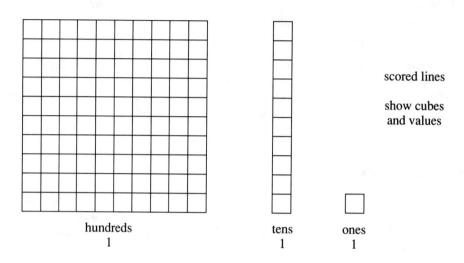

scored lines

show cubes
and values

hundreds
1

tens
1

ones
1

3. Draw the hundreds, tens, and ones pictures again but without filling in all the
   small squares. These shapes will help children concentrate on understanding
   place value.

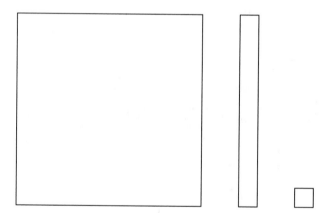

4. Use numerals to write the abstract form: 111.

To build beyond 111, children can select additional concrete materials, such as:

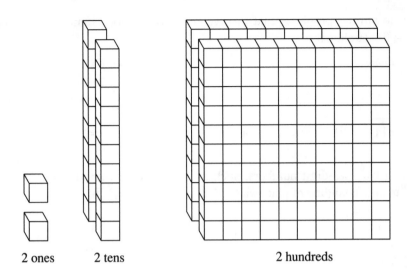

| 2 ones | 2 tens | 2 hundreds |

to add to 111. Then, following the steps just given, they will reach the number 222 and add it to 111:

$$
\begin{array}{r}
111 \\
+\ 222 \\
\hline
333
\end{array}
$$

With the extension of place value from tens to hundreds, seven-year-olds are ready to explore many new number concepts involving the use of money and consumer-oriented mathematics.

Addition of Whole Numbers

Addition for seven-year-olds involves a continuation of the work completed in first grade. Although some children will still be learning addition combinations through 9 + 9, the teacher can extend addition operations to include adding a one-digit and a two-digit number, using easy combinations such as 14 + 4. To do this new work, children must understand place value. A child may add 14 + 4 in one mental operation, thinking "14 + 4 is 18." Have children demonstrate their understanding of place value using base ten blocks or play money. After doing 14 + 4 = 18, children can move on to similar problems that involve regrouping. For example, they can add $14 + 7 = 21$, as shown:

Tens	Ones		Tens	Ones	
			1		(move 10 ones to tens place;
1	4	$\longrightarrow$	1	4	becomes 1 ten)
+	7		+	7	
	11 $= 10 + 1$ (regroup ones)		2	1̶1̶ $= 10 + 1$	
				1	

Adding two two-digit numbers, such as $15¢ + 13¢$, without regrouping, also requires an understanding of place value:

Tens	Ones
1	5¢
+ 1	3¢
2	8¢

Some children will use their own strategies for finding the sum, such as $15¢ + 13¢ = (10¢ + 10¢) + (5¢ + 3¢)$, with the sum $20¢ + 8¢ = 28¢$. Or they may think $15 + 10 + 3 = 25 + 3 = 28$.

Expanded notation may help children better understand place value. For example:

		Tens		Ones			
25		20	+	5			25
+ 14	=	10	+	4	=		+ 14
		30	+	9	= 39		39

The use of regrouping in the addition of two two-digit numbers requires cognitive development usually found in eight-year-olds, although some seven-year-old children will also have reached this level, especially the older seven-year-olds — those who, due to entrance requirements for kindergarten were $6\frac{1}{2}$, when they entered school. Introduce this regrouping process during the last part of the school year, after children have demonstrated both an understanding of place value and an ability to make exchanges with money, such as $16¢ =$ one dime, one nickel, and one penny or $10¢$ and $6¢$. The following is an example of a lesson teachers can use to introduce regrouping with two two-digit numbers.

AIM

Children give oral responses and use play money to show their understanding of regrouping in the addition of two two-digit numbers.

MATERIALS

Display table for play money
Place-value chart showing tens and ones
Apple and orange with price tags attached

ACTIVITY

1. Show two objects: an apple with a price tag showing 16¢ and an orange tagged at 25¢. "If you buy these two pieces of fruit, how much money would you need to give the clerk?"
2. Some children will probably say 41¢. Ask, "How did you get this amount?" or "Let's see if 41¢ is the correct amount to give to the clerk."
3. Use the play money to show 16¢ for the apple and have children agree that the amount shown is correct. Then show 25¢ for the orange and have them agree.
4. Arrange the money as follows:

Tens	Ones		Tens	Ones			
			X				
X +	000000 = 16¢		X	000000	0	Regroup to	16¢
X X +	00000 = 25¢		X X	00000		get 1 ten	+ 25¢
			4		1	and 1 one	41¢

Other objects can be used in the problem, such as a ball for 58¢ and a candy bar for 35¢. How much for both?

5. Follow-up lessons should come later in the day or on another day. First give a brief review. Then have children work in small groups with play money and pictures of articles to buy, with the prices marked. Encourage children to make up word problems in addition to doing the ones shown on the worksheets.

Although **column** addition is better suited to third-grade children, it is commonly introduced in second-grade textbooks, in problems three digits high, such as:

$$
\begin{array}{r}
3¢ \\
4¢ \\
+\ 2¢ \\
\hline
\end{array}
\quad \text{or} \quad
\begin{array}{r}
3 \text{ bounces and catch} \\
4 \text{ bounces and catch} \\
+\ 2 \text{ bounces and catch} \\
\hline
\end{array}
$$

New skills are involved in column addition. For example, in the money problem, adding from the bottom, the child must think "2 + 4 are 6," and then must remember the 6 and think "6 + 3 are 9." This new operation requires teachers to provide considerable practice with mental addition: "Listen to the numbers I give—2, add 3 (pause), add 4. What did you get? When I said, '2, add 3,' what did you think?" Children who cannot hold the *unseen number* in their minds will probably count the addends with their fingers or make dots with a pencil as they count. This mental operation is used repeatedly in column addition.

When children understand place value and can add two two-digit numbers, teachers can extend column addition to three two-digit numbers — for example,

$$
\begin{array}{r}
15\cent \\
21\cent \\
+\ \ 25\cent \\
\hline
\end{array}
$$

Children at this age begin to use three fundamental postulates (assumptions) that apply to the addition and multiplication of whole numbers. For teacher clarification, we state them here and show how they apply to addition, and then, in Chapter 7, we apply them to multiplication.

The commutative law	$a + b = b + a$
The associative law	$(a + b) + c = a + (b + c)$
The law of closure	For every pair of numbers, a and b, there exists a unique number $(a + b)$ that is called the sum of a and b.

For the example

$$
\begin{array}{r}
4 \\
3 \\
+\ \ 2 \\
\hline
\end{array}
$$

the child can think $2 + 3 = 5$ or $3 + 2 = 5$ (the commutative law). Then she can add up: $(3 + 2)$ [or $(2 + 3)$] $+ 4 = 9$, or she can start at the top and add down: $(4 + 3) + 2 = 9$ (the associative law).

Subtraction of Whole Numbers

Seven-year-old children have had numerous opportunities to learn and use basic subtraction facts in connection with addition facts — for example, $9 + 9 = 18$ and $18 - 9 = 9$. However, many children will not have memorized these basic facts. We recommend using a variety of gamelike activities and hands-on materials connected with worksheets to help children think about all the basic subtraction facts and build a foundation for remembering them. Teachers can reinforce the learning of basic facts by introducing "mental math games" or other related brief activities to fill in free time before or after a lesson.

Games such as the following can go for as long or as short a period of time as there is available. Have children work in pairs using a shaker and a group of 12 disks. One child uses the shaker and disks while the other says and then records the answers. The children exchange roles after an agreed upon number of shakes.

The child with the shaker decides how many disks to subtract from 12 after each shake or follows a list that tells him how many disks (1 through 11) to subtract. For example, the child shakes out the 12 disks onto a mat and takes away 7. The other child then responds, "7 from 12 leaves 5," and writes

$$
\begin{array}{r}
12 \\
-7 \\
\hline
5
\end{array}
$$

A variation on this uses a set of cards along with a shaker and 12 beans to tell which number is to be subtracted from 12. On one side of the cards is the number to subtract (-8, for example), and on the other side is the entire problem:

$$
\begin{array}{r}
12 \\
-8 \\
\hline
4
\end{array}
$$

Again the children can play the game in pairs. The child with the shaker shows a card — for example, -5 — then rolls the beans onto a mat, and takes away five beans. The other child then says, "$12 - 5 = 7$" and writes the problem. After a while, the children change roles. They may remove cards for the facts they know and then concentrate on unknown facts. Children can play this game at their seats or at a center after finishing their other work.

Worksheets for individual practice should include pictures and word problems, and should call for the use of hands-on materials. These will help children who are having difficulty learning the basic subtraction facts.

Before extending subtraction operations to include subtracting a two-digit number from a two-digit number without regrouping, teachers must ensure that children understand place value and are able to compare and relate the operation to addition in order to check answers — the taking apart and putting together process. The following example illustrates this: If a child has 35 blocks and gives 12 blocks to a friend, how many blocks are left? The problem can be laid out using multilink blocks:

Tens	Ones		Tens	Ones
3	5		XXX	00000
− 1	2		− X	00
2	3		XX	000

In expanded notation, the problem is:

$$
\begin{array}{rcl}
35 &=& 30 + 5 \\
- \quad 12 &=& 10 + 2 \\
\hline
&& 20 + 3 \;=\; 23
\end{array}
$$

A variation is:

$$
\begin{array}{r}
35 \quad \text{take away 2 ones} \\
- \quad 12 \\
\hline
3
\end{array}
$$

$$
\begin{array}{r}
- \quad 20 \\
\hline
23 \quad \text{take away 1 ten}
\end{array}
$$

This last example shows the standard algorithm:

$$
\begin{array}{r}
35 \\
- \quad 12 \\
\hline
23
\end{array}
$$

Subtracting a two-digit number from a larger two-digit number with regrouping is difficult for many seven-year-olds. We recommend not introducing this work until the last part of the second grade, and then providing numerous applications of it in the third grade. An introductory lesson involving two two-digit numbers follows.

AIM

Children use play money to show how to regroup a two-digit number in subtraction and analyze results to check the answer.

MATERIALS

Play money — 10¢, 5¢, 1¢ pieces — to make exchanges
Display table or area
Classroom materials with price tags attached, such as scissors 55¢, crayons 35¢, pencil 15¢, pen 37¢, and so on
Place-value chart for tens and ones

ACTIVITY

1. Make up a word problem: "On the table are things we use in our classroom with prices marked on them. If you have 44¢ and you buy a box of crayons for 35¢, how much money would you have left?"
2. Use the chart to show

	Tens	Ones	
Money we have:	XXXX	0000	44¢
Money we spend:	XXX	00000	35¢

3. Ask, "How can we begin to subtract the ones?" There are several answers. Then show the regrouping so that XXXX + 0000 becomes XXX + X0000 or 14 ones:

Tens	Ones		Tens	Ones			
4	4	(44¢)	XXX +	0000000	14 ones		44¢
		=		0000000			
− 3	5	(35¢)	−XXX +	00000	−	5 ones	− 35¢
				9			9¢

4. Next ask, "How can we tell if this is the correct answer?" There are a variety of answers, such as 9 + 35 = 44 or 30 + 5 + 9 = 44.
5. Finally say, "How would a store clerk give you change if you bought 35¢ worth of candy and gave him 44¢? Yes, he would count out the change like this — 35¢, gives you a nickel and says 40¢, then gives you four pennies and says 44¢. You would have in your hand a nickel and four cents."
6. Children make up other word problems, such as:

	Tens	Ones		Tens	Ones
You have 50¢:	5	0¢	You have 85¢:	8	5¢
You buy something for 18¢:	− 1	8¢	You buy something for 37¢:	− 3	7¢
You have left:	___	___	You have left:	___	___

Teachers should do follow-up work with small groups at another time. Be sure worksheets have spaces for children to show how much money they have, how much they spend, and how much they have left. Play money should be available to help with regrouping.

Some textbooks at this level present subtracting three-digit numbers with and without regrouping. However, we recommend that this subject only be introduced — and only at the end of the year. We leave examples of this type of work for Chapter 7 and the eight-year-olds.

Multiplication of Whole Numbers

Multiplication is introduced at this age level because of its relationship to addition. Multiplication is based on addition. In addition, the addends may be unequal, as in 2 + 4 + 5 = 11. In multiplication, the addends must be equal. For example, 3 × 2 means 3 twos. The reverse fact 2 × 3 means 2 threes:

$$
\begin{array}{cc}
2 & 2 \\
 & 2 \\
= & 2 \\
\times\ 3 & 2 \\
\hline
6 & 6
\end{array}
$$

Since multiplication is based on addition, and addition is based on counting, it follows that multiplication is based indirectly on counting.

Multiplication and addition are direct processes (they put things together) while division and subtraction are inverse processes (they take things apart). We showed subtraction as the inverse of addition earlier in this chapter. Division as the inverse of multiplication is discussed in Chapter 7.

Multiplication work for seven-year-olds includes learning the facts through 5 × 5 = 25.

Although there are three interpretations of multiplication (repeated addition of equivalent sets, the ratio comparison of number pairs, and the Cartesian product of two sets), only repeated addition will be developed for this age group.

We begin multiplication with a familiar activity: the repeated addition of equivalent sets. This is an extension of addition concepts. Since addition and multiplication are combining operations, teachers can introduce the work in this way. Begin with a whole-class lesson. With the use of unifix cubes, make an array such as:

$$X \ X \ X$$
$$X \ X \ X$$
$$X \ X \ X$$
$$X \ X \ X$$

Ask the children to identify the number of stacks (three) and the number of blocks in each (four). "How many stacks are threre?" Children answer, "Three." "How many blocks are in each?" "Four." "How many blocks are there in all?" "Twelve." "Yes, there are three stacks with four blocks in each. We can write":

$$4 + 4 + 4 = 12 \qquad \text{and} \qquad \begin{array}{r} 4 \\ \times \ 3 \\ \hline 12 \end{array}$$

"Now let's arrange these 12 blocks in another order, such as:

$$X \ X \ X \ X$$
$$X \ X \ X \ X$$
$$X \ X \ X \ X$$

"How many stacks are there?" "There are four." "How many blocks are in each?" "Three." "How many blocks are there in all? "Twelve."

$$3 + 3 + 3 + 3 = 12 \quad \text{and} \quad \begin{array}{r} 3 \\ \times \quad 4 \\ \hline 12 \end{array}$$

Guide the children to learn that one number (factor) names the number of groups or sets and that the second number (factor) names the members in each group. The product is the set that results from the combining action. We state the multiplier first — for example,

$$3 \times 4 = 12 \quad \text{or} \quad \begin{array}{r} 4 \\ \times \quad 3 \\ \hline 12 \end{array}$$

To show the relationships between addition and multiplication, teachers can set up this type of arrangement:

		Add		*Multiply*	
2 sets of 5: XXXXX XXXXX	$5 + 5$		5	2×5	5
3 sets of 2			$\underline{+ \quad 5}$		$\underline{\times \quad 2}$
4 sets of 3			10		10
5 sets of 3					

PROPERTIES (LAWS OR PRINCIPLES) APPLYING TO MULTIPLICATION

Five properties, or laws, apply to the multiplication operation: (1) closure, (2) the identity element, (3) the commutative law, (4) the associative law, and (5) the distributive law. The first three laws apply to multiplication at this learning level. The last two are used in third- and fourth-grade multiplication.

■ CLOSURE The product of two natural numbers is a natural number. This is the law of closure for multiplication. Thus, $2 \times 3 = 6$. The product 6 is a natural number. We say that the set of natural numbers is closed with respect to multiplication. This law applies to addition as well: The sum of two natural numbers is a natural number.

■ IDENTITY ELEMENT The product of any whole number and 1 is that whole number ($2 \times 1 = 2$, $10 \times 1 = 10$, and so on) and the product of 1 and any whole number is that whole number ($1 \times 3 = 3$, $1 \times 25 = 25$, $1 \times 100 = 100$, and so on).

■ COMMUTATIVE LAW The product of two numbers is the same regardless of the order in which the numbers are given: $a \times b = b \times a$, or $2 \times 5 = 10$ and $5 \times 2 =$

10. The facts are different (that is, the order *does* determine which is the multiplier and which the multiplicand), but the product is the same.

RATIONALIZING THE USE OF ZERO IN MULTIPLICATION

Most textbooks for this age group show multiplication facts involving zero, such as $1 \times 0 = 0$, $5 \times 0 = 0$, $0 \times 0 = 0$, $0 \times 4 = 0$. We discussed the use of zero in connection with addition facts. But we need to rationalize the use of zero.

Any number times zero is zero. This may be explained by interpreting multiplication as cumulative addition. For example, $6 \times 0 = 0$ can be explained by saying that it means six zeros, or $6 \times 0 = 0 + 0 + 0 + 0 + 0 + 0$. An individual's score throwing darts at a target and missing each time could be recorded as six tries without any hits, or $6 \times 0 = 0$.

Rationalizing the fact $0 \times 6 = 0$, we say that 0×6 means not any sixes, which is zero. The commutative law may be used thus: $0 \times 6 = 6 \times 0$; since $6 \times 0 = 0$, then $0 \times 6 = 0$.

Zero facts should be left out of worksheets, however, unless they are part of specific applications. In the third grade, there will be ample opportunity for children to use zero in multiplication work, such as in 2×105, 3×100, or 20×40. In these cases, zero is used as a placeholder.

LEARNING MULTIPLICATION FACTS THROUGH 5 × 5

We recommend the use of hands-on materials to help children beginning to learn multiplication facts. Have them master the 2s before they move on to the facts for 3s, and so on.

To introduce multiplication facts, begin with a whole-class lesson to help children discover the multiplication facts for the 2s. Use multilink cubes, attaching them in sets of 2. After children have made several sets of these, have them show two sets of two:

$$\begin{array}{r} 2 \\ \times\ 2 \\ \hline \end{array}$$

Record $2 + 2 = 4$ and $2 \times 2 = 4$:

$$\begin{array}{r} 2 \\ \times\ 2 \\ \hline 4 \end{array}$$

Move to the next set (3×2). After children make this set, have them tell what they have done. For example, they may say, "We made three groups of two, and that makes 6." Then ask, "Can you help me write this on the chalkboard?" As before, write $2 + 2 + 2 = 6$ and $3 \times 2 = 6$:

$$\begin{array}{r} 2 \\ \times\ 3 \\ \hline 6 \end{array}$$

Continue this procedure through four 2s and five 2s.

At another time, have children work in pairs with multilinks to make and record all four of these 2s facts themselves: 2×2, 2×3, 2×4, and 2×5. Teachers may choose to have children work on only two of the four facts at a time, including applications for them. The identity element applies to the 1s in each set of facts, and children quickly learn $1 \times$ after their introduction to multiplication with $2 \times$.

These same procedures may be used for the 3s, 4s, and 5s. However, for each set relate the new facts to the known facts. For example, when working on the 3s, bring to the children's attention that they have already learned $2 \times 3 = 6$ and now they are learning the other part of the combination: $3 \times 2 = 6$ (the commutative law). For the 4s, the new facts are 4×4 and 4×5, and for the 5s, the new fact is 5×5. The other facts have already been learned. To summarize, the new facts for each group are:

3s: 3×3
3×4
3×5
4s: 4×4
4×5
5s: 5×5

We do not recommend requiring children to write multiplication tables. Children spend too much time on repeating and writing facts they already know. After they have learned all the new facts, children can organize them into table or chart form to discover relationships such as the following:

x	1	2	3	4	5
1					
2					
3					
4					
5					

Fill in this chart; then find the correct number fact for each of the groups named below.

1. 5 rows, 5 squares each row = $5 \times 5 = 25$
2. 5 rows, 3 squares each row = $5 \times 3 =$
3. 1 row, 5 squares each row =
4. 3 rows, 5 squares each row =
5. 5 rows, 1 square each row =
6. 5 rows, 2 squares each row =
7. 2 rows, 5 squares each row =
8. 4 rows, 5 squares each row =
9. 5 rows, 1 square each row =
10. 5 rows, 4 squares each row =

Children can use a calendar in the same way to show:

Days   *Weeks*
5 days of school $=$ $1 \times 5 = 2$
5 days of school $=$ $2 \times \_ =$
5 days of school $=$ $3 \times \_ =$
5 days of school $=$ $4 \times \_ =$
Total weeks $\times$ days
    ___ $\times$ ___

Fractions

Seven-year-olds use fractions in their daily activities at home and at school. Teachers should concentrate on these activities, which include telling time to the half hour, measuring, and cutting pies or cakes, to help children learn about fractions appropriate for their development.

Children should learn the meaning of *common fractions* — those fractions commonly used in daily life: $\frac{1}{2}$, $\frac{1}{4}$, and $\frac{1}{3}$. Begin by teaching that one whole can be cut or broken into several parts, but ensure that the parts are equal. The word *fraction* (Latin, *frangere*) means to break, or a small part. The symbol $\frac{1}{2}$ means one of two parts, or one part of a whole cut into two equal parts. The 2 tells the number of cuts or pieces, and the 1 tells how many parts are being used.

At first, children can use the words *top part* and *bottom part* to identify specific parts of the fraction. Then teachers should introduce the words *numerator* (the number of parts being used) and *denominator* (the number of pieces into which the whole is divided).

Help children use fractions in connection with numerous school activities. They should learn to mark off parts of a clock face into halves ($\frac{1}{2}$) and fourths ($\frac{1}{4}$) in order to tell time. They use one cup, one-half cup, and one-fourth cup measures to measure sand or liquid. In linear measurement, using standard units on a ruler, they discover how to measure to the nearest inch, then to the nearest half-inch, and finally to use the quarter-inch.

Emphasize identifying and using fractions rather than having children make and color fractional parts of a variety of figures. Children at this level will not be able to cut a circle into three equal parts. In general, they have considerable difficulty making fractional parts that are equal.

Seven-year-olds should be introduced to common fractions, helped to understand the meaning of a fraction, and be given many opportunities to use fractions in a variety of daily activities.

PROBLEM SOLVING

In terms of problem solving, we continue with the multiple approach introduced in preceding chapters, and extend it for seven-year-old children.

1. *Environmental activities.* Seven-year-olds should be able to tell time to the hour, half hour, and quarter hour and allot time intervals for their daily activities. Problem solving is involved in answering questions such as "How much time is needed? Did we need more time or better organization? How many school days are in this month?"

   For size and weight problems, children can use a balance beam to make estimates (heavier, lighter, or the same as). They can compare size with weight.

   For problems involving quantity of liquids, children can measure amounts such as cup, pint, quart, and gallon. For linear measurement involving growth patterns, they can record and compare heights over given periods of time.

   Problems involving money have either one step or two steps: Children can find out how much two items would cost (addition); or they can start with a certain amount, spend part of it on two items (addition), and then find the amount left (subtraction).

2. *Daily lessons.* Word problems are used to extend addition and subtraction concepts and to show the meaning of place value.

   The teacher plays an important role in creating an environment that encourages problem solving in daily work. Teachers need to help children select their own techniques with which to combine, separate, and compare the data needed to solve a problem.

3. *Daily activities.* There are many opportunities for problem solving at this age level. Children can find the pages used in reading (sequence and number); plan how to use new materials; organize groups for playground activities; establish a new science center; collect lunch money; order supplies for a snack or for lunch; and collect and record money for savings or school projects. For each activity, children need to first plan how to solve the problem. The teacher must guide this process and strive to promote higher-order thinking skills.

4. *Teacher intervention.* Teacher intervention means helping children at a crucial, "just right" time by asking a question or exploring alternative solutions. It also means introducing creative projects and activities.

In her book *Counting and Measuring,* Eileen Churchill (1961) reported on a teacher who provided an environment where children could operate at their own level and find experiences to challenge their interests. The seven-year-olds in this class put together a small book in which they recorded interesting mathematical discoveries. The following are excerpts from the book:

The smallest thing I know is one small tuft of moss. The sea is the largest thing I know.

Michael is the tallest boy in our class. Margaret is the tallest girl in the class. Jacqueline is the smallest girl in our class. I am tall but I am not as tall as Margaret.

On Saturday, April 21st, they put the clocks forward (one) hour.

The narrowest thing I know is a piece of cotton.

CALCULATORS

Extensions in using the calculator at this level should be based on whatever new math concepts and skills the children have learned. The calculator should help children increase the speed and accuracy with which they do each basic operation. For example, children can use calculators to:

1. Read and write numerals and increase or decrease a number by adding one number at a time or subtracting one number at a time
2. Explore and practice basic addition and subtraction facts
3. Estimate and check answers
4. Show how multiplication works by using repeated additions
5. Make shopping lists and then find the costs
6. Make change for purchases and check answers

See Chapter 9 for suggested exercises.

COMPUTERS

By this time, seven-year-olds should have had some experiences with a computer, including beginning work in programming. We now need to extend these experiences.

One program that will extend them is *Instant Logo (Logo: Planning with Turtle Graphics)*, 1983. IBM. This is a simplified version of LOGO. The program helps children create computer drawings using single-keystroke commands, such as F, R, L, and B. About 60 activity cards created by classroom teachers are combined into an instructional unit for second-grade children.

Two other software programs that can be used as part of computer instruction in mathematics are the following.

Children help each other explore basic number concepts through computer games.

First Shapes by Mary Cron, from First Byte, Long Beach, California, 1986. Macintosh Apple II GS. This program consists of a set of four activities, some drill-oriented and some game-oriented, designed to develop beginning concepts about shape and form. Children identify, match, and compare five basic shapes and three sizes, and use shapes to build objects.

Math Rabbit by Teri Perl, from Learning Co., Menlo Park, California, 1986. Apple II family, 64K; IBM version available. This program is designed to aid and inspire young children (preschool to second grade) as they explore basic number concepts. It has three levels of ascending difficulty. Teacher or parent may help to choose target numbers, game speed, and mathematical operation. The activities are built around a circus theme that includes: a *clown's counting* game (three game options), where players make music as they count numbers from 1 to 8; a *tightrope walker,* for matching sets of objects with numerals; and a *circus train,* to help in problem solving and in practicing adding and subtracting.

How computers are used with seven-year-olds depends on each school's computer program. When a computer laboratory is available, small groups of children can be introduced to and given instruction in using new software programs. Then children can use these programs at learning centers in the classroom. Without a computer laboratory, the classroom teacher has to introduce the program and monitor its use. Parents and a teachers' aide should be available to help as well.

EVALUATION

Evaluation techniques used in this chapter have centered around the use of behavioral (measurable) objectives for sample lessons and the use of hands-on materials to assess children's understanding of each new math concept.

Working in pairs or small groups, the children check each other's work and compare answers to see if they are correct. Worksheets used for follow-up and for work at a math station allow children to check themselves and allow teachers to develop sample problems that will show children's thinking and the strategies they use.

Math textbooks have chapter check-up and chapter review pages. The teacher should study these pages, deleting examples that are not appropriate for the children or for the level of instruction that has been given. Additional items may be added to test children's understanding.

Paper and pencil test items to measure children's thinking and understanding are found in Chapter 8 of this book. Each of these items may be used in an interview (teacher–pupil) situation that will enable the teacher to explore a child's thinking processes, use of strategies, and mathematics vocabulary.

SUMMARY

Seven-year-old children have made important developmental changes that enable them to participate in a wide variety of mathematical activities. Increased cognitive development allows them to use a variety of strategies for solving problems.

In this chapter, we continued and expanded the addition and subtraction operations to include numbers with and without regrouping. We also discussed adding three two-digit numbers during the last part of the school year. We introduced the multiplication facts through 5×5 and showed their relationship with addition. We discussed new applications for fractions ($\frac{1}{2}, \frac{1}{4}, \frac{1}{3}$) centering around children's environment. Problem-solving skills were emphasized and extended.

We discussed using the components of children's environment to provide opportunities for: using standard measures in a meaningful way; telling time; using money for problem-solving activities and to aid in presenting place values; making patterns; and discovering basic geometric concepts relating to space, surface, and area.

We also gave suggestions for using the calculator and computer. We used evaluation techniques in sample lessons, whole-class presentations, small-group work, and one-on-one interview situations.

ACTIVITIES FOR TEACHER INSIGHT

1. Prepare a set of work cards or plans that children can use at a learning center with a scale or balance beam to compare:
   a. different objects (size and weight)
   b. sand and water (in same-size containers)
   c. sand and a material, such as wheat or corn, that occupies more space than the sand
2. Make a place-value chart showing tens and ones. Then plan on how to use the chart and U.S. coins or play money to help children understand regrouping. Restrict the numbers to 80 or less.
3. Prepare a set of cards and clock faces to assess seven-year-olds' understanding of time. Use both pictures and clock faces with movable hands so the children can demonstrate their understanding of time concepts.
4. Make a set of paper and pencil evaluation items to determine a child's understanding of:
   a. ordinal numbers
   b. the commutative law for addition and multiplication facts
   c. place values for ones, tens, hundreds
   d. ways to cover surface to show more than, less than, and the same as
   e. expanded notation for two two-digit numbers in addition, with and without regrouping and with sums less than 70

REFERENCES

BARATTA-LORTON, M. (1976). *Mathematics their way*. Menlo Park, CA: Addison-Wesley.

BURK, D., SNIDER, A., & SYMONDS, P. (1988). *Box it or bag it mathematics*. Salem, OR: Math Learning Center.

BURNS, M. (1975). *The I hate mathematics book*. Boston: Little, Brown.

CARPENTER, T. P., & MOSER, J. M. (1984). The acquisition of addition and subtraction concepts in grades one through three. *Journal for Research in Mathematics Education, 15,* 179–202.

CHURCHILL, E. (1961). *Counting and measuring* (pp. 124f.) Toronto: University of Toronto Press.

CLITHERS, D. (June 1987). Learning LOGO instantly. *Arithmetic Teacher,* pp. 12–15.

Creative Publications. (1988). *Early childhood* (Manipulatives preschool through second grade). Oak Lawn, IL: Author.

KAMII, C., & DE VRIES, R. (1976). *Piaget, children, and numbers*. National Association for Education of Young Children: Washington, DC.

LABINOWICZ, E. (1985). *Learning from children*. Menlo Park, CA: Addison-Wesley.

MYERS, B. K., & MAURER, K. (July 1987). Teaching with less talking: Learning centers in the kindergarten. *Young Children, 42*.

PIAGET, J. (1964). Development and learning. In R. Riffle & V. Rockcastle (Eds.), *Piaget rediscovered*. Ithaca, NY: Cornell University.

SMITH, N. J., & WENDELIN, K. K. (1981). Using children's books to teach mathematical concepts. *Arithmetic Teacher, 29*(3), 10–15.

SPIKER, J., & KURTZ, R. (February 1987). Teaching primary-grade mathematics skills with calculators. *Arithmetic Teacher, 34*(6), 24–27.

WILLOUGHBY, S. S. (1981). *How deep is the water?* La Salle, IL: Open Court.

CHAPTER 7

Mathematics for Eight-Year-Old Children

The growth and development of eight-year-olds, especially in the cognitive domain, enables them to expand their understanding of many new mathematics concepts as well as make rapid strides in school. An eight-year-old with normal physical, cognitive, and social-emotional characteristics is generally a healthy child with a great deal of physical energy and good eye-hand coordination who can concentrate for longer periods of time than a seven-year-old, reason logically about data (objects) that are present (the concrete operational stage), has skill in working and playing with others and accepting responsibilities in group activities, and needs to participate in games, activities, and vigorous exercise.

Teachers should understand the importance of the fact that eight-year-olds are in the concrete operational stage of development. The clearest sign that they have reached the concrete level of reasoning is their ability to conserve. Conservation, as we discussed earlier, is the ability to reverse internally, to take into account more than one feature at a time, and to focus on the transformation between one state and another, as well as to understand that quantity remains the same even in a different container or in another shape.

An important feature of conservation is its wide applicability to properties such as quantity, length, two- and three-dimensional space, area, weight, and volume. In this chapter we discuss conservation in relation to each of these and point out the fact that conservation does not come suddenly. In addition, it is not achieved for each conceptual level. Children attain conservation following a definite progression with respect to quantity, weight, and volume. In the scope and sequence charts we have been presenting, the mathematical and environmental concepts reflect the develop-

159

mental patterns of children. Conservation of quantity develops first, and so is covered first in many math programs. Concepts pertaining to weight and volume develop more slowly; thus, in preceding chapters, we merely introduced them.

The underlying logical structure that provides the foundation for conservation is, according to Piaget, the structure of "groupings." The child who is capable of thinking in terms of groupings knows in advance that a whole will be conserved when broken into parts.

In the math program for six- and seven-year-olds two major kinds of groupings were discussed: (1) *combining* two operations to a third operation — for example, $4 + 2 = 6$ — and (2) *reversibility* — for example, $3 + 2 = 5$ and $5 - 3 = 2$. A third kind of grouping — *associativity* — is appropriate for eight-year-olds. According to the principle of associativity, when three terms are combined, it does not matter which two are combined first — for example, $(3 + 4) + 2 = 3 + (4 + 2)$.

Eight-year-old children, who understand these groupings, have advanced in logical thinking and are able to reason in ways that were not possible in the intuitive stage.

Although eight-year-olds have made impressive gains at the beginning of the concrete operations stage, the quality of their thinking is still developing. Thinking is related to objects and to the relations between objects. Organization is inseparable from the content. At this stage of development, the concrete operational child does not have a unified logical system that would enable him or her to explore abstract relations independent of content.

Two powerful tools should be used with eight-year-olds. First, eight-year-olds still need to use hands-on materials to solve math problems and problems centering around their environment. Experimenting, handling, manipulating are integral parts of learning by doing.

The second is *models*, which enable children to combine the experiences they learn through manipulating concrete materials with new concepts. This ability will continue to be useful as mathematical learning is extended. Materials such as cubes, squares, flat sheets, and containers, can be used to construct models. The main units for measurement will be the square, for working with area; the line segment, for linear measuring; and the cube, for measuring mass and volume. Architects use all three of these to build miniature models for a new structure. With this model, prospective buyers can move objects in space, rearrange space, and create additions and new designs. Not only can they visualize and handle the model, they can apply "standard units" of measurement and develop patterns for improving existing structures.

We believe that the best environment for the development of cognitive structures is also best for the development of language. Such an environment provides for (1) general experience, self-regulation, and cognitive match; (2) intrinsic motivation as well as novelty in learning; (3) interpersonal interaction and discussion; and (4) activity, discovery, and opportunities to develop understanding as cognitive structures are being built.

MATHEMATICS PROGRAM FOR EIGHT-YEAR-OLDS

The scope and sequence chart that follows presents the mathematics program for eight-year-old children. Components included in the program for seven-year-olds will be extended and new topics introduced. Standard algorithms for addition, subtraction, multiplication, and division, based on our base ten numeration system, are presented. Place values are extended to include thousands. The relationship between multiplication and division is shown, but division work is limited to one-digit divisors and two-digit dividends, with regrouping and a remainder.

SCOPE AND SEQUENCE CHART FOR MATHEMATICS: EIGHT-YEAR-OLDS

Scope	Sequence				
Math components	Time (Days)	Whole-class activity	Small-group activity	Daily	Special events
Numeration: • reading and writing 1000 • place values to thousands • roman numerals (time)	16	x	x	x	x
Addition of whole numbers: • basic facts • two- and three-digit, with regrouping • three- and four-digit • column addition • understanding algorithm • environmental components (shown in next chart)	25	x	x	x	x
Subtraction of whole numbers: • basic facts • two- and three-digit, with regrouping • three- and four-digit • two-step problem solving • understanding algorithm	25	x	x	x	x

SCOPE AND SEQUENCE CHART FOR MATHEMATICS: EIGHT-YEAR-OLDS
(*Continued*)

Scope	Sequence				
Math components	**Time (Days)**	**Whole-class activity**	**Small-group activity**	**Daily**	**Special events**
Multiplication of whole numbers: • basic facts • 9×5 and 9×9 • multiplying by 10s • relation to addition • two-digit by one-digit	33	x	x	x	x
Division of whole numbers: • basic facts • by 2–3, 4–5, 6–9 • relation to multiplication — two-digit by one-digit • estimation quotients and r • understanding algorithm	36	x	x	x	x
Fractions: • $\frac{1}{2}, \frac{1}{4}, \frac{1}{8}, \frac{1}{3}, \frac{1}{6}$ • parts of regions, sets • equivalent, comparing tenths and hundredths	13	x	x	x	x
Problem solving: • finding data • estimating, checking • two-step • four situations	15	x	x	x	x
Calculators: • estimating • problem solving	10	x	x	x	x
Computers: • using commands in programs • paths and maps • writing programs for paths and treasures	10	x	x	x	x

With children's growth in cognitive structures and achievement in reading and writing, there will be numerous opportunities to use calculators and computers. The chart defines the main content of the eight-year-olds' math program, but the time allotments should be considered only suggestions since topics will overlap a great deal during instruction.

LANGUAGE DEVELOPMENT

Eight-year-old children grow rapidly in reading and writing skills. However, in most cases, reading and writing programs do not contain either mathematical content or vocabulary. Thus, teachers must provide direct instruction for reading and writing mathematical material such as word problems as well as for developing new math vocabulary. As noted in Chapter 6, the teacher has two important tasks: (1) examining the child's mathematical language for clarity and accuracy and rebuilding it when necessary, and (2) helping children learn new vocabulary. The teacher must model mathematical vocabulary and communicate mathematical ideas.

COMPONENTS OF CHILDREN'S ENVIRONMENT

For eight-year-olds, we continue and extend over those of seven-year-olds the mathematical concepts and skills relating to components of children's environment. Because eight-year-olds are in the concrete operations stage and have made considerable growth in cognitive structures, they can explore geometric figures and concepts. They also understand larger numbers — thus, extending place value from tens and hundreds to thousands enables them to work with larger numbers as well as a variety of new word problems connected with environmental components. Their understanding of and use of fractions such as one-eighth and one-tenth will provide new experiences in measurement. Also, their understanding of regrouping in addition and subtraction enables them to explore the use of money for buying, selling, and opening savings accounts.

The chart that follows identifies these extensions of mathematical concepts and their applications to children's everyday living. The synthesizing of environmental and mathematical components is quite pronounced at this learning level — making a distinct contribution to the mathematics program.

COMPONENTS OF CHILDREN'S ENVIRONMENT

Mathematical concepts and vocabulary

Measurement
- time: hour, half-hour, minute
- temperature: degrees, freezing, recording
- linear: line segment, inches, feet
- area: square unit, surfaces, uses in home
- perimeter: borders, blocks, enclosures (around)
- volume: introduction, nonstandard units
- capacity: unit of measure, liquid, nonliquid
- weight: grams, kilograms, ounces, pounds

Money
- coins: 1¢, 5¢, 10¢, 25¢, 50¢, $1.00
- bills: $1, $5, $10, $20, $50, $100
- decimal for cents
- making change, buying, selling, saving

Geometry (nonmetric)
- solids
- plane figures
- congruent shapes
- lines of symmetry

Measurement

In order to achieve at a higher level, eight-year-olds need stimulating activities in their daily life. Because they need to be able to order their daily activities, measurement becomes important, and teachers and parents must apply it regularly at school and at home.

In this section, we discuss measurement in terms of time, temperature, linear, area, perimeter, volume, capacity, and weight. A good resource book for teachers is Sylvia Horne's *Learning about Measurement* (1970).

TIME   For this age group, we extend what children learned about time during the last year in school to mastering the telling of time, including to the hour, half hour, quarter (one-fourth) hour, and minute. Children learn to state time before and after the hour in various ways, such as "a quarter to," "a quarter past," and in terms of smaller intervals using minutes. They learn how to read an electric digital clock. They learn to use the calendar and record time by the day, week, month, and year. They learn that they can check the accuracy of a clock, and then discover ways to tell when a clock is slow or fast. Children should also learn that time may be changed to daylight savings

Children tell time to the minute and describe what they do during each part of the day.

time to accommodate seasons of the year. Children can show their understanding of time by telling what they did during one day, such as a holiday, Sunday, or Saturday.

In an earlier discussion of time, we suggested using the 12 numerals on a clock face to make a number line to show the movement of the minute hand. This same technique can be used with eight-year-olds to help them learn the fractional parts of an hour:

12	1	2	3	4	5	6	7	8	9	10	11	12	60 minutes

$\frac{1}{4}$ hour $\frac{1}{2}$ hour $\frac{3}{4}$ hour   1 hour   1 hour

Given this number line, children can work in pairs to ask questions and make story problems about it for each other, or they can use it to demonstrate their understanding of the parts of an hour and the minutes in an hour to the teacher.

Ordering their day can be an interesting learning experience for children. They can take turns reading and telling the time for each part of the day. Teachers may give children a sheet of clock faces such as that shown in the figure and have them tell what they do at each of those times.

I got up.

I washed and dressed.

I had breakfast.

I went to the store.

I went to the pizza shop.

I played soccer.

I took a rest.

Supper was ready.

I watched TV.

I went to bed.

I had a funny dream.

Then morning came.

TEMPERATURE As with time, eight-year-olds learn to read, record, and use temperature data better and with more enjoyment if activities at school and at home are interesting and necessary for the child's daily activities. They should become familiar with and use both the Celsius and Fahrenheit scales. They should also learn the degree sign °—for example, 70°. Children can make a vertical number line to show zero, above zero, and below zero.

The children may keep records for a week or month of high and low daily temperatures. They can use weather reports to decide what clothing to wear to school, for a camping trip, or for other scheduled activities. If the classroom has an aquarium, the teacher can initiate a discussion about water temperatures and the need for a thermometer to ensure temperatures appropriate for a variety of fish and plants.

Children like simple science experiments, and temperature is often important in such experiments. Teachers should help children learn the concept of temperature control—for example, controlling room temperature during an experiment.

Temperatures are important in cooking, such as in preparing yeast for recipes, and for adding a starter to hot milk to make yogurt. Teachers may wish to consider doing these as classroom activities. Temperatures are also important for keeping food, boiling water, freezing (making ice or storing food), and keeping a car radiator from boiling or freezing. The eight-year-old child should be involved in activities where decisions must be made for each of these situations.

Eight-year-olds need to know how to read and record body temperatures when they are sick. Knowing about the use of alcohol and mercury in a thermometer is important, especially since the mercury in some of the bulbs is poisonous.

LINEAR MEASURE Eight-year-old children use linear measurement in numerous ways. In the beginning, they measure in nonstandard units. When a child says to a friend, "I can jump farther than you can," I can throw a ball farther than you can," or "I am taller than you are," the pair will probably use nonstandard units to see if the statements are true. At school, teachers should also begin with nonstandard units. They can use pieces of string or a stick to measure height, the length of a table, or the width of a door. The child soon sees the need for accurate measurement and for an instrument with units of measure accurately shown.

The unit of measurement for length is a *line segment*. The teacher can demonstrate this unit with two pieces of string 36″ long. Drop the two pieces on a table top. Have two children each take an end of one piece of string and draw the string taut. Compare the two pieces of string. The taut string is a line segment; the string lying on the table will form some type of open curve. The taut string can be held alongside a yardstick and marked in inches to 36″.

A number line such as the following illustrates various fractions of a line segment:

Children first learn to measure in a straight line. Then they learn that the line may be marked off into segments. Children can explore different ways to mark off these segments, such as by halves or quarters. They can learn about units such as inches, feet, yards, rods, and miles and when to use each of them. These measures are part of the English system of measurement.

As children explore the English system of measurement, they can be introduced to the metric system, which is built on multiples of ten. The basic unit of the metric system is the meter, which is about $39\frac{1}{2}$ inches long. A meter can be segmented into smaller parts called decimeters (tenths of a meter), centimeters (hundredths of a meter), and millimeters (thousandths of a meter):

1 dm = 10 cm	1 cm = 10 mm

Metric Units of Length
1 meter (m)

1 decimeter (dm)	=	$\dfrac{1}{10}$ m
1 centimeter (cm)	=	$\dfrac{1}{100}$ m
1 millimeter (mm)	=	$\dfrac{1}{1000}$ m

Introduce and use a metric ruler along with a standard ruler. In order to learn the metric system, children would have to use it daily at home, at school, and in the community. However, since the United States has been reluctant and slow in changing to the metric system, this is not really possible. We recommend that teachers take a realistic view of this situation and help children learn to apply the metric system where they can — on road signs, gasoline pumps, odometers on foreign-built cars, and on labels on liquid and dry measures. They will not completely learn the metric system until it is used in all parts of daily life. Even in high school and college, where students use metric measures in science courses, they will probably learn the system only for this specific use.

Children need to learn that *all measurement is approximate*. Accuracy depends on the instrument, the system used, and the individual doing the measuring. This fact may be demonstrated by having a child use several instruments to measure a table top, record the data, and then compare the measurements. Have several children measure a table top and then compare their measurements.

AREA   The unit for finding the area of a surface is the square. The use of a "square unit" grows out of the experiences children had as seven-year-olds. They should have learned that surfaces (floors, walls, shelves in cupboards, desktops) may be covered with paint, carpet, contact paper, leather, blotters, plastic, and linoleum. They also should have had experiences using nonstandard measures of surface: least surface, same surface, covers, covers most, and covers least. Review these concepts.

Having mastered the concept of surface, children should be ready to learn about ways to measure surface and to gradually learn that the square unit can be named — square foot or square yard, for example — and given number names for measurement.

Teachers can obtain pieces of carpet or floor tile one foot square and help children count the number needed to cover a given surface (space). The following are some activities teachers can do.

How many dark colored tiles have been laid? How many more tiles can be laid?

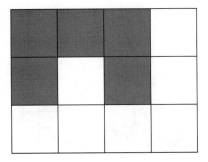

How many square units are there in A? How many in B?

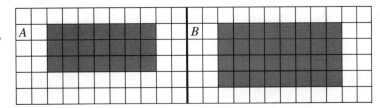

Can you find a quick way to tell how many squares there are in C, in D, and in E?

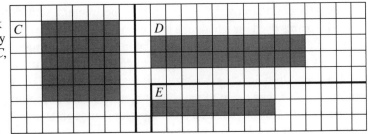

After several lessons using pieces of tile or carpet, children may be ready to discover a quick way to count the squares in a surface.

How many squares wide is this?

How many squares long?

How may squares are in the whole piece?

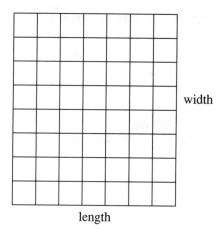

width

length

A = _____ long
A = _____ wide
   length (l) x width (w) = _____
B = _____ long and wide,
   so l x w = _____ x _____
C = l x w = _____ x _____

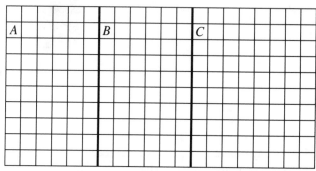

PERIMETER The eight-year-old child, who has had numerous experiences with linear measurement and who understands standard units of measurement (inch, foot, yard, or metric units), should be able to find the perimeter of familiar geometric shapes.

Help the child discover practical uses for perimeters, such as fencing for the school grounds, plants used for a hedge, a border made of bricks, redwood strips for a garden area, moldings used to frame pictures, mop board encircling a room where the walls and floors meet, and facing used on the edge of some table tops.

Have children decide what size line segment to use as the unit of measure (inch, centimeter) and then use it to measure a picture frame or molding. They can measure the perimeter of a room with a steel tape long enough to reach from one end of the room to the other. Avoid having them count too many small units. Help children estimate and make approximate measurements.

Children need to learn what a polygon is—a plane figure with three or more vertices and sufficient line segments to form a closed curve. After the children identify several kinds of polygons around the room, such as table tops or box surfaces, they should understand that the word **polygon** describes a *closed curve figure*. They can use a ruler to measure the line segments on each side of a figure:

P (perimeter) $= 1'' + 1'' + 1'' + 1'' = 4''$

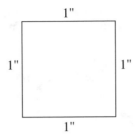

After they have measured several squares, children can make a rule for finding perimeter. Their statements will vary: "Add the measurements for all sides," "All of the inches or feet all the way around." Help them develop an equation:

Perimeter of

Rectangle:	$P = l + w + l + w$
Triangle:	$P = s + s + s$ or $P = 3s$
Square:	$P = s + s + s + s$ or $P = 4s$

VOLUME AND CAPACITY   The method used to measure volume and capacity (three-dimensional space) is an extension of that used to measure two-dimensional space (area). The child must learn that, instead of covering space (as in area), we fill a space with some type of "building block" or fluid.

The child must understand the concept that volume applies only to a closed figure in three dimensions that has an "inside" region. This concept is difficult to learn and must be taught slowly.

The concept of capacity is much easier to learn. Most children have already had experiences in measuring liquids (air, water, milk, syrup, oils) at home. The capacity concept is used to measure dry ingredients as well — flour, salt, sugar, grains, and spices.

Children learn to measure capacity by using a variety of containers. The child pours water and sand into these containers to arrange them in order of volume or amount held. Mature children are able to conserve quantities and can show that one cup of sand poured into a larger container is still one cup. Changing the shape does not change the amount of sand.

Standard units, such as quart, pint, half pint (milk), and cup, are easily learned; they are used in cooking, planning for a party, or buying for lunch. The following activities may be initiated by asking questions such as "What do we buy by the pint?" "How much milk do you drink each day at school?" "What do we measure with cups?" "If three children drink a carton of milk at school, how much milk will they drink altogether?"

In the metric system, the liter is the basic unit. It can be used to measure either dry or liquid volume. Since some service stations sell gasoline by the liter, the eight-year-old child can learn that a liter is larger than a quart and is a little more than a fourth of a gallon. The capacity of large soft drink bottles is measured in liters. Children can pour from the bottle to convert the liquid measure to cups and then to gallons.

Introduce volume measurement by investigating the use of nonstandard units to fill a box. Begin by using blocks of varying sizes and gradually move to blocks of the same size. Show by counting and by placing the blocks that volume can be measured with a "cube," a three-dimensional unit.

Extending this concept further is not recommended for eight-year-olds. Some would even say that the concept should not be presented to this age group. Piaget, for example, considers this concept too difficult for the average primary school child.

WEIGHT Weight is an important mathematical topic in the instructional program for eight-year-olds. During the first two or three years of school, children have had experiences with balance scales, using nonstandard units of measurement, and learning the words *heavy, light, heavier,* and *lighter*. They are now ready to discover and apply standard units to measuring weight. Both metric and English systems should be used, and children should be given many opportunities to use calibrated scales to weigh a variety of objects.

Children working in a classroom store center can learn to weigh objects and record the results in grams or kilograms, as well as in ounces and pounds. They can learn to read the labels on cans and packages to determine amounts and to compare the cost of these items according to weight. This can be done in conjunction with a cooking project, including planning the purchase of ingredients.

Other meaningful activities involving the measurement of weight include keeping charts of children's weight in order to record changes or growth patterns and help determine team sport categories, and weighing paper collected for a school paper drive. Other practical activities that involve measuring and recording weight are collecting for a food drive and collecting recyclable material to help the environment.

These experiences will enable children to learn the basic skills of measuring weight as well as to apply fundamental mathematical skills and concepts.

Using Money

Eight-year-olds should be able to state the value of all U.S. coins and common bank notes, including $1.00, $2.00, $5.00, $10.00, $20.00, $50.00, and $100.00. They must also learn appropriate symbols (¢, $, .). The children must learn to work with equivalent sets of coins in order to make change. They can learn these skills along with the regrouping, as in the following examples:

$$
\begin{array}{r@{\;}l}
50 \;=\; 40 + 10 \\
-\;25 \quad\; 20 + 5 \\
\hline
20 + 5 = 25
\end{array}
\qquad
\begin{array}{r@{\;}l}
40¢ + 10¢ \\
-\;20¢ + 5¢ \\
\hline
20¢ + 5¢ = 25¢
\end{array}
$$

An additive approach is used by many store clerks when they make change. For example, when given a $1.00 bill in payment for a 25¢ purchase, the clerk will say "25¢," then give the customer three quarters, saying, "50¢, 75¢, and $1.00." The decimal point separates dollars and cents and shows cents.

Children learn the value of money and its uses by: making lists for shopping; keeping allowances; having a savings account; planning for weekly lunch money; budgeting for activities requiring money; saving to buy a wide variety of toys and materials; and doing jobs for pay around the home or community.

The eight-year-old child will be ready to work in a classroom store as a clerk or as a buyer, making and giving change. Related work cards and activities are suggested in Chapter 10.

Dramatic play in pretend store provides many useful math experiences.

Work cards can be prepared first without regrouping, and then gradually with regrouping. For example,

I have	39¢	58¢	79¢
I buy	25¢	50¢	35¢
I have left	—	—	—

I have	$1.00	75¢	50¢
I buy	75¢	56¢	35¢
I have left	—	—	—

Children can make up their own money problems after they complete the examples. They can share them with a friend or group, orally.

Geometry (nonmetric)

Third-grade children should be familiar with common geometric shapes (circle, square, rectangle, triangle). Their experiences with linear measurement and perimeter should have developed their understanding of the line segment as well as introduced them to simple equations. Now they are ready to expand their geometric knowledge. They should learn to identify plane figures, congruent figures, lines of symmetry, and open and closed curves; use two and three attributes to classify triangles, circles, rectangles, spheres, cones, and cylinders; and identify and name points, lines, rays, and angles.

Teachers must use an informal, intuitive approach when introducing geometry. We want the child to become acquainted with the terminology, some relationships, properties common to all geometric figures, and some new geometric shapes (sphere, cylinder, cone, and rectangular solid).

SOLIDS AND PLANE FIGURES   The first activity in geometry should be to introduce the **plane**. A plane can be illustrated by the top of a desk or table. Teachers can describe the desktop in terms of **lines** and **points**: "This plane (desktop) is a rectangle and is made up of many points." The children's experiences with perimeter, area, and points used on a number line will enable them to "see" the desktop in geometric terms.

Children can be asked to think about taking the desk away. Then what points could be used to show the surface of the desktop? They can be asked to name other familiar planes or surfaces, such as a piece of paper, book cover, chalkboard, or floor covering. If they can imagine, without seeing a physical representation, how each of these would look, they are imagining a geometric plane.

Having established the concept of points and lines to identify a familiar **space,** teachers can direct the eight-year-olds to think about paths between points, such as between *A* and *B,* a path between two points. This is a *simple* **curve**—the line does not pass through the same point twice.

In a **closed curve,** the line segment returns to its starting point without crossing itself at any point. Simple closed curves may be formed with the use of one or more points—for example:

Children can be taught to think about the space inside the curve and outside the curve (undefined) or a space that has certain limits, such as a basketball court, with playing area, foul line, and boundary lines. The teacher can ask, "What is outside the lines of a basketball court?" After many responses, the teacher can add, "Can we call this undefined space?"

With these concepts and terms, children can begin to use simple nonmetric geometry and to talk about a variety of geometric figures, such as congruent figures or shapes.

CONGRUENT SHAPES   Two figures or shapes are congruent if they have the same shape and size. Their location and orientation may be different. For example, panes of glass in a window may be congruent (have the same shape and size), but be in different locations in the frame. We are surrounded by congruent articles—cars of the same model, toys, and clothing.

The principle of congruence is applied when patterns are repeated on wallpaper, on clothing, or in flower garden borders. Children can identify congruent triangles, rectangles, and other shapes on ink pad stamps and use them to make patterns. They can use graph paper to identify and make congruent shapes. Without such paper, their shapes would not be accurate and they would not be able to see the identity.

LINES OF SYMMETRY   Teachers can help a child develop some basic ideas about geometry by introducing figures that show symmetry and geometric transformation. These figures should be drawn by an adult since an eight-year-old would find them difficult to draw and they would lack the accuracy to demonstrate the basic geometric ideas. Duplicate the figures on a worksheet and have the child trace the figures, cut them out, and fold them along the dotted lines to see if the parts on each side of the line match perfectly—that is, to see if they are an exact fit. This may be called "flipping the image." More formally, it is known as *geometric transformation*. Study these figures, which show symmetry about a line:

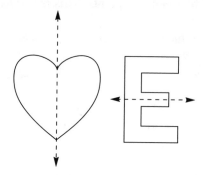

Teachers can demonstrate symmetry with respect to a line by presenting a figure such as the following:

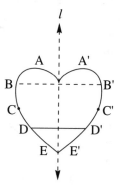

A figure is symmetric with respect to a line (l) if, for each point on the figure, there is a matching point on the other side of the line (l), and the line l bisects BB', the line joining the points, and is perpendicular to it.

Numerous activities will help children identify and understand line of symmetry: paper-folding, making ink blots, showing a pinwheel (rotational symmetry), and translation (moving a figure such as a rectangle successively in one direction and through a certain distance to make a pattern). Have children name things around them that could be used to show lines of symmetry, such as two wings of a butterfly, two halves of an apple, and two halves of a leaf.

NUMBER AND NUMERATION

Eight-year-olds can read and write whole numbers to 9,999, and beyond when needed, and understand the numbers. Children need to understand the base ten numeration system and to discover that the four fundamental operations of arithmetic ($+$, $-$, $\times$, $\div$) are built on this system.

Teachers can use the following hands-on materials to help children understand place value and to provide practice in working with groups of ten:

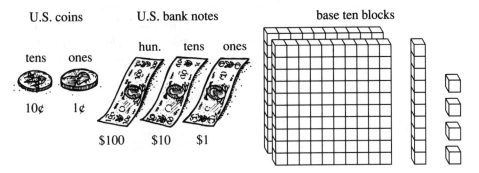

We explore the use of place value in detail when we discuss standard algorithms for basic operations. Various symbols may be used as placeholders to represent a numeral:

$$\underline{\quad\quad} \; , \; \boxed{\quad\quad} \; , \; \text{or } ?$$

Expanded notation, such as $604 = 450 + 100 + 50 + 4$, should be used in all mathematics work with eight-year-olds. This process helps children understand place value.

ADDITION OF WHOLE NUMBERS

Teachers must review and have children practice basic addition and subtraction facts through $9 + 9 = 18$. Some children will have mastered these facts; others will still depend on manipulative materials and their fingers.

A variety of devices and materials to help children master these basic facts was presented in previous chapters. At this level, teachers can introduce the function machine.

■ THE FUNCTION MACHINE A **function** is a rule that assigns to each element of one set (an input set or domain) exactly one element of another set (the output set, or range). The concept of functions helps children learn the basic facts of the four fundamental operations of arithmetic. Through the use of a *function machine* — either a picture or an actual machine made from a cardboard box — children can explore a variety of interesting and meaningful rules pertaining to an ordered pair of numbers. The picture of the machine shown below is similar to those found in many children's textbooks.

In the following function machine, there is a place for input, a place to indicate the function, and an output. With the window showing " + 2" open, children see that any number placed in the input must be added to 2 — for example, 5 + 2 = 7 or 7 + 2 = 9. When the window in the middle of the machine is closed, children must *discover* the function (+ , − , × , or ÷ and the number) producing the output number.

the number to be
placed (input)

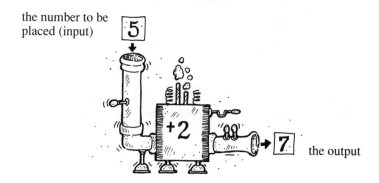

the output

Similar exercises can be used for other operations with ordered pairs of numbers. Children can work in pairs or in small groups to discover correct responses when only the input number and output number are shown. They input a card with a number on it and when it comes out the other end, they turn the card over to check their answer. For example, when 5 shows in the input slot and 11 in the output slot (with the window closed showing " + 6"), children discover that the function is " + 6" (5 + 6 = 11). Other single-digit numbers can be placed in the input slot and 6 added to each to give the correct sums.

Tables such as the following are useful for children who need more time and practice to master basic addition facts. In the first table, have children add 3 to each top number:

+	6	7	5	8	9
3	9				

For this, more difficult magic square, have children fill in the empty squares to total 15 in each direction:

8		
	5	
		2

Teachers can introduce addition of two-digit numbers without regrouping with problems like this:

$$35$$
$$+\ 22$$

Or they can use with expanded notation:

$$40 = 40 + 0$$
$$22 = 20 + 2$$
$$60 + 2\ =\ 62$$

You had			
10¢ 10¢ 10¢ 10¢ = 40¢			
You earned			
10¢ 10¢ 1¢ 1¢ = 22¢			
You now have 62¢			

Teachers can demonstrate regrouping, beginning with ones and gradually advancing to hundreds, with examples like these:

Complete each example:

	Add *1s*	*Add* *10s*	*Add* *100s*
	$3\overset{1}{6}5$	$\overset{1}{2}65$	$\overset{1}{5}45$
	226	254	+ 534
	_ _ 1	_ 1 9	_ 0 7 9

In the following problem, children must use several shortcuts. Learning how shortcuts are related to our base ten number system and how they are used is the basic problem children have in addition. This example shows what is added using the mechanical shortcut:

355	15	ones
465	17	tens
+ 265	+ 9	hundreds

If the child simply works the problem without understanding the place value represented by the numbers, difficulties will arise later. Use base ten blocks to help demonstrate the problem.

$$\begin{array}{r} \overset{11}{355} \\ 465 \\ +\ 265 \\ \hline 1{,}085 \end{array}$$

Add ones to get 15 ones: write 5 (ones) and carry 1 ten to the tens column
Add tens to get 18 tens: write 8 (tens) and carry 10 tens to the hundreds column
Add hundreds to get 10 hundreds: write 10 (hundreds) in the hundreds and thousands columns. (This may be thought of as no hundreds and 1 thousand).

This example shows what was added.

$$\begin{array}{rl} 15 & \text{ones} \\ 17 & \text{tens} \\ +\ 9 & \text{hundreds} \\ \hline 1{,}085 & \end{array}$$

SUBTRACTION OF WHOLE NUMBERS

As with addition, teachers begin work in subtraction for eight-year-olds by reviewing basic addition and subtraction facts and subtraction of one- and two-digit numbers without regrouping. Children who have not yet mastered these skills must be given particular attention.

The new work begins with regrouping, using hands-on materials to show the work.

You have	25¢	55¢
You buy	8¢	9¢
Have left	17¢	

The first example involves changing 25¢ to one dime (10¢) and 15¢. This may be shown as:

$$25\cent = \begin{array}{r} 10\cent + 15\cent \\ -\ 8\cent \\ \hline 10\cent +\ 7\cent = 17\cent \end{array} \qquad \text{or} \qquad \begin{array}{r} 25\cent \\ -\ 8\cent \\ \hline \end{array}$$

Teachers can use coins to help present this work. The use of hands-on materials help children better understand the process. The coins can be followed with plastic money and work cards for buying things at a school supply store. Children can make a small class store to provide many opportunities for buying, selling, and making change.

The operation of subtracting a two-digit number from another two-digit number with regrouping in the tens place may be approached with the same pattern:

You had	25¢	41¢	33¢	63¢	70¢
You buy	− 19¢	− 35¢	− 15¢	− 25¢	− 25¢
Have left	6¢				

Children can work several examples and then use expanded notation to show that they understand the steps. The teacher may say, "Now show the subtractions with expanded notations."

$$
\begin{array}{ll}
73¢ = 70¢ + 3¢ & \text{becomes} \\
- 25¢ = 20¢ + 5¢ & \text{becomes}
\end{array}
\qquad
\begin{array}{l}
60¢ + 13¢ \\
- 20¢ + 5¢ \\
\hline
40¢ + 8¢ = 48¢
\end{array}
$$

Careful teaching and use of hands-on materials will help reduce the number of errors. However, children should learn to check their answers. They do this by adding the difference and the number subtracted (subtrahend). If the result is the number subtracted from (minuend) the answer is correct.

$$
\begin{array}{r}
36 \\
- 24 \\
\hline
\end{array}
\qquad \text{by adding these numbers:} \qquad
\begin{array}{r}
12 \\
+ 24 \\
\hline
\end{array}
$$

check this answer: 12 $\qquad\qquad\qquad\qquad$ 36: the answer is correct

Teachers can introduce regrouping involving three-digit numbers by setting up problems in this way:

$$
\begin{array}{r}
548 \\
- 173 \\
\hline
\end{array}
\qquad
\begin{array}{r}
\overset{4}{\cancel{5}}\overset{14}{\cancel{4}}8 \\
- 173 \\
\hline
375
\end{array}
\qquad
\begin{array}{l}
3 \text{ from } 8 = 5 \\
7 \text{ tens from } 14 \text{ tens} = 7 \text{ tens} \\
1 \text{ hundred from } 4 \text{ hundreds} = 3 \text{ hundreds}
\end{array}
$$

$$
\begin{array}{ll}
548 = 500 + 40 + 8 = & 400 + 140 + 8 \\
173 = 100 + 70 + 3 = & - \ 100 + \ 70 + 3 \\
& \hline
& 300 + \ 70 + 5 = 375
\end{array}
$$

Using play money bills from $1.00 to $100.00 will help children understand the use of zero as a placeholder and strengthen their understanding of place value. Teachers can present problems like these:

$10	$40	$50	$100	$300	$5,000
− $5	− $10	− $20	− $50	− $100	− $2,000

If bank notes and coins are both used, children can do problems such as the following:

You had	$3.50	$5.75	$6.35
You spent	$1.60	$3.80	$3.54
Have left	$1.90		

In expanded notation, this problem becomes:

$$\$3.50 = \$3.00 + \$.50 \quad = \quad \begin{array}{r} \$2.00 \quad \$1.00 \\ \$3.00 \quad \$ .50 \end{array}$$

$$- \$1.60 = \$1.00 + \$.60 \quad = \quad \begin{array}{r} \$1.50 \\ - \$1.00 + \$ .60 \end{array}$$

$$\$1.00 + \$ .90 = \$1.90$$

MULTIPLICATION OF WHOLE NUMBERS

Teachers begin work in multiplication by reviewing the facts through $5 \times 5 = 25$. Extend multiplication facts beyond 5×5 gradually, allowing children to learn one fact at a time and including division facts.

Multiplication and division are related. When children learn one multiplication fact, they can also learn two division facts. For example,

$$5 \times 6 = 30 \longrightarrow 30 \div 5 = 6 \quad \text{and} \quad 30 \div 6 = 5$$

Then, altogether as a family,

$$5 \times 6 = 30$$
$$6 \times 5 = 30$$
$$30 \div 5 = 6$$
$$30 \div 6 = 5$$

Terminology should be reviewed. For example, the numbers 5 and 6 in the above example are called *factors* and 30 is the *product* of these two factors. When 1 is a factor, the product is the other factor — $5 \times 1 = 5$. When 0 is a factor, the product is 0.

Have children learn the more difficult facts, such as 5×6, 5×7, 5×8, and 5×9, one at a time, as they arise. When facts are presented in table form, children spend about 80 percent of their time practicing known, easy facts. Teachers can use the following devices to help children learn these multiplication facts:

$\times$ 5	
9	45
6	—
8	—
8	—
7	—

Multiply by 6

$\times \rightarrow$	0	1	2	3	4	5	6	7	8	9	. . .
$\uparrow$ 6	0	6	12	—	—	—	36	—	—	—	

These devices avoid the sequencing of facts, which children often memorize. They also require children to work each problem separately.

Eight-year-old children need to understand that the multiplication algorithm is based on three rules:

1. *Commutative property.* The product of two numbers is the same regardless of the order of multiplication: $3 \times 4 = 12$ and $4 \times 3 = 12$. The two factors (3 and 4) are used differently, but the product is the same. Each order of these factors produces a different arrangement: $4 \times 3 = 4$ threes and $3 \times 4 = 3$ fours.

2. *Associative property.* The product of three numbers is the same, no matter how the numbers are grouped:

$$
\begin{aligned}
4 \times 5 \times 3 &= 60 \\
(4 \times 5) \times 3 &= 4 \times (5 \times 3) \\
20 \times 3 &= 4 \times 15 \\
60 &= 60
\end{aligned}
$$

3. *Distributive property.* This is the basis for the multiplication operation. We distribute the multiplier over the terms of the other factor (multiplicand) — that is, we multiply the multiplier by each term of the other factor — and add to find the product. For example, to multiply 2×123, we multiply to find the product of the ones (3), the tens (2), and the hundreds (1) and then add:

$$
\begin{array}{r}
123 = \quad 100 + 20 + 3 \\
\underline{\times \quad 2} \quad \underline{\times \qquad\qquad 2} \\
200 + 40 + 6 = 246
\end{array}
$$

Multiplication of a two-digit number by a one-digit number without regrouping involves basic multiplication facts. In the following example, simple facts (5 × 1 and 5 × 3) are used. Teachers can introduce this work with an interesting, practical problem.

If we have 5 classrooms in a parade and there are 31 children in each room, how many children will be in the parade?

$$
5 \times 31 = \begin{array}{r} 31 \\ \times\ \ 5 \\ \hline 5\ \ (5 \times 1) \\ 150\ \ (5 \times 30) \\ \hline 155 \end{array}
$$

Teachers may also introduce multiplication of a two-digit number by a one-digit number involving carrying so that children become familiar with the process — for example,

$$
\begin{array}{r} 35 \\ \times\ \ 5 \\ \hline \end{array} = \begin{array}{r} 30 + 5 \\ \times\ \ \ \ \ \ \ \ \ \ 5 \\ \hline 150 + 25 \end{array} = \begin{array}{r} 35 \\ \times\ \ 5 \\ \hline 25 \\ 150 \\ \hline 175 \end{array} = \begin{array}{r} 35 \\ \times\ \ 5 \\ \hline 175 \end{array}
$$

Multiplication of three-digit numbers by a one-digit number can be presented with practical problems. This work extends the algorithm and shows its relationship to addition. The following example uses U.S. money:

$$
\begin{array}{r} \$1.25 \\ \times\ \ \ \ 3 \\ \hline \end{array} \qquad \begin{array}{r} \$1.00 + 20¢ + 5¢ \\ \times\ 3 \\ \hline \$3.00 + 60¢ + 15¢ \end{array} \qquad \begin{array}{r} \$3.00 \\ 60¢ \\ +\ \ \ 15¢ \\ \hline \$3.75 \end{array}
$$

A child may also think 3 × $1.00 is $3.00 and three × 25¢ is 75¢ — then, $3.00 + 75¢ is $3.75.

DIVISION OF WHOLE NUMBERS

Although division facts may be learned along with multiplication facts, a systematic presentation of the meaning of division is necessary. Children should learn that division is a quick way to take a large number apart and that it involves repeated subtractions; division is the inverse of multiplication; division may be interpreted as the process of measurement (showing how many); and division may be interpreted as partition (showing the size of each part). Division employs the basic skills used in multiplication, subtraction, and addition. Because division involves all of these operations, *the process is difficult for many children.*

There are 90 primary facts in division, and division by zero is not possible. The facts include those used in multiplication up to and including $9 \times 9 = 81$ and $9\,\overline{)81}$. The following examples illustrate ways in which teachers can introduce division:

Repeated subtraction

$$
\begin{array}{r}
5\,\overline{)25} \\
-\ 5 \\
\hline
20 \\
5 \\
\hline
15 \\
5 \\
\hline
10 \\
5 \\
\hline
5 \\
5 \\
\hline
0
\end{array}
$$

There are 5 fives in 25.

Taking groups out (such as multiples of 5: 5, 10, 15, 20)

$$
\begin{array}{r}
5\,\overline{)25} \\
-20 \quad 4 \\
\hline
5 \\
-\ 5 \quad 1 \\
\hline
0 \\
\hline
5
\end{array}
$$

Child estimates: "How many fives can I take out of 25?" Tries: $4 \times 5 = 20$. Because there is a remainder of 5, child tries again; $5 \times 5 = 25$.

$$
\begin{array}{r}
5 \\
5\,\overline{)25} \\
-25 \\
\hline
0
\end{array}
$$

Basic operation

$$
\begin{array}{r}
5 \\
5\,\overline{)25} \\
25 \\
\hline
0
\end{array}
$$

"What must I multiply 5 by to get 25?"

When division is interpreted as measurement, children may ask, "How many groups of the divisor are in a number?" For example, using hands-on material, teachers may present the following:

<u>0   2'   4'   6'</u>   *Three* 2-foot pieces are in 6 feet.

When division is interpreted as partition, it shows the size of each part. In the last example, for instance, the pieces (cloth or other material) are 2 feet long.

Teachers can create a variety of division examples based on the situation of buying at the store. The following involve dividing by 6 or 7 with no remainders.

You have	36¢	24¢	28¢	42¢	63¢	49¢
Each candy costs	6¢	6¢	7¢	6¢	7¢	7¢
You can buy						

The next examples involve dividing by 7, 8, or 9 to buy cookies at a school bake sale. In these examples there are remainders.

You have	18¢	25¢	45¢	51¢	45¢	63¢	70¢
Cookie costs	8¢	8¢	9¢	7¢	8¢	7¢	9¢
You can buy	2						
Money left	2¢						

Teachers will have to use their own judgment concerning the "just right" time to teach the terms associated with division: **divisor, dividend,** and **quotient**. We suggest introducing the terms one at a time.

In some of the examples shown, children are faced with remainders. We do not recommend showing a remainder in the quotient in a format such as

$$\begin{array}{r} 2 \text{ r}2 \\ 8\overline{)18¢} \end{array}$$

This implies that the remainder is a fraction, and we cannot justify writing remainders as fractions at this level. Even in the upper grades it should be done only rarely.

The word problem itself should help to determine how a remainder will be used. In the examples just given, the children keep the change, the pennies left over. They might then consider how many more pennies would be needed to buy another cookie. In working with wood or other materials, children would probably throw small pieces away.

FRACTIONAL PARTS OF WHOLE NUMBERS

Fractional parts of a whole as well as the concept of part-whole relationships have already been introduced and used in connection with time, measurement, and area, and with combining parts to form a whole (the set) when working with the four basic operations of addition, subtraction, multiplication, and division.

Telling time to the hour, half hour, quarter hour, and minute is a major learning task for eight-year-old children. Teachers should begin to extend work with fractions by using children's understanding of a clock face. Divide the face into fractional parts: one whole, one-half, one-fourth.

Concentrate on the common fractions, those used most in daily life: $\frac{1}{2}, \frac{1}{4}, \frac{1}{8}$. These fractions constitute over 80 percent of the fractions used by adults. Some textbooks and curriculum guides also recommend teaching one-third. However, children have difficulty using one-third and making and cutting objects into thirds. Teachers may want to use colored rods to demonstrate one-third (three white rods which equal one red rod) since children can see that one red may be cut into three one-thirds.

Some of the uses for common fractions that children can understand are: folding paper into halves or fourths, cutting apples or fruit, sharing one-half a candy bar, and marking off playing areas, such as a tether ball circle or four-square court. They can also show how to fraction a whole by working with circles and rectangles; using a one-foot ruler marked off into inch, $\frac{1}{2}$ inch, $\frac{1}{4}$ inch; and using a table to show related and equivalent fractions, such as $\frac{1}{2}$ and $\frac{2}{4}$, $\frac{1}{3}$ and $\frac{2}{6}$:

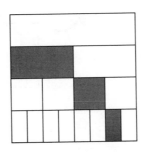

Teachers should develop the following concepts:

- The parts must be equal (one-fourth is one of four equal parts).
- The part of a fraction below the line (the denominator) tells the size of the fraction used.
- The number above the line (the numerator) tells how many equal parts are being used.
- A fraction may be cut into equal parts.

Teach the fractions that are important parts of the components of the child's environment. We do not recommend adding and subtracting fractions at this learning level.

Teachers can have children do the following sample exercises using sets of tagboard or felt cut into circles, squares, rectangles.

Make these shapes with the pieces you have. Now label them with a fraction for each shaded part.

Shade these two squares to show equivalent fractions. Then complete the written forms.

$$\frac{1}{2} = \frac{}{4}$$

Compare and show less than, greater than, or equal to. Can you write a fraction for each part?

Teachers can also discuss fractions in terms of food. For example, when cutting a pie or a rectangular-shaped cake, start with the whole and cut it into smaller parts. To cut a pie into fourths, first cut one-half and then cut each of the halves into fourths. To cut eighths, repeat the first two steps and then cut the fourths into eighths. Restaurants have special marked cutters to place over a pie or cake to make each cut accurate and easy. Ask, "Have you ever tried cutting a pie into thirds, fifths, sevenths, or tenths?"

However, do not ask children to draw thirds, fifths, sevenths, ninths, or tenths. If these fractions are to be used, draw, on ditto pages, appropriate figures and shapes that are accurate and easy to use.

Some textbooks for third grade discuss fractions of a number — for example,

$$\text{Find } \tfrac{1}{4} \text{ of} \qquad \circ \circ \circ \circ$$
$$\circ \circ \circ \circ$$

$$\text{Find } \tfrac{1}{3} \text{ of} \qquad \circ \circ \circ$$
$$\circ \circ \circ$$

We do not recommend this work for eight-year-olds. Leave problems such as $\tfrac{1}{3}$ of 6 or $\tfrac{1}{4}$ of 8 for the upper grades.

PROBLEM SOLVING

We used a multiple approach to problem solving in this chapter. In extending the components of children's environment, we used time to order and show how a child's day begins and ends, used money to buy things and to make change, measured children's growth in height, discovered how floor surfaces are covered and measured with the use of square units and graphing paper, estimated quantities and then measuring, and made approximate measurements. Problem-solving skills were an integral part of these math problems.

We used money to illustrate the algorithms for the four basic operations because children are interested in money and because money is an easy-to-see application of place value. We made suggestions for using money to solve problems relating to buying at a store. Children can prepare a shopping list and determine, using newspaper ads, the items they can purchase with a given amount of money, such as $5.00 or $10.00.

Children can use calculators to help them make estimates, solve problems involving large numbers, compare prices of items at a store, and help the cashier total the cost of items purchased. Both buyer and cashier are involved in adding and subtracting the amounts for coupons.

Eight-year-olds can also use computers for problem solving — to estimate, determine travel times and schedules, and make programs for locating treasures, using maps, and playing a variety of games.

CALCULATORS

Eight-year-olds are ready for extensive and enriched instruction using a hand-held calculator. Calculators should be used after the children have mastered the basic math concepts. Calculator work should supplement and follow the mathematics work being taught. Having gained an understanding of the four fundamental operations in arithmetic, children can use the calculator to work a variety of problems quickly and accurately. Any difficulties that arise due to the appearance of decimal numbers in the display can be overcome by working problems that come out even and by using multiples of ten to discover the meaning of larger numbers or to show place value. Teachers can introduce rounding off.

With their mathematics background and mental development, eight-year-olds can use the calculator to:

- Add and subtract one-, two-, and three-digit numbers
- Make patterns by using the = and + by 2s, 5s, and 10s
- Show the commutative property for addition and multiplication
- Display numbers that are greater than or less than the one shown
- Estimate answers and then check for accuracy with the calculator
- Add several terms to make 20 or 30, or to find the cost of items on a shopping list

See the calculator exercises in Chapter 9. All are appropriate for eight-year-olds.

COMPUTERS

The importance of beginning computer instruction at an early age is being recognized more and more. Computers have already made inroads into schools — into computer centers and even individual classrooms.

At the Brentwood Magnet School, a public school in Los Angeles, the third grade has a computer program funded by the Educational Compensatory Act (ECIA). During the first part of the school year, children learn the keyboard in the school's computer center. During the second part of the year, the teacher uses the Apple IIe computers for a variety of learning activities. Software includes that for teaching the symbols for basic operations (+ , − , *, /); *Math Is Easy* (multiplication facts); *How Computers Work Problems* (input and output for basic facts); *Bits and Bytes* (number computer patterns and magic squares); *Computer Math Magic* (guess the magic number 4); and software with a grid for exploring the 100 basic facts. Children work in pairs at computer stations. They have access to the computer two or three times each week for 30 to 40 minutes each time.

Many modern math textbooks include instruction on using computers. For example, one series includes exercises to help children learn how to input and output basic facts and to do operations on these facts; learn the commands (to follow a path or a map, take and leave, jump, go back); and write simple math programs.

The following software provides specific instruction on important math concepts, such as shapes, place value, problem solving, and using a cash register connected with buying at a store.

Inside and Outside Shapes, developed for Apple II with 64K by Random House, 1986. The program provides a *User's Guide* and *Teacher's Guide* with blackline masters. It helps children learn six shapes by matching: rectangle, triangle, square, diamond, star, and circle. Children are introduced to concepts such as inside and outside the boundaries of shapes.

Place Value, developed for Apple II with 48K by Educational Materials Equipment Company, 1985. This program uses cubes and two- and three-digit numerals with pictures of base ten blocks. As the blocks are shown, the child types in the associated number. If a numeral is shown, the child orders the correct number of base ten blocks.

Blockers and Finders by O'Brien. Sunburst Communications, 1987. Apple II family, 64K. For ages 5 to adult. Within a 4 × 4 grid, "finders" (small, curiously shaped animals) are sent by students on invisible paths with starting and ending points revealed. "Blockers" alter paths and are hidden in the grid. The object is to guess the finder's path. Levels of play include 1 to 12 blockers.

The Magic Cash Register, Metacomet Software, 1986. Apple II series, 64K. For grades 3 through 6. The program involves buying with the use of a cash register. Package includes a program disk, one page of documentation, play money (reproducible), and a story booklet. The "Wizard" explains the four required categories of input for a store purchase: item name, number of items purchased, individual item price, and a calculated total of the items.

SUMMARY

In this chapter, we stressed the importance of teachers recognizing the pronounced changes that have occurred in the growth and development of eight-year-old children, especially in the cognitive domain. These children are well into the stage of concrete operations. Thus, they can conserve important mathematical concepts and consolidate them into an understanding of the standard algorithms connected with the four fundamental operations in arithmetic.

The eight-year-olds can concentrate and work for longer periods of time than seven-year-olds. They are active, curious, interested in working and playing with others of their own age, and ready for considerable achievement in school. They accept responsibilities for working with others as well as for planning their own learning activities.

The new mathematical work for this age group has centered around: understanding the basic algorithms and the shortcuts involved in each operation; extending the meaningful use of place value; beginning division work and relating it to multiplication; and synthesizing the environmental strands with the mathematical strands to provide many opportunities for applying mathematical concepts to everyday living.

We made suggestions for helping the teacher plan for special events, establish a problem-solving center for science or other subjects, use the calendar for recording days in school, and plan for a variety of class and school activities that require practical problem solving.

We also made suggestions for more intensive use of calculators and computers. These include using new programs that go beyond doing practice exercises to problem solving, reference to concrete materials, and program writing.

ACTIVITIES FOR TEACHER INSIGHT

1. Plan for one or two interviews with third-grade children to discover their ability to count forward and backward by 5s and 10s. Use different starting points, such as having them count ahead by 5s beginning at 53 (odd) or 55 (even). Then have them count backward by 10s from 120 or 115.

2. Study this example:

$$\begin{array}{r} 6 \\ 4\overline{)24} \\ 24 \end{array}$$

How would you help a third-grade child learn the correct place values for this example? What might happen if the 6 is left in the tens place?

3. Use a clock face that has the numerals 1 through 12. Interview several children, one at a time, to see if they understand the use of $\frac{1}{2}$ and $\frac{1}{4}$ in telling time.

4. Visit one or more third-grade classrooms where calculators or computers are being used. Try to determine the appropriateness of their use in terms of child involvement in making decisions, problem solving, and understanding math concepts. Interview one or two children to get their reactions to using computers and calculators.

REFERENCES

BARATTA-LORTON, M. (1976). *Mathematics their way*. Menlo Park, CA: Addison-Wesley.

BRUNER, J. S. (1967). *Toward a theory of instruction*. Cambridge, MA: Belknap Press, Harvard University.

BURNS, M. (1975). *The I hate mathematics book*. Boston: Little, Brown.

California State Department of Education. (1987). *Mathematics: Model curriculum guide (K-8)*. Sacramento, CA: Office of State Printing.

HORNE, S. (1970). *Learning about measurement*. Sacramento, CA: California State Department of Education.

KRULEK, S., & RUDNICK, J. (1984). *A sourcebook for teaching problem solving*. Newton, MA: Allyn and Bacon.

LABINOWICZ, E. (1985). *Learning from children*. Menlo Park, CA: Addison-Wesley.

National Council of Teachers of Mathematics. (1976). *Yearbook: Measurement in school mathematics*. Reston, VA: Author.

———. (1978). *Yearbook: Developing computational skills*. Reston, VA: Author.

RICHARDSON, K. (February 1988). Assessing understanding. *Arithmetic Teacher, 35*.

SCHULTZ, K. A., COLARUSSO, R. P., & STRAWDERMAN, V. W. (1989). *Mathematics for every young child*. Columbus, OH: Charles E. Merrill.

SHADE, W. H., & SHADE, D. W. (1988). Developmentally appropriate software for young children. *Young Children, 43*(4), 37–43.

SPIKER, J., & KURTZ, R. (February 1987). Teaching primary grade mathematics skills with calculators. *Arithmetic Teacher, 34*.

STENMARK, J. K., THOMPSON, V., & COSSEY, R. (1986). *Family math*. Berkeley: University of California Press.

STONE, J. I. (1987). Early childhood math: Make it manipulative! *Young Children, 42*(6), 16–23.

CHAPTER 8

Evaluation

In Chapter 2, we listed seven principles for guiding the learning activities of children. These principles provide a framework for selecting, organizing, and presenting mathematics programs for children. We have condensed these principles in order to apply them to instruction and evaluation. They become the important intellectual or cognitive outcomes that educators strive to help children achieve through their experiences with mathematics. To judge the effectiveness of math programs, teachers and schools must periodically evaluate children's progress toward achieving these outcomes, which are as follows:

1. *Attitudes* that influence positively all aspects of mathematics instruction and learning
2. *Understanding* of each new aspect of mathematics instruction as well as of the structure of the subject
3. *Basic skills* that help children do computation accurately and easily
4. *Intellectual development* — growth in and development of cognitive structures

The mathematical content and learning described in Chapter 2 [selected from the components of children's environment, *Essential Math for the 21st Century* (NCSM, 1988), and the structure of mathematics] are woven into the math program for each learning level and are evaluated as part of the four larger outcomes described above.

The term **evaluation** is used in this book to describe a process for identifying a child's progress toward mastery of measurable objectives established for specific skills, understandings, knowledge, and attitudes. The evaluation process is broader than testing and provides data that helps educators assess children's understanding of a concept, diagnose areas of difficulty, discover a child's readiness for new learning, and appraise instructional practices.

EVALUATION RELATED TO THE SEQUENCING OF INSTRUCTION

Evaluation plays an important role in determining the amount of time spent on a particular mathematical concept. It also helps determine the pacing of instruction throughout the year to cover the course of study, and the appropriate sequence of instruction for the learner and the mathematics program.

The time spent on mathematics, each day and throughout the year, is a major factor in high pupil achievement. Evaluation procedures can make an important contribution to this factor by providing data on how well a child is progressing in learning new math skills and concepts based on his or her maturity and ability. Instruction should move along at appropriate rates — neither too fast nor too slow.

Pacing involves breaking a yearly plan down into smaller units so that the appropriate instruction is given for each new mathematical concept or skill and adequate time is allowed to complete the work.

The sequencing of instruction takes into account the ability and maturity of the children as well as the structure of mathematics. Children should be guided through mathematical learning experiences at their own rate — that is, they should move on only after they understand each new concept. Teachers must ensure that children follow a continuum based on the structure of our base ten number system. Without a planned and monitored sequence, time can be wasted on irrelevant games and activities and gaps created in children's understanding of the number system.

SELECTING AND USING EVALUATION TECHNIQUES

Two important factors must be considered in selecting and using evaluation tests and procedures: (1) their validity or suitability to measure specific pupil behavior, and (2) their reliability or consistency.

For this discussion of the validity of evaluation techniques, we concentrate on the relevance and suitability of the procedures used. We will refer to validity again in connection with standardized tests, which are used extensively by many school systems.

To ascertain validity, we need to determine that a test not only measures defined pupil behaviors, but that it is appropriate for the child's level of development as well. We often use the terms *behavioral objectives* and *criterion-referenced* objectives. In sample lessons throughout this book, we have stated most objectives in behavioral form — that is, in specific, measurable terms, such as "With the use of base ten blocks the child will show an understanding of the place values used in writing 25 — two strips of ten and five cubes (ones)." The tests presented in this chapter are valid because they fit the concepts to be measured for each age group, they have been used in experimental classroom situations, and they agree with concepts presented in other modern textbooks. To be valid for a particular child or group of children, the tests have to fit the specific objectives of the teacher and the instruction used. Teachers wishing to use any of these test items can select those suitable for the children in their own teaching situation.

Each measuring device used should be reliable. Reliability is influenced by the way the measure is administered as well as by the way the device has been constructed. The classroom teacher will have to try different test items or techniques with children to see if similar results are obtained when the tests are administered several times in the same or similar situations. If such results are obtained, the device can be judged reliable. With practice and refinement of procedures, teachers will find themselves able to select and use numerous reliable test items (oral and written).

EVALUATION TECHNIQUES

The main evaluation techniques used with young children are oral testing, observation, written tests, and interviewing. Standardized tests are discussed along with written tests and in a separate section on evaluating a school program or a new instructional program.

Oral Testing

Oral testing is especially useful for gaining information from young children who are learning to read and have difficulty with vocabulary and symbols. The teacher can probe into the child's thinking process to see if new concepts are being internalized and understood. The technique involves some of the procedures used in Piaget-type interviews, but concentrates on testing one skill rather than many, as in interviews.

For example, while observing a third-grade math group at work, a teacher sees one child shake a number of two-colored beans, roll them on the desk, and record the results. The recording is not accurate or consistent. In this case, the teacher can ask, "What did you roll?" "What did you record?" "Would you like me to show you another way?" The teacher can then shake, roll the beans out of the container, count the beans in each group one by one, and record the results. The child can then repeat the procedure.

The teacher can use oral testing as part of a class or group lesson to get feedback. Based on the feedback, the teacher can continue the lesson, move into follow-up work, or wait for another time to present additional instruction.

Observation

Teachers continuously observe children's work — individually, as a class, and in groups. The teacher should search for information based on the quality of answers given, the vocabulary used, how materials are used, work habits, ease of solving a problem, recording data, and general attitude toward math. With practice, teachers can learn to record accurate, objective information. However, they should withhold their reactions and judgments until enough data are collected to make important decisions and to plan for changes in instruction.

Written Tests

Several kinds of written tests are used with young children: the textbook or workbook tests, which basically review a topic or chapter; check-up pages, which test for mastery of basic facts; cumulative tests, which cover several topics, such as time, money, and place value; and teacher-prepared, follow-up work, which tests pupil understanding of the math concepts presented in a lesson. Each of these written tests has been discussed at appropriate places throughout this book.

STANDARDIZED TESTS   Other written tests include standardized achievement tests, which are used to test children's progress in learning a certain subject such as mathematics or their overall progress in all school subjects. The results of these tests have been used for a variety of purposes, including general assessment of instruction, children's readiness to enter or leave programs at each learning level, and support for existing programs and instructional practices.

In their latest publication, *Achievement Testing in Early Grades: The Games Grown-ups Play,* edited by Constance Kamii (1990), the National Association for the Education of Young Children has called for a rethinking of the use of achievement tests. These tests are also being challenged by classroom teachers, leading educators, and other national organizations such as the Association for Childhood Education International (ACEI) (Perrone, 1977), the Association for Supervision and Curriculum Development (ASCD, 1987), and the National Council of Teachers of Mathematics (NCTM, 1989).

We agree. Achievement testing in grades K–3 must end. We must rethink assessment procedures as well as our educational goals and methods of teaching. We must stop drilling children on isolated mathematical facts, skills, and problem-solving skills — which achievement testing necessitates and encourages.

The National Association of State Boards of Education (1988) has taken a strong stand on the use of standardized achievement tests:

> Preschool, kindergarten, and primary grade teachers report an increasing use of standardized tests, worksheets, and workbooks, ability grouping, retention, and other practices that focus on academic skills too early and in inappropriate ways . . .
>
> Thinking in young children is directly tied to their interactions with people and materials. Young children learn best and most by actively exploring their environment, using hands-on materials and building upon their natural curiosity and desire to make sense of the world around them. (pp. 3–5)

In this chapter, we have prepared sample tests covering basic mathematical concepts for ages five through eight. These tests are only one part of an appropriate evaluation program. They measure children's understanding of specific math concepts, and teachers may use them as models in constructing tests appropriate for their children and their own unique style of instruction.

The teacher gives oral directions when administering the tests and shows the children where to begin to write a response for each question. Children are tested individually or in small groups of four or five children. We recommend that formal evaluation begin at the kindergarten level with a two-part evaluation: prenumber concepts at mid-term and beginning number concepts at the end of the year.

EVALUATING PRENUMBER CONCEPTS

The prenumber evaluation test that follows is designed to assess children's understanding of fundamental concepts relating to size, weight, shape, color, measurement, surface (area), capacity, patterns, attributes joined together, sets, curves, and one-to-one correspondence.

We have already suggested several ways for teachers to use this test. Children need to be familiar with the term *frame,* and with the pictures, and know how to make an X or draw lines to show their responses. Directions are given in the space next to each item. The test may be used one page at a time, or in its entirety at appropriate times during the instructional program. The whole test covers half a year of instruction for kindergarten children.

1. Mark X on the largest figure.

2. Mark X on the smallest figure.

3. Mark X on the balloon with the longest string.

4. Mark X on the heavier box.

5. Mark X on the largest apple.

Circle the smallest apple.

6. Find another pattern the same as the first one.

Circle the two that are the same.

7. Mark X on the leaf covering the most surface.

8. On A, mark an X on a square; on B, on a circle; on C, on a triangle.

A.

B.

C.

9. Mark X on the pitcher with the most water in it.

10. Mark X on the ball with the shortest rope.

11. Make more circles to repeat the pattern.

12. The girl and boy each want as many balloons as the other. Add as many balloons as you need to give the boy and girl each the same number. Draw lines to show "the same as."

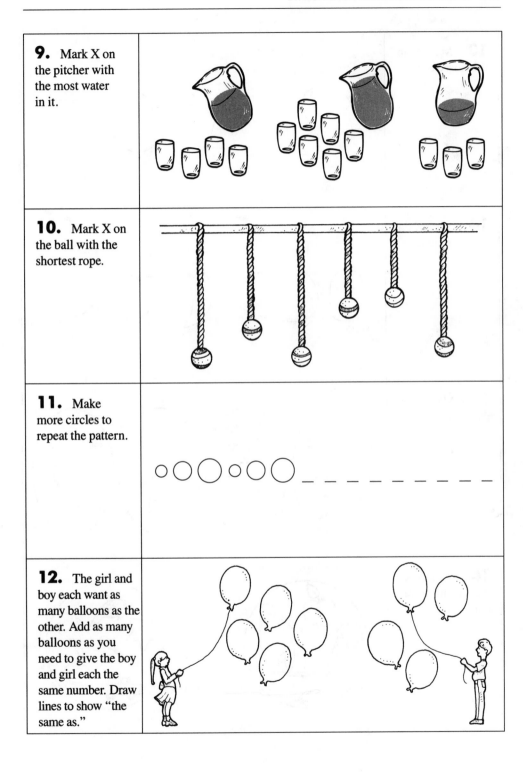

13. Mark X on the closed curve.

14. Mark X on the open curve.

15. Mark X on the set of cars.

16. Mark X on the set with more things in it.

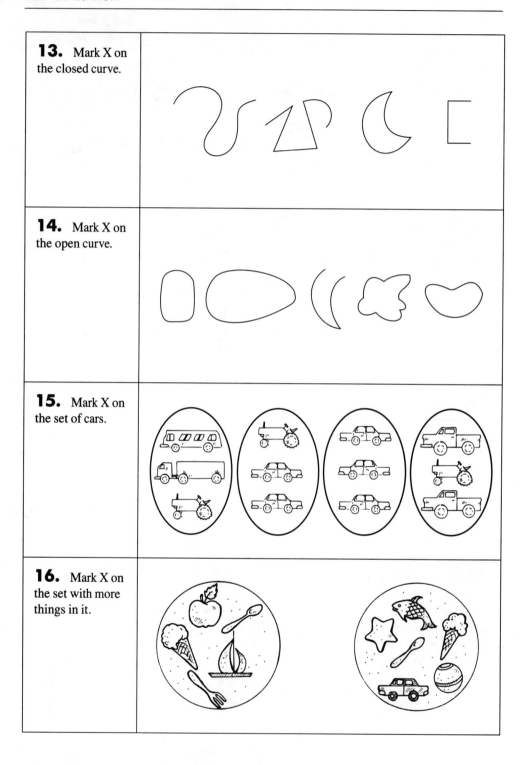

17. Mark X on the container that holds the same amount of water as the first container.

18. Put your finger on the picture to show me the time to: get up, go to school, play.

19. Circle the thing that does not belong.

20. Mark X to show outside the circle.

21. Mark X to show all the things inside the closed curve.

22. Mark X on the set with the most elements.

23. Circle the number that tells how many.

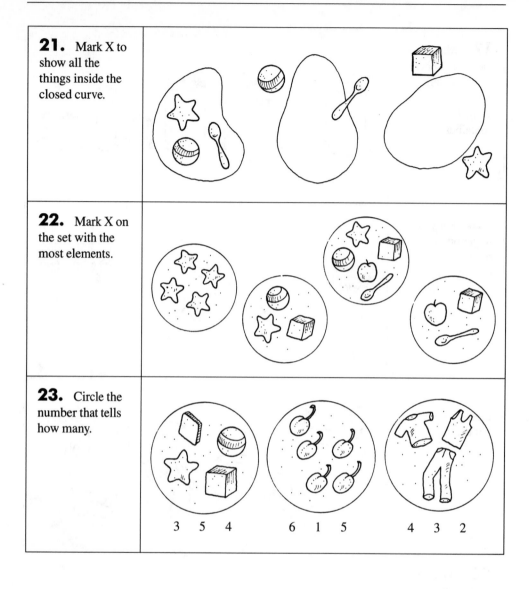

3   5   4   6   1   5   4   3   2

EVALUATING BEGINNING NUMBER CONCEPTS

The next evaluation test covers the last half-year of instruction in kindergarten. Children at this level will have learned to read and write the numbers 1 through 10. The mathematical concepts covered include: joining numbers in a sequence; matching sets of 5, 7, 9; matching sets with the same number of elements; ordinal fifth; thin and thick objects; repeating a pattern; coins: 1¢, 5¢, 10¢; number to select and name sets; shapes; using time during the day; greater than and less than; putting together on a number line; and putting together 5¢ + 5¢.

This test may be used in first grade following prenumber work.

1. Join the numbers from 1 to 10. (in order)

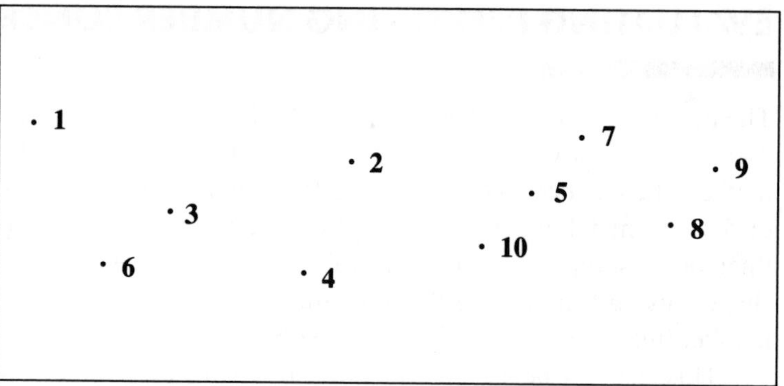

. 1

. 2   . 7

. 3   . 5   . 9

. 6   . 4   . 10   . 8

2. Draw a line from the number to a set with the same number of elements.

| x | * * * | # |
| x x x x x | * * * * | # # # # |

@ @ @   0
@   0 0

7   6   3   4   5

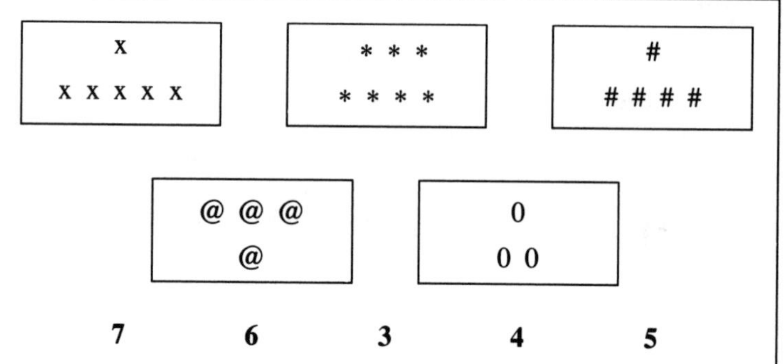

3. Add Xs to each set to get the number shown.

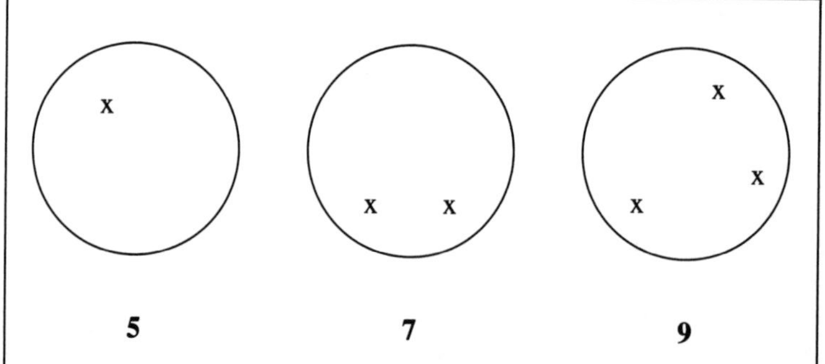

x

x   x

x   x

x

x

5   7   9

4. Draw a line to connect sets with the same number of elements.

x
x   x
x

&
&   &

C C C
C C C C

△△ △
△
△△△

. .
. .

*   *
*   *   *
*

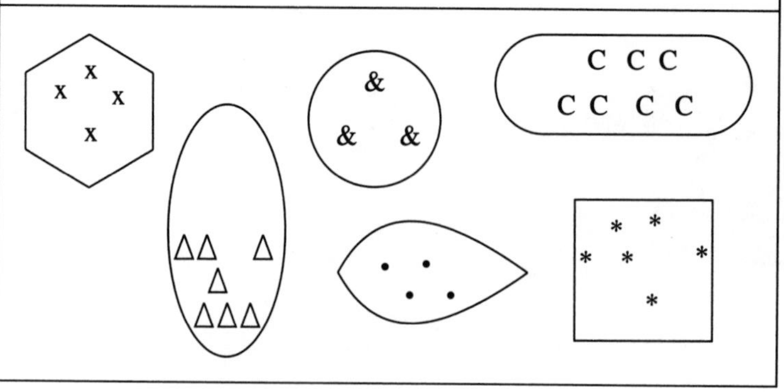

5. Mark the fifth circle.

6. Put an X on the object that is thin.

7. Put an X on the person who has grown the tallest.

8. Put an X on the object that does not belong in the kitchen.

9. Put an X on the thickest object.

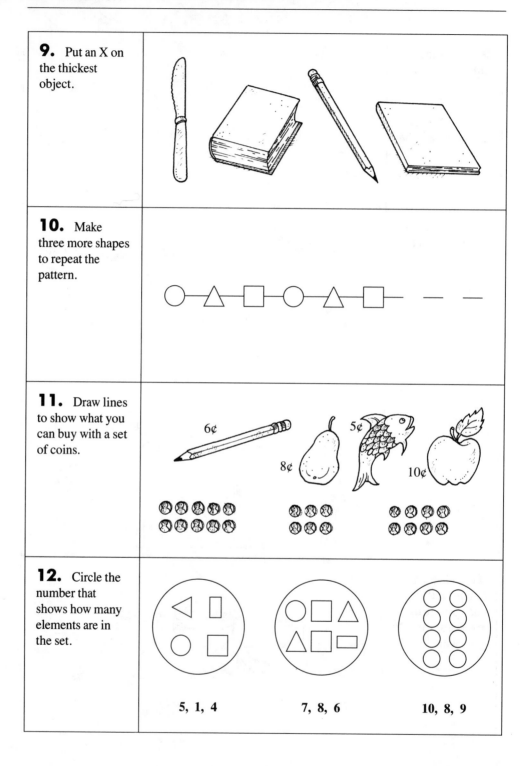

10. Make three more shapes to repeat the pattern.

11. Draw lines to show what you can buy with a set of coins.

6¢

8¢

5¢

10¢

12. Circle the number that shows how many elements are in the set.

5, 1, 4

7, 8, 6

10, 8, 9

13. Write a number to name the number of elements in each of the sets.

_____   _____   _____

14. Write a number to name the number of elements in the set.

_____   _____   _____

15. From a pile of attribute blocks, show me a . . .

blue
triangle

thin
green
circle

thick
red
square

yellow
circle

16. Draw a line to connect each picture to the words it goes with.

Play.   Get up.   Go to school.

17. Draw a line to connect the cost in words with the object that costs that much.

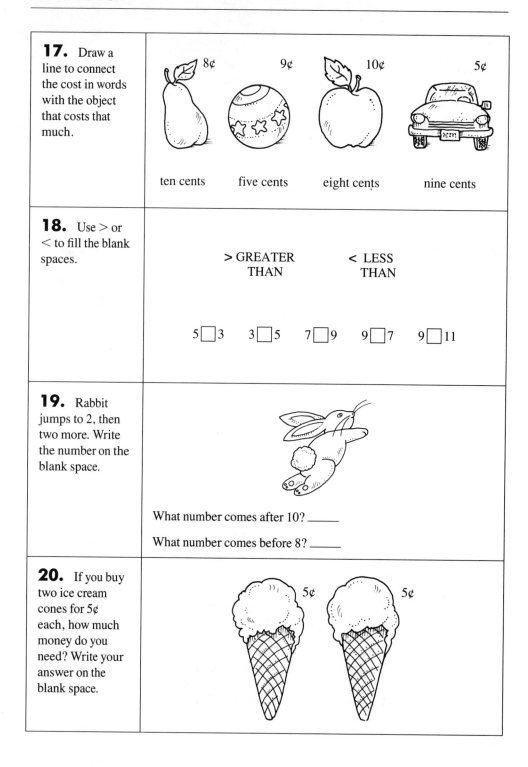

8¢   9¢   10¢   5¢

ten cents   five cents   eight cents   nine cents

18. Use > or < to fill the blank spaces.

> GREATER THAN   < LESS THAN

5 ☐ 3   3 ☐ 5   7 ☐ 9   9 ☐ 7   9 ☐ 11

19. Rabbit jumps to 2, then two more. Write the number on the blank space.

What number comes after 10? _____

What number comes before 8? _____

20. If you buy two ice cream cones for 5¢ each, how much money do you need? Write your answer on the blank space.

5¢   5¢

EVALUATION CONTENT: SIX-YEAR-OLDS

Components of child's environment and basic operations for six-year-old children that are covered in the test questions are as follows:

1. Money, coin denomination value
2. Pattern recognition and sequence
3. Time on hour, half hour, quarter hour
4. Concept of half, area
5. Concept of half, quantity
6. Concept of one-fourth
7. Place value: hundreds, ones, tens
8. Number sequence
9. Place-value understanding
10. Number sequence
11. Set recognition
12. Set concept understanding
13. Counting by 2s, 5s and 10s; writing numbers
14. Measuring with ruler
15. Addition, including regrouping
16. Counting by 2s, 3s, 5s, and 10s
17. Multiplication
18. Subtraction
19. Money, subtraction of one-digit numbers without regrouping
20. Money, subtraction problem solving
21. Place value to thousands

1. Draw a line from the money to the coin of the same value.

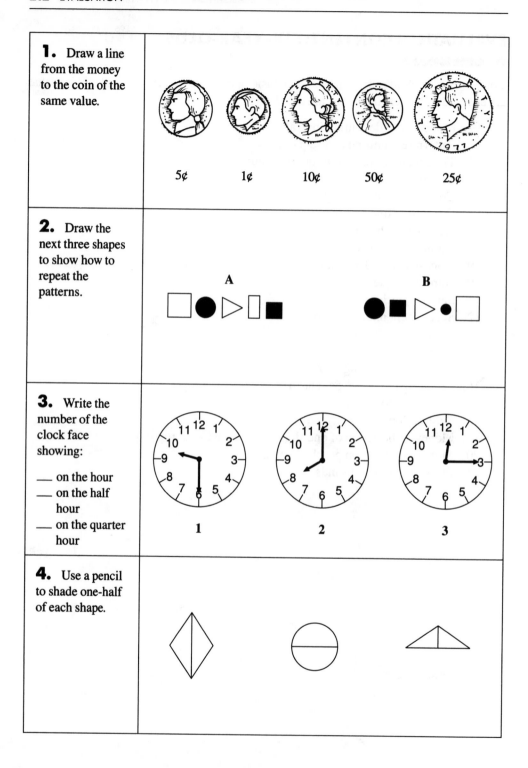

5¢   1¢   10¢   50¢   25¢

2. Draw the next three shapes to show how to repeat the patterns.

A

B

3. Write the number of the clock face showing:

___ on the hour
___ on the half hour
___ on the quarter hour

1   2   3

4. Use a pencil to shade one-half of each shape.

5. Use a pencil to shade one-half of each group of shapes.

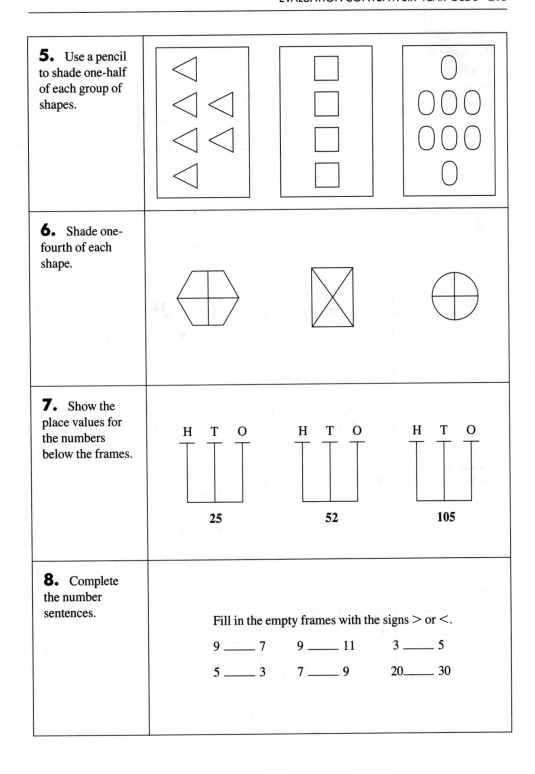

6. Shade one-fourth of each shape.

7. Show the place values for the numbers below the frames.

H T O H T O H T O

25 52 105

8. Complete the number sentences.

Fill in the empty frames with the signs > or <.

9 _____ 7   9 _____ 11   3 _____ 5

5 _____ 3   7 _____ 9   20_____ 30

9. Name the tens, ones, and hundreds for each example.

A.   35 = _____ tens and _____ ones

B.   75 = _____ tens and _____ ones

C. 115 = _____ hundreds, _____ tens, and _____ ones

10. Connect the numbers starting with one (in order).

• 1
• 2   • 16   • 13
• 15
• 5   • 14   • 12
• 4   • 10
• 8   • 18
• 7
• 9   • 17
• 3   • 6
•
11

11. Circle the number for each set that says the number of elements in that set.

3 8 6 5   3 7 6 5   5 3 2 4

12. Write the number naming the elements in each set.

_____   _____   _____

13. Count by 2s, 5s, and 10s to fill in the blanks.

2s: 2   4   6   ___ ___ ___ ___ ___

5s: 5   10   15 ___ ___ ___ ___ ___

10s: 50 60   ___ ___ ___ ___ ___ ___

14. Use a ruler to measure each line to the inch or half-inch.

_____ = ___ inches

_____ = ___ inches

_____ = ___ inches

15. Fill in the blank spaces under each number by adding 8 each time.

4	5	3	8	9	7	6	2
12							

+8

16. Fill in each blank space.

2 + 2 + 2 = ___ and 3 × ___ = 6

3 + 3 + 3 = ___ and 3 × ___ = ___

5 + 5 + 5 = ___ and 3 × ___ = ___

10 + 10 + 10 = ___ and 3 × ___ = ___

17. Fill in each blank space.

$4 \times 5 =$ _____ $4 \times 4 =$ _____

$5 \times 5 =$ _____ $3 \times 6 =$ _____

$2 \times 6 =$ _____ $2 \times 5 =$ _____

18. Fill in each blank space by subtracting the number 7.

	12	14	16	15	9	11	10
-7	5						

19. Write in the money you have left in the blank spaces.

You had	You lost	Have left
10¢	5¢	_____ ¢
25¢	15¢	_____ ¢
15¢	6¢	_____ ¢

20. Write in the amount you need to make each purchase.

You have	You want	You need
5¢	10¢	_____ ¢
15¢	25¢	_____ ¢
6¢	15¢	_____ ¢

21. Use the number frames to show the place values for each number shown below the frame.

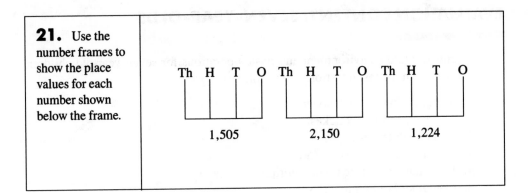

EVALUATION CONTENT: SEVEN-YEAR-OLDS

Components of child's environment and basic operations for seven-year-old children that are covered in the test questions are as follows:

1. Weight. How much heavier?
2. Longest, shortest, thickest
3. Story problem (weight)
4. Covers the most surface (area)
5. How many tiles (area) and multiplication facts
6. Container holding the most
7. Days of the week, number of weeks in a month, days in month, number of school days
8. Time on the hour; half-past; 15 minutes past the hour, or quarter hour
9. Time for events, TV time to the minute
10. Money, subtraction of two one-digit numbers without regrouping
11. Adding 10s (10¢)
12. Adding coins to make 25¢
13. Adding coins to make 50¢
14. Coins in one dollar
15. Addition facts
16. Subtraction facts, one-digit numbers from two-digit numbers, no regrouping
17. Adding one-digit to two-digit numbers
18. Place values, two-digit addition
19. Place values, two-digit numbers in subtraction
20. Place values using bundles of tens and ones
21. Place values in hundreds
22. Multiplication using repeated additions on a number line
23. Problem solving, finding the facts that are not needed
24. Problem solving

1. Mark an X on the heavier box.

2. Use a ruler to find the longest line, the shortest line, and the thickest line. Write the letter of each line in the blank space.

A _____

B ━━━━━━━━━━━━━━━━━━━

C _____

Longest _____   Shortest _____   Thickest _____

3. How many sacks of sugar are there? How heavy is each sack? How many pounds does each weigh?

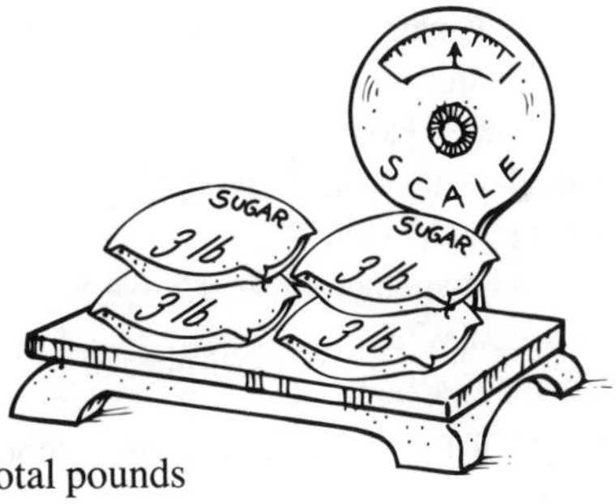

Number of sacks _____

Weight of each sack _____

_____ × _____ = _____ total pounds

4. Circle the tile covering the least surface. Mark an X on the tile covering the most surface.

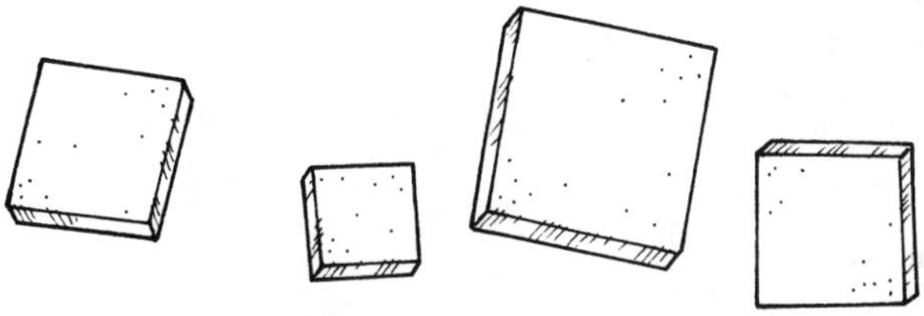

5. How many rows are there? How many tiles are in each row? How many tiles are there altogether?

Rows _____

Tiles in each row _____

_____ × _____ = _____ number of tiles

6. Mark X on the container that holds the most.

7. How many weeks in this month have 7 days? How many days are there in this month? How many days are there in a school week? How many school days are in this month?

Days in each week _____

Number of weeks _____

How many days _____ × _____ = _____

Days in a school week _____

Number of full school weeks _____

How many school days _____ × _____ = _____

1988   May

SUN	MON	TUE	WED	THU	FRI	SAT
1	2	3	4	5	6	7
8	9	10	11	12	13	14
15	16	17	18	19	20	21
22	23	24	25	26	27	28
29	30	31				

8. Write the letter of the clock that shows:

half past the hour _____

on the hour _____

15 minutes past the hour _____

A   B   C

9. Tell time to the minute.

What time is she watching TV?

_____

10. Work each example to find how much money is left after buying.

You have	A. 45¢	B. 56¢	C. 85¢
You buy	30¢	45¢	55¢
You have left	_____	_____	_____

11. Combine the coins in each row to find how much money there is.

2 dimes + 7 dimes = _____ ¢

5 dimes + 3 dimes = _____ ¢

4 dimes + 5 dimes = _____ ¢

12. Use the coins in the circle to show different ways to make 25¢.

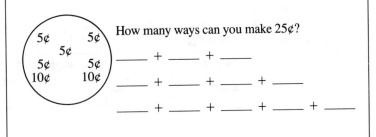

How many ways can you make 25¢?

_____ + _____ + _____

_____ + _____ + _____ + _____

_____ + _____ + _____ + _____ + _____

13. Use the coins in the circle to show different ways to make 50¢.

25¢   10¢
10¢
10¢
25¢   10¢
5¢   5¢

How many ways can you make 50¢?

_____ + _____ + _____

_____ + _____ + _____ + _____

_____ + _____ + _____ + _____ + _____

---

14. Fill in the number of coins to show how many are needed to make $1.

$1 dollar

= _____ nickels

= _____ dimes

= _____ quarters

= _____ half dollars

= _____ pennies

---

15. Using the number line, finish the chart by having rabbit start at the top number and hop ahead the number of spaces given.

0 1 2 3 4 5 6 7 8 9 10 11 12 13 14 15 16 17 18 19 20

Starts at	9	8	7	4	6	3	5
Hops ahead	5	6	8	7	9	3	4
Lands on	14						

---

16. Finish the number chart by having rabbit hop back, starting at the top number in each box.

Starts at	10	12	14	16	18	20
Hops back	5	4	6	6	8	10
Lands on	5					

17. Finish the first number chart by adding 6 to each number on the top. Then in the next chart add 12 to the top number.

+	13	23	33	53	63
6	19				

+	8	15	13	14	16	18
12	20					

18. Add the numbers, then write the number of tens and ones.

52 = 4 tens, 2 ones
+ 35 = _____tens, _____ones
_____ = _____tens, _____ones

64 = 6 tens, 4 ones
+ 24 = 2 tens, 4 ones
_____ = _____tens, _____ones

19. Fill in the blanks to complete the problems.

```
  70        3_        86        _8
+ __      + _2      - _2      - 2
  90        55        5_        60
```

20. Find how many tubes are in each bundle. Write the number of tubes altogether.

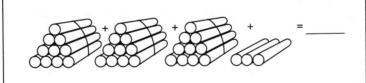

+   +   +   = _____

21. Show the place values of each number on the number frame.

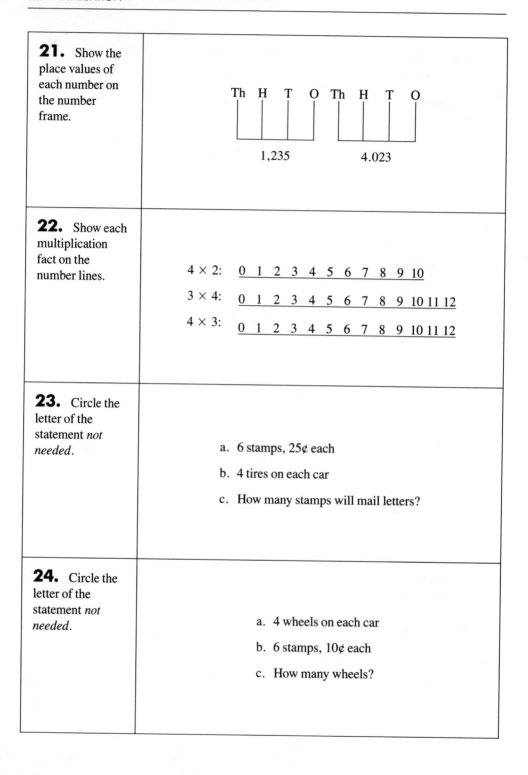

Th H T O   Th H T O

1,235   4.023

22. Show each multiplication fact on the number lines.

4 × 2: 0 1 2 3 4 5 6 7 8 9 10

3 × 4: 0 1 2 3 4 5 6 7 8 9 10 11 12

4 × 3: 0 1 2 3 4 5 6 7 8 9 10 11 12

23. Circle the letter of the statement *not needed*.

a. 6 stamps, 25¢ each

b. 4 tires on each car

c. How many stamps will mail letters?

24. Circle the letter of the statement *not needed*.

a. 4 wheels on each car

b. 6 stamps, 10¢ each

c. How many wheels?

EVALUATION CONTENT: EIGHT-YEAR-OLDS

Components of child's environment and basic operations for eight-year-old children that are covered in the test questions are as follows:

1. Surface (area)
2. Distance around (perimeter)
3. Measurement (standard or metric), line segments
4. Liquid measurement, pints, quarts, gallon
5. Reading a chart
6. Time to 15 minutes to the hour, 10 minutes past the hour, and 20 minutes past the hour
7. Temperature, night and morning
8. Patterns and square tiles
9. Covering a surface, width $\times$ length
10. Subtraction with U.S. money, three digits

11-15. Story problems

16. Making change with chart, 50¢, 25¢, 10¢, 5¢, 1¢
17. Fractions, identifying $\frac{1}{2}, \frac{1}{3}, \frac{1}{4}$
18. Shading $\frac{2}{4}, \frac{3}{4}$
19. $>$, $<$, or $=$ with $\frac{1}{2}, \frac{1}{3}, \frac{1}{4}$
20. Telling time to the hour, 15 minutes after, half past
21. Telling time, number line to minutes
22. Weight, heavier than, and how much?
23. Addition facts for 7 and 8
24. Place value, two-digit numbers
25. Place values, three-digit numbers
26. Adding two two-place numbers
27. Subtraction with money (buying)
28. Multiplying odd numbers by 6 and 7
29. Weight of sacks of grain, total weight
30. Multiplying by 6 and 7
31. Multiplying by 8 and 9
32. Combining multiplication and division
33. Combining
34. Finding quotients and recording a remainder

1. Use a ruler to find how many square inches there are in this rectangle.

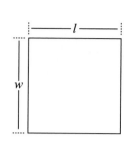

How many square inches in the figure?

$l =$ _____ inches, $w =$ _____ inches

l _____ $\times$ w _____ $=$ _____ sq. in.

2. Use a ruler to measure the distance around the rectangle (perimeter).

top = _____

side = _____

bottom = _____

side = _____

distance around = _____ inches

3. Use a ruler to measure each line to the inch, half-inch, or one-fourth inch (or metric).

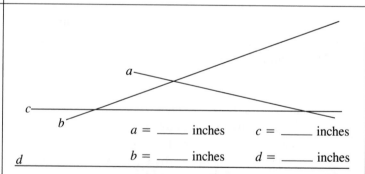

$a =$ _____ inches $c =$ _____ inches

$b =$ _____ inches $d =$ _____ inches

4. Circle one pint.

How many pints in one quart?

Place an X on one quart.

How many quarts in one gallon?

5. Fill in the blanks to describe the results of the throwing game.

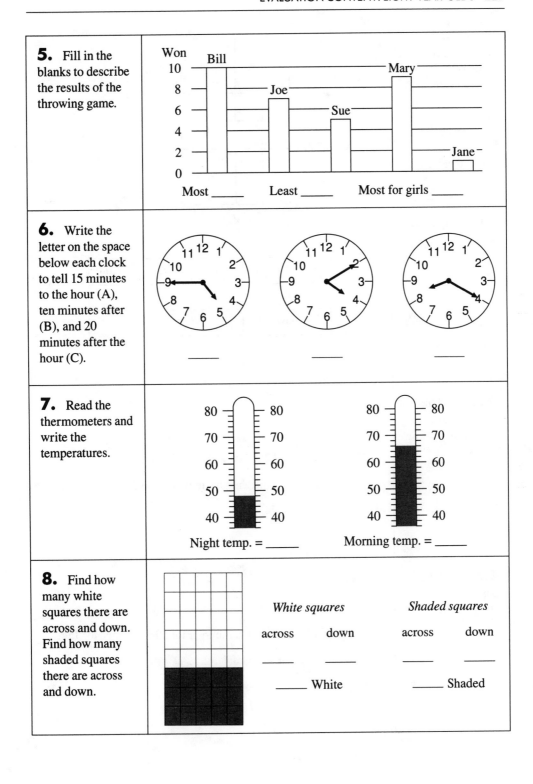

Won

Bill

Joe

Mary

Sue

Jane

Most _____   Least _____   Most for girls _____

6. Write the letter on the space below each clock to tell 15 minutes to the hour (A), ten minutes after (B), and 20 minutes after the hour (C).

_____   _____   _____

7. Read the thermometers and write the temperatures.

Night temp. = _____   Morning temp. = _____

8. Find how many white squares there are across and down. Find how many shaded squares there are across and down.

White squares

across   down

_____   _____

_____ White

Shaded squares

across   down

_____   _____

_____ Shaded

9. How many tiles wide is the bathroom floor? _____ How many tiles long is it? _____ How many tiles are there altogether? _____ Then _____ × _____ = _____

10. Fill in the blanks.

You have	$1.46	$4.50	$7.08
You buy	.75		
You have left			

11. Find the answer to the story problem.

Jane saved 25¢ last week and 33¢ this week.

How much did she save in two weeks? _____

12. Find the answer to the story problem.

You have 75¢ and buy a hamburger for 50¢ and juice for 15¢.

How much do you have left? _____

13. Find the answer to the story problem.

Mary had 95¢.

She spent 35¢ for fruit and 50¢ for a doll.

How much does she have left? _____

14. Find the answer to the story problem.

How many 25¢ stamps can you buy for $1.00? _____

15. Find the answer to the problem.

You have a one-dollar bill.

You buy a toy for 75¢.

What change will you get back? _____

16. Using the chart, how many ways can you make 85¢? Use one coin no more than three times.

50¢	25¢	10¢	5¢	1¢
1	1		0	0
0	2			
1	0			
0	3			

17. Write the fraction for each shaded part.

A   B   C

_____   _____   _____

18. Shade the parts for each written fraction.

$\frac{3}{4}$ $\frac{2}{4}$

19. Use >, <, or = to make true statements.

$\frac{1}{2} - \frac{1}{4}$ $\frac{1}{3} - \frac{1}{4}$ $\frac{1}{2} - \frac{1}{3}$

$\frac{1}{2} - \frac{2}{4}$ $\frac{2}{3} - \frac{1}{2}$

20. Write the letter on the blank space to show time on the hour, half past, and quarter past the hour.

A   B   C

Which clock shows half past? _____

Which clock shows on the hour? _____

Which clock shows quarter past? _____

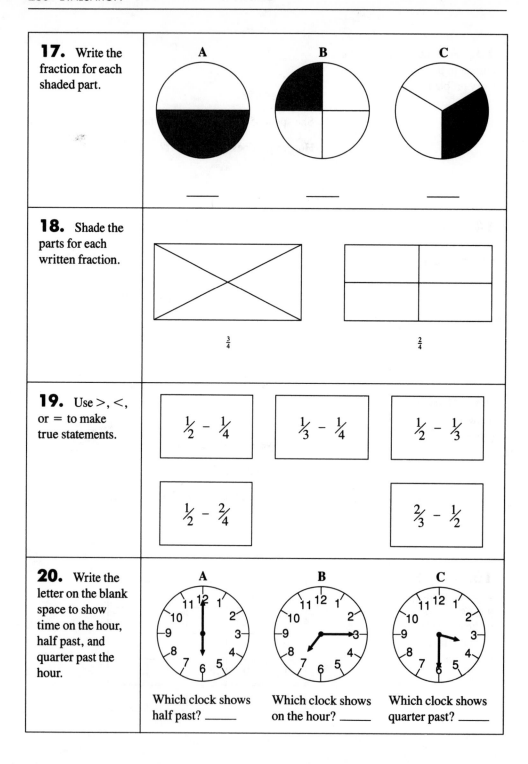

21. Numbers on the clock face have been made into a number line. There are 5 minutes between each pair of numbers. Answer the problems by filling in the blanks.

0   1   2   3   4   5   6   7   8   9   10   11   12

How many numbers on the clock face? _____

How many minutes in one hour? _____

Write a multiplication fact to show how many minutes.

_____ × _____ = _____

22. Make an X on the heavier box. How much heavier is it?

How much heavier? _____

75

8|

23. Rabbit wants to add 7 and 8 to the numbers on the number line. Fill in the blanks in each row.

+		1	2	3	4	5	6	7	8	9	10	11	12
+ 7→													
+ 8→													

24. Show the place values and add.

4 1 = _____ tens and _____ ones   4 6 = _____ _____

+ 1 8 = _____ tens and _____ ones   + 3 6 = _____ _____

__ __ = _____ tens and _____ ones   __ __ = _____ _____

25. Show the place values and add.

214 = _____ hundreds _____ tens _____ ones
+ 355 = _____ hundreds _____ tens _____ ones
___ = _____ hundreds _____ tens _____ ones

378 = _____ hundreds _____ tens _____ ones
154 = _____ hundreds _____ tens _____ ones
+ 312 = _____ hundreds _____ tens _____ ones
___ = _____ hundreds _____ tens _____ ones

26. Add the examples.

47	38	124	135
+ 52	+ 25	+ 43	+ 56

27. Fill in the blanks to show how much money is left.

You have	28¢	45¢	75¢
You buy	10¢	25¢	21¢
You have left			

28. Multiply the numbers on the number line as indicated.

0   1   2   3   4   5   6   7   8   9   10

Multiply each number by 6:

_____, _____, _____, _____, _____, _____, _____, _____, _____, _____

Multiply each number by 7:

_____, _____, _____, _____, _____, _____, _____, _____, _____, _____

29. Weigh these sacks of grain.

How many sacks are there? _____

What is the weight of each sack? _____

What is the total weight? _____

____ × ____ = _____

30. Multiply each number on the top line by 6 and then by 7.

×	4	6	5	8	9	7
6						
7						

31. Multiply each number on the top line by 8 and then by 9.

×	5	7	4	9	6	8
8						
9						

32. Fill in the blank spaces.

____ × 3 = 9   9 ÷ 3 = ____

____ × 4 = 24   24 ÷ 4 = ____   or   4) 24

5 × ____ = 25   25 ÷ 5 = ____

6 × ____ = 30   or   6) 30

33. Complete the examples.

If $3 \times 6 = 18$, then $18 \div 3 =$ _____

If $7 \times 5 = 35$, then $35 \div$ _____ $=$ _____

34. Complete the problems and show the remainder with "r." Look at the example.

Find the quotient:

$$\begin{array}{r} 3 \\ 5\overline{)16} \\ \underline{15} \\ 1r \end{array}$$

$5\overline{)35}$ $7\overline{)63}$ $8\overline{)64}$ $6\overline{)36}$ $9\overline{)45}$

$4\overline{)12}$ $6\overline{)38}$ $7\overline{)50}$ $8\overline{)65}$ $9\overline{)65}$

EVALUATION USING INTERVIEW METHOD

Piaget used the clinical interview method to study children's thinking. In this method, an adult interviewer engages a child in conversation, verbally asking questions and presenting problems in a setting where concrete, hands-on materials are used. The main purpose of the interview is to get the child to talk freely and interact with objects related to mathematics. In this section, we discuss three interview situations that can be used for short periods of time, such as while the class is working at activity centers or in small groups. These interview situations are:

1. Informal teacher–pupil interviews in which one mathematical concept is explored
2. Interviews that use two dolls or puppets to explore the child's thinking about one or two math concepts

3. The clinical-type interview, which is structured and strives to secure objective data for a detailed study of a child

The Informal Interview

The teacher can conduct informal interviews in second or third grade while the class is working at activity centers or in groups. The interview should take place at a table near the front or back of the class. If a teacher's aide is available to assist, the teacher may prefer a more secluded spot. Try to do two or three short interviews with each child so that no one child feels embarrassed or singled out.

The teacher can initiate the interview by asking the child to bring a worksheet (multiplication facts) to the table. The teacher can then ask the child to show and tell about the concepts involved, for example, in $3 \times 4 = 12$ and $4 \times 3 = 12$. The teacher might say, "Show me what these facts mean" (using concrete materials).

Or the teacher might initiate the interview by asking about a paper from the previous day's work, a workcard from the math center, or a problem relating to telling time.

Teachers can use this type of interview throughout the year to gain important information about children's thinking. In addition, children appreciate the personal, friendly contact.

Interviews with Puppets or Dolls

In a second type of interview, the teacher uses two attractive playthings, such as puppets or dolls, that the child can relate to and think about. The puppets are important as a means of describing materials (for example, "Tell me how many the rabbit has"), helping the teacher ask questions, and making the teacher's role more objective. Children are less inhibited when responding to the puppet. Children watch the puppets — they do not look at the teacher for approval, disapproval, or reactions. This procedure is an important part of the Australian TRIAD math program for five-year-old children (see Rawlinson, Phillips, & Yabsley, 1974). The following example identifies the important aspects of this type of interview.

AIM

The child uses a set of counters to show an understanding of one-to-one correspondence in forming equivalent sets.

MATERIALS

16 counters

One 5" × 8" card with sets of circles the same size as counters

ARRANGEMENT FOR INTERVIEW

Teacher

J.J. Puppet   •   •   •   So So Puppet

•   •

Child

Allowing the child to tell the answer to the puppet encourages participation because it is less risky from the child's perspective.

TEACHER COMMENTS AND QUESTIONS

1. "Can you give So So as many counters as J.J. has?" Point to the counters on the J.J. card.
2. "Has J.J. as many as So So? How do you know?"
3. Teacher moves J.J.'s counters closer together; So So's are spread out.
4. "Has J.J. as many as So So has? Why do you say that?"
5. Spread J.J.'s counters out so that they "appear" to be more than So So's.
6. "J.J. says he has more than So So. What do you think?"

The teacher can explore the child's thinking and ability to confirm equivalent sets. Vocabulary needed in this interview includes *as many as, more than, less than, fewer than*. Questions and steps may be repeated if a child does not seem to understand. The interview may stop when a child shows an inability to conserve the changes in groupings. The teacher must then decide where to begin teaching or to reteach certain aspects of one-to-one correspondence.

The Clinical-Type Interview

Piaget used the clinical-type interview with a limited number of children. We reported Piaget's research in Chapter 2, in our discussion of his theories about mathematical education. In a recent book, *Learning from Children,* Labinowicz (1985) adapted Piaget's open method of exploration — the clinical interview method — to the study of school-related tasks with first-, second-, and third-graders.

For teachers interested in children's thinking or in doing research work in this area, we recommend Labinowicz's provocative, practical book.

EVALUATION OF ATTITUDES – THE AFFECTIVE DOMAIN

Throughout the mathematics program, we emphasize the development of children's cognitive structures. However, the affective aspects are important, too, and are closely related to and influence intellectual development.

Attitudes are the emotions of children for or against something — in this discussion, mathematics. Anderson, in a classic statement (1949), defined *attitudes*:

> The term 'attitudes' includes not only the negative attitudes, such as prejudice, bias, and the like, but also positive attitudes (sometimes called sentiments) which include our attachments and loyalties to persons, objects, and ideals. An attitude, then, is a system of ideas with an emotional core or content. . . . You can be sure that the normal nine-year-old child will learn that 'two plus two' equals four and rattle if off without difficulty. But you cannot be quite so sure whether he will like or dislike arithmetic or will like or dislike his teacher. (pp. 282–283)

In several studies of the attitudes of prospective elementary school teachers and children (grades 3–8) toward arithmetic, Dutton (1951) identified the factors that influenced their development. Unfavorable attitudes center around these factors: lack of understanding, teaching disassociated from life, pages of word problems, boring drill, poor teaching, lack of interest, and fear of making mistakes. Favorable attitudes center around: proficiency in arithmetic, good teachers who explained the work and made it meaningful, appreciation of the subject as a vital part of school work, and enjoyment of advanced work in math.

A scale for evaluating children's attitudes toward math is given in Chapter 10.

Characteristics of Affective Behavior

The teacher can collect important information on children's attitudes when interviewing them and by looking for relevant characteristics during periods of observation. The following are some characteristics to look for:

Positive	Negative
Active when doing math	Listless, inattentive
Enthusiastic	Unenthusiastic
Confident	Not sure of self
Persistent	Easily distracted
Shows initiative	Lacks initiative
Creative, imaginative	Unimaginative, plodder

Although other characteristics may emerge, these are the important ones to look for. Start by finding one or two characteristics and try to collect corroborating evidence to support a judgment. Then include one or two more to your observation list.

To help children develop favorable feelings toward math, as well as overcome any negative feelings, the teacher should:

- Stimulate math exploration in everyday activities.
- Make math interesting and enjoyable.
- Use hands-on materials, structured and unstructured.
- Encourage pupil interaction — encourage them to help each other to succeed and to discover.
- Encourage children to concentrate on the work to be done and on seeking a variety of answers.
- Model enthusiasm for math activities.
- Provide positive, helpful assistance at appropriate times.

EVALUATION STRUCTURED INTO MATH PROGRAMS

The National Council of Supervisors of Mathematics believes that evaluation at each administrative level should align the objectives of the curriculum. They recommend caution in using standardized tests to monitor pupil progress and to evaluate effectiveness of instruction: "Existing standardized tests could perpetuate the domination of the mathematics curriculum by lower-order skills. . . . There is need for new tests that shift the focus from computation to problem solving and reasoning" (NCSM, 1988).

The National Diffusion Network (NDN) is a nationwide system established to help schools improve their educational programs through the adoption of already developed, *rigorously evaluated,* exemplary education programs.

Many programs accepted and funded by NDN contain evaluation components and provisions for determining the effectiveness of the programs, require parent involvement, and provide for in-service teacher preparation.

Most programs determine effectiveness by demonstrating statistically significant growth in children's knowledge of mathematics relative to national norms on standardized tests or in comparative experimental designs.

Parent involvement in NDN programs must be applauded. Lines of communication are established with parents, who then reinforce school instruction by providing carefully designed homework, reviewing math concepts, and providing enrichment experiences.

We close this section with the admonition voiced by the National Council of Supervisors of Mathematics: "that evaluation at each administrative level should be aligned with the objectives of the curriculum." This view challenges all who make and use evaluation instruments to provide an appropriate match between instruction and the learning that takes place and what is measured and reported as achievement in mathematics.

SUMMARY

In this chapter, we identified the main objectives for instruction in mathematics for children four through eight years of age. We also defined the role of evaluation in assessing children's understanding of math concepts, diagnosing areas of difficulty, discovering readiness for new learning, and appraising instructional practices.

The main evaluation techniques discussed included: oral testing, interview situations, observations, and a variety of appropriate written tests. We covered in detail test items that measure children's understanding of the main mathematical concepts for each learning level. The test items are based on the objectives established for each level. They can be used as separate test items to measure one basic math concept; in readiness tests for beginning instruction at another, higher level; in diagnostic tests after instruction on a unit of work; and in achievement tests at the end of the year or semester.

We carefully evaluated children's attitudes toward mathematics and learning, identifying favorable and unfavorable attitudes and making suggestions for instruction that would foster favorable feelings toward math.

Finally, we discussed the NCSM view that evaluation at each administrative level should be aligned with the objectives of the school's curriculum.

ACTIVITIES FOR TEACHER INSIGHT

1. Study the following test items to determine if they measure thinking and understanding of math concepts:
   a. In 2,5___4, the tens digit is missing. What is the greatest digit that we can place there: 0, 8, 9, 10, or 90?
   b. 256 is the same number as:
      i. 250 tens + 6 ones
      ii. 25 hundreds + 56 ones
      iii. 20 tens + 56 ones
      iv. 2 hundreds + 56 tens
   c. True or False: If the order of multiplying two whole numbers is changed, their product is changed.
   d. Which of these can we weigh: a child, a leaf, a feather, a car, all of these?
2. Develop several test items covering specific objectives for lessons in which new concepts are introduced.
3. Using two dolls or two puppets, try out the interview lesson on one-to-one correspondence with several five-year-olds. Can they understand the vocabulary and conserve the changes in groupings?
4. Select an elementary school in your area and arrange for an interview with the principal. What provision does the school make for evaluating its math program? How does the school measure and report pupil achievement in math?

REFERENCES

ANDERSON, J. E. (1949). *The psychology of development and personal adjustment*. New York: Henry Holt, pp. 282–283.

Association for Supervision and Curriculum Development. (1987). Testing concerns. In *Forty years of leadership: A synthesis of ASCD resolutions through 1987* (pp. 17–19). Alexandria, VA: Author.

California State Department of Education. (1987). *Mathematics: Model curriculum guide*. Sacramento, CA: Department of Education.

CARPENTER, T. P. (1988). Results of the fourth MAEP assessment of mathematics: Trends and conclusions. *Arithmetic Teacher, 36,* 38–41.

DUTTON, W. H. (October 1951). Attitudes of prospective teachers toward arithmetic. *Elementary School Journal, 52,* 84–90.

———. (1961). University students' comprehension of arithmetic. *Arithmetic Teacher, 8,* 60–62.

———. (1964). *Evaluating pupils' understanding of arithmetic*. Englewood Cliffs, NJ: Prentice-Hall.

KAMII, C. (1990). *Achievement testing in early grades: the games grown-ups play*. Washington, DC: National Association Education of Young Children.

LABINOWICZ, E. (1985). *Learning from children: New beginnings for teaching numerical thinking. A Piagetian approach*. Menlo Park, CA: Addison-Wesley.

National Assessment of Educational Progress (NAEP). (1987). *The third national mathematics assessment: Results, trends, and issues, 13-MA-01*. Denver, CO: Educational Commission of the States.

National Association of State Boards of Education. (1988). *Right from the start, birth to 8 year-olds (a report)*. Alexandria, VA: Author.

National Council of Supervisors of Mathematics. (1988). *Essential mathematics for the 21st century*. Minneapolis, MN: Author.

National Council of Teachers of Mathematics. (1989). *Curriculum and evaluation standards for school mathematics*. Reston, VA: Author.

National Diffusion Network (See United States Department of Education)

PERRONE, V. (1977). *Standardized testing and evaluation*. Wheaton, MD: Association for Childhood Education International.

RANDALL, C. (1987). *How to evaluate progress in problem solving*. Reston, VA: National Council of Teachers of Mathematics.

RAWLINSON, R. W., PHILLIPS, R. D., & YABSLEY, K. B. (1974). *TRIAD mathematics laboratory*. New South Wales, Australia: Jacaranda Press.

United States Department of Education. (1987). *Profile*. Washington, DC: National Diffusion Network, pp. 1–2.

CHAPTER 9

Computing Technology and School Mathematics

Computers have had a tremendous impact on education. In this chapter, we discuss the importance of computers, standards for their use, their characteristics, and selecting appropriate software. We end the chapter with suggestions for the meaningful use of calculators in math work.

THE IMPORTANCE OF COMPUTERS

In *Mindstorms* (1980), Seymour Papert writes on the importance of computers as carriers of powerful ideas and of the "seeds of cultural change, helping people form new relationships with knowledge of the self."

Instead of "computer-aided instruction," Papert believed that *the child should program the computer* and acquire a sense of mastery over a piece of the modern and powerful technology as well as establish an intimate contact with some of the deepest ideas of science, from mathematics, and from the art of intellectual model building (p. 5). He describes learning paths to help children become programmers. Programming a computer helps children communicate with it in a language the computer and the child can both understand. Since language is easy for children to learn and use, they should be able to learn to talk to a computer.

Two fundamental ideas were developed by Papert: (1) Computers can be designed so that learning to communicate with them is a natural process — like learning a foreign language by living in the country; and (2) learning to communicate with a computer may change the way other learning takes place. Computers can be a mathematics-speaking and an alphabetic-speaking entity. Mathematical communication can be transformed from something alien and difficult for most children into something easy and natural.

Over a ten-year period (1970–1980), Papert worked at the Massachusetts Institute of Technology (MIT) with the LOGO group in the Artificial Intelligence Laboratory to create a programming environment in which children could learn to communicate with computers. "The name LOGO was chosen for the new language to suggest the fact it is primarily symbolic and only secondarily quantitative," said Papert (1980, p. 210). The work on LOGO by the MIT community of researchers at the Artificial Intelligence Laboratory resulted in discoveries and commitments involving epistemology and aesthetics in computers.

We have been especially interested in Papert's commitment to Piaget theories. Prior to his work at MIT, Papert spent five years living and working at Piaget's Center for Genetic Epistemology in Geneva, Switzerland. His work there laid the foundation for his work in the uses of LOGO with young children.

Papert's Development of LOGO and Turtle

Papert and his colleagues at MIT made two monumental contributions to helping children communicate with computers. First, they developed a powerful computer language, LOGO. Second, they invented the "Turtle," a computational "thing-to-think-with" within the LOGO environment. Papert defined the Turtle as a "computer-controlled cybernetic animal. It exists within the cognitive minicultures of the LOGO environment, LOGO being the computer language in which communication with Turtle takes place." Children manipulate the Turtle — which moves and draws — by giving commands on the computer. Because of the Turtle, they see the direct results of their computer commands.

Papert started developing the Turtle in the LOGO environment in 1968 in an experimental program with 12 average seventh-grade students. The program was set up to see if these "novices" could learn the language of LOGO. They worked with LOGO during the school year instead of attending their regular mathematics class. The students wrote a variety of programs to play games of strategy, translate English to "Pig Latin," and create poetry. With the success of this test program, Papert proposed that the Turtle was a programming tool that could be used by individuals of all ages. Other research workers at MIT confirmed this belief, showing that even four-year-old children could learn to control the mechanical Turtles.

Through his work on LOGO and the Turtle, Papert showed that all children, under the right conditions, can become proficient in programming. He also showed that schools needed a new computer language and different computers from those they were using that were not based on children's thinking style.

Financial Support for LOGO and NSF

Financial support for the LOGO Project was provided by the National Science Foundation (NSF), which also made the country aware of and responsible for educational reform. The importance of the computer was spelled out in the NSF publication *Educating America for the 21st Century* (1983). This publication nurtured the work of the National Council of Supervisors of Mathematics in their preparation of *Essential Mathematics for the 21st Century* (1988), which we discussed in Chapter 1.

The NSF stated that the educational uses of microcomputers fell into three categories:

1. *Learning about computers:* how to use them and how they benefit society. Computer literacy at advanced stages is a marketable skill; it encourages students to think algorithmically as well as to develop problem-solving skills.
2. *Learning through computers:* a tool for drill, practice, diagnostic testing, and question-and-answer tutorials
3. *Learning with computers:* a tool for instruction and an environment within which learning can take place

Computers contribute to mathematics education for young children in several important ways, according to the NSF.

1. They allow children to explore real-world phenomena.
2. They provide tools children can use, including graph-plotting, routines, word processing, spreadsheet programs, and general-purpose problem-solvers.
3. They allow the use of special-purpose computer languages such as LOGO, which permits the creation of learning environments that foster the development of children's intellect.
4. They provide simulations, which create flexible universes so students may experimentally discover properties of the real world.
5. They allow discovery learning in mathematics, which provides for an active, self-directed learning environment.

The NSF closes this discussion of computer contributions to mathematics education with the admonition that producers of computer materials must provide software appropriate to teacher's needs, as well as provide them with the training necessary to apply this computer technology effectively.

STANDARDS FOR SCHOOL MATHEMATICS

In keeping with the recommendations of the NSF, the National Council for Teachers of Mathematics (NCTM) has prepared a list of standards for school mathematics K–12 that includes the use of computers.

The NCTM began this work in 1987, when it established a Commission on

Standards to prepare a working draft of the standards that should influence both curriculum writing at state and local levels and the content of textbooks prepared for school districts. Greater emphasis was to be placed on concept development, mathematical reasoning, and problem solving. The final version of this report, *Curriculum and Evaluation Standards for School Mathematics* (1988), enlarges on the 1987 report. In September 1989, the NCTM began a series of articles in the *Arithmetic Teacher* that focuses on these newly written standards for curriculum improvement and evaluation.

At all grade levels, the standards recommended by the NCTM are affected by the capabilities and availabilities of new technology in the form of calculators and computers. Both are widely available in the classroom for mathematics instruction as well as available outside the classroom in the home.

In this book, we have identified the appropriate mathematical concepts, reasoning skills and abilities, and problem-solving experiences for each learning level — four through eight years of age. The scope and sequence charts for each age group were prepared to guide teachers in the development of these important factors as well as to provide a continuum for their development. These same scope and sequence charts provide a sound framework within which teachers can select and use calculators and computers.

The basic principles of learning, content selection, grade placement of topics and concepts, recommendations for delivery of instruction, and evaluation that we present throughout this book agree with the standards set by the NCTM. However, the NCTM makes certain recommendations that teachers should consider regarding the delivery of appropriate instruction when computers and appropriate software are used. We feel these recommendations are important enough to repeat, and we do so here:

1. There should be a balanced curriculum and introduction of new topics.
2. Place value should be presented in the second grade.
3. Basic addition and subtraction facts should be mastered by third grade.
4. Basic multiplication and division facts should be mastered by fourth grade.
5. Smaller numbers should be used in paper-and-pencil computational work; proficiency with two- and three-digit numbers should be achieved by third grade.
6. Pen-and-pencil computation with fractions should be delayed until after fourth grade.
7. There should be more time available for other mathematical content.
8. Greater emphasis should be placed on problem solving, mathematical reasoning, measurement, geometry, and estimation.

In addition to these recommendations, several general themes have a direct bearing on the use of calculators and computers:

1. Problem solving should be the main focus of the mathematics curriculum.
2. Mathematics should be communicated through the use of representational

models, such as physical models, oral language, pictures and diagrams, written symbols, and mental images.

3. Mathematical reasoning and the statement of logical conclusions should be emphasized.

4. Teachers should have pupils justify and validate their thinking and solutions.

CHARACTERISTICS OF COMPUTERS

Modern computers have large memory systems. Mathematical operations and calculations can be completed with split-second speed and almost flawless accuracy. Computers can accept data, process it according to prearranged plans, and give out the results.

The typical computer system comprises several units: a central processing unit (CPU) and input and output devices (see Figure 1). These latter devices are connected to the computer by electric cables. Figure 2 shows how data are input, processed, and output.

These two views of the computer represent structural and functional views. However, neither gets down to the level of functional behavior needed for a discussion of elementary math or its teaching and learning. For that, we must look in detail at the

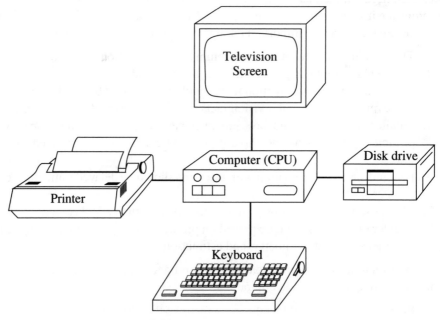

Figure 1 Typical Computer System

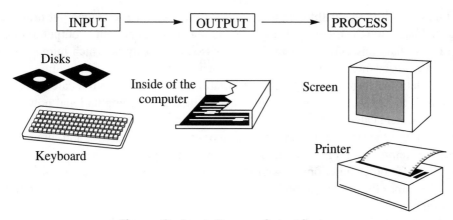

Figure 2   Input, Process, Output System

central processing unit (CPU) of a computer. We do that now, and show, by analogy, how students solve problems — both with and without the aid of calculators or other computing devices.

The top of Figure 3 shows schematically the three essential components of the CPU and its interface to input/output devices. These components are: (1) a control unit, (2) a memory system, and (3) an arithmetic-logic unit (ALU).

The CPU accepts data and instructions from the input devices and channels them to memory for storage. The control function in CPU can call data from the memory

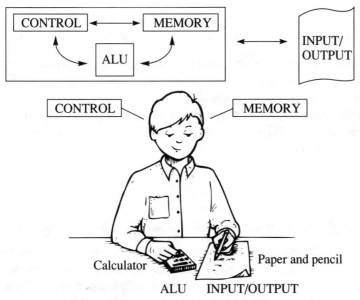

Figure 3   Basic Units of CPU and Human Problem Solving
with and without Computation Aids.

unit and send it to the arithmetic-logic unit for processing. It can then put processed material back into the memory. Data stored in memory can be sent to output devices.

Direct parallels exist between this process and the way in which humans solve problems. Based on a learned method stored in human memory, the individual collects needed data, performs the required computations (with or without a calculator) and "outputs" the results. The simplest first step in increasing computational power is to use a hand-held calculator. When we use a calculator, the computation is done by the calculator but the storage of data, execution of command sequence, and input/output processes remain human functions. As we begin to use computers, however, we can transfer these other functions as well to the computer. The challenge at this point is how to enhance the growth of intelligence and not allow it to diminish through reliance on computers.

To illustrate how the calculator and human function together to find answers to problems, we will take a simple example and go through the calculations. Figure 4 shows the steps necessary to compute the product of 2×8. The two operations that "enter" data correspond to taking information from (human) memory; the "multiply" and "equal" statements are the control operations with which the human tells the calculator what functional operation it is to perform on the data (factors).

Clear old result	(C)
Enter 2	(2)
State multiplication operation	($\times$)
Enter 8	(8)
Ask for result	(=)
New result is outputted	(16)

Figure 4   Calculator Operation to Obtain Multiplication Function

As we noted, as we move up in computation power to a computer, we transfer the control and memory storage functions to the computer. The transfer is formalized in the use of a so-called high-level language.

One of the oldest high-level languages is FORTRAN, which stands for *FORmula TRANslation* language. Figure 5 shows how a FORTRAN input would look for the same example shown in Figure 4.

$$A = 2$$
$$B = 8$$
$$C = A * B$$

Figure 5   High-Level Language (FORTRAN) Statements for Multiplication Function

The locations for data in memory are A, B, C. The first two statements say that 2 and 8 are located in A and B; the next statement has the ALU perform the calculation and store the result in location C. This simple example has taken us from a situation where memory and control are provided by the user to a situation in which they are provided by the CPU through the means of a high-level language.

Dozens of high-level languages have been developed over the last two decades. FORTRAN was developed for specialists interested in mathematical computations. However, the language is cryptic and not particularly "user friendly." More recent languages that are easier to use and are used extensively for educational purposes are BASIC and LOGO.

BASIC (Beginners All-purpose Symbolic Instruction Code) is relatively easy to learn and is used extensively for first courses in computer programming. LOGO, a newer programming language, is particularly useful for geometric and graphical activities. LOGO, developed by Papert, is used at all learning levels, but especially in elementary schools.

Computer languages are different for each major manufacturer. Computer manufacturers modify BASIC and LOGO to fit their own particular equipment. For example, the Apple IIe computer has Applesoft BASIC and Terrapin LOGO.

The following illustrates how LOGO, designed primarily for young children, is used in a school setting. At the Corrine Seeds Elementary School, University of California, Los Angeles, the primary grades use the Terrapin LOGO program. Twenty Apple IIe's are available in a computer laboratory. The program used is LOGO MICRO: The Wonderful World of Paws and some Data Base. In groups of 20, children undergo six weeks of instruction; this continues until all 120 children have completed the program.

The Terrapin LOGO language package for Apple II, II + , and IIe includes: one LOGO language disk; one utilities disk containing demonstration and utility programs; one documentation manual containing a Terrapin LOGO Tutorial; and one technical manual.

The LOGO Tutorial uses three LOGO mascots (elephant, rabbit, and snail), all drawn with LOGO Turtle, to teach children how to use the language. LOGO has basic programs for graphics, computation, words and lists, and music.

The LOGO utilities disk includes a collection of procedures that makes LOGO Turtle graphics accessible to young children. An INSTANT system uses single-character commands that are equivalent to longer LOGO commands. Colored stickers may be used to identify appropriate keys. The system is for children who have not learned to read.

COMPUTERS AND YOUNG CHILDREN

Douglas Clements (1987), codirector of the Logo-based Geometry Project at Kent State University, has written a timely and definitive article reviewing the research being done on computers and young children. The article covers such basic questions as: Are young children physically and cognitively ready to use computers? Will such use inhibit social development? Can computers help build skills or develop problem-solving ability? Research has made important contributions toward answering these and other questions.

Beeson and Williams, for example, looked at the computer readiness of young children and concluded: "There is little evidence that computers should not be introduced to younger children. No major differences were found between the way computers were used by younger and older pre-schoolers" (1985).

Binder and Ledger found that adults play a significant role in successful computer use: "Children are more attentive, more interested, and less frustrated when an adult is present" (1985). Teachers may need to place the computer where they can easily help children.

Three- to five-year-old children will spend approximately the same amount of time playing in the computer center as drawing, talking, or playing in other centers such as with blocks or art (Hoover & Austin, 1986). "The computer, then, is an interesting but not engrossing activity for young children" (Lipinski, 1986).

Clements points out two critical elements in having young children use the computer for mathematics and problem solving: (1) "Children should not work with such programs until they understand the concepts, then, practice may be of real benefit"; and (2) "the teacher must play an active role — encouraging, questioning, prompting, modeling, and, in general, mediating children's interaction with the computer" (Clements, 1987, p. 41).

Drawing upon Clements's conclusions, we find that several important research findings have implications for primary-level teachers:

- Computers are neither panacean nor pernicious.
- Children do not need computers any more than they need other potentially valuable learning centers.
- There are potentially rich benefits to acquire through the desirable use of computers with young children.
- Effectiveness depends upon the quality of the software, the amount or time it is used, and the way it is used.
- The field is changing rapidly, and inflexible conclusions should be avoided.
- The goal, according to Clements, is to develop problem solvers, communicators, and fulfilled children.
- The strength of good computer use is that it allows the teacher to focus on the human aspects of teaching.

SELECTING APPROPRIATE SOFTWARE

A great variety of software is available for use in early childhood mathematics education. However, from a developmental education perspective, it is not all high-quality software. Teachers will need assistance in securing software that is high quality, appropriate for their group of children, and compatible with the computers available for use in the classroom. Publishers of math textbooks for primary levels are beginning to include sections on getting ready for computer programming. Such sections include using commands in programs, making commands, completing programs, and writing appropriate programs for their learning level.

Throughout this book, we have advocated and used Piaget's developmental approach to learning and the growth of mental structures, and have searched for computer programs incorporating his theories. Haugland and Shade (1988) identified computer programs for young children that follow Piaget's developmental approach. They also defined criteria for the preparation of developmentally appropriate software and applied them to eight commercial software programs.

Their report begins with a description of Papert's work (see Papert, 1980). Papert applied Piaget's developmental theory of learning to children's experiences with computers. Papert follows a discovery approach to computers. According to him, children are in control of the computers and act on software to make things happen. He calls this interaction with computers "microworlds."

Haugland and Shade go on to identify four microworld programs prepared for young children: Lawler (1982) designed *Beachworld* for his three-year-old daughter; Watson (1987) designed software for three-year-olds on classifying objects according to inside and outside concepts; Chaille and Littman (1985) designed *Process Highlighters* to discover cause and effect relationships; and Papert (1980) designed software to teach mathematical concepts.

Based on these four microworld programs, Haugland and Shade developed a set of ten criteria for identifying software that is developmentally appropriate for young children. Briefly, these criteria are:

1. It is age appropriate — it reflects realistic expectations for children.
2. The child is in control — the child initiates and decides the sequence of events.
3. Instructions are clear.
4. It has expanding complexity — children build structures and knowledge and gain ideas.
5. It allows independent exploration.
6. It offers a process orientation — children learn through discovery, intrinsic motivation.
7. It has real-world representations.
8. It has good technical features — colorful, realistic, durable disks.
9. It allows trial and error — children have opportunities to test alternatives.
10. Transformations are visible — children have an impact on the software, changing objects and situations. (1988, p. 39)

Haugland and Shade used these ten developmental criteria to evaluate eight programs for primary-level children. On a rating scale of 0 to 10, three programs were given high scores of 9.0, 8.5, and 7.5. Although these programs received high ratings, the authors concluded that

> When carefully evaluated according to educational criteria, most software does not reflect a developmental approach to teaching and learning. Teachers who reject all other types of drill and practice find themselves using drill and practice software because it is readily available. (1988, p. 42).

The following are the three software programs that received the highest ratings according to these criteria:

1. Davis, D. (1983). *Kindercomp*. Spinnaker Software, Cambridge, MA. Ages 3–8. Developmental ratings of 9.0. *Kindercomp* has six program options: Draw, Scribble, Names, Sequences, Letters, and Math.
2. *Panda Workout: How to Weigh an Elephant* (1985). Educational Technologies, Dallas, TX. Ages 4–8. Developmental rating of 8.5. Panda Workout is an innovative program that helps children experiment and discover using their own creativity and problem-solving skills.
3. Davis, D. (1986). *Facemaker*. Spinnaker Software, Cambridge, MA. Ages 4–12. Developmental rating of 7.5. Program allows children to build a face using different mouth, eyes, ears, nose, and hair options. Allows children to explore, discover, and use their creativity and problem-solving skills.

The work of Haugland and Shade is exceedingly important and their article should be read in its entirety. Two conclusions come out of the article: (1) The "microworlds" approach and the experimental programs developed by Lawler (1982), Shade and Watson (1987), and Papert (1980) represent the direction of the future in software development; and (2) the criteria established by Haugland and Shade for distinguishing developmentally appropriate software will help direct the development of future microworlds.

Warren Buckleiter and Kerry Olson (1989) have written an excellent article entitled "Kids at the Keyboard," which lists the attributes of good early childhood software and gives tips for introducing software to young children. We briefly list these attributes below, and recommend the reading of their timely article to obtain a detailed discussion of each attribute.

1. Matches developmental level — matches needs, abilities, interests
2. Easy to use — simple language, reading, on-screen help
3. Child controlled — child's own pace, reaccessed menu, choices
4. Interactive — child's individual actions
5. Strong in content — age appropriate
6. Versatile — designed to grow with the child
7. Appealing — fun to use, holds child's interest
8. Crashproof — without lockups
9. Designed with features for adults

INNOVATIVE COMPUTER PROJECTS

Many school systems throughout the United States have innovative mathematics projects that involve the use of computers. In the following sections, we describe several of these projects to show how these schools are exploring the use of modern technology.

A Head Start Project

Tsantis, Wright, and Thouvenelle (1989) explored the use of computers with preschoolers. Their Head Start, IBM Partnership Project, involved integrating computers into the preschool curriculum. They worked with two hundred Head Start children and reported that children benefitted from the use of computers in three ways: equity, empowerment, and enrichment.

1. *Equity.* Computers gave the children a technological head start, an information source, and communication tool.
2. *Empowerment.* The program created interest centers, with two computers side by side, where children and teachers could exchange ideas about how to use a particular software package. They shared insights while exploring alternatives.
3. *Enrichment.* In addition to enhancing problem-solving skills and building self-confidence and self-esteem, the use of computers complemented other goals of early childhood education, such as supporting open-ended discovery-oriented tasks, stimulating language comprehension learning and development, avoiding the fear of failure, and enhancing creativity.

Tsantis and her colleagues emphasized choosing the right software. They selected *Facemaker,* produced by Spinnaker, and *Fantastic Animals,* by Firebird. Both of these support open-ended learning and allow children to make logical choices or create fanciful solutions. The researchers also emphasized the need for developing software that reflects the diversity of Head Start.

Parents were used in the project as classroom volunteers.

A State-Financed Project

In 1987, the State of California selected five sites as Model Technology Schools (MTS). (Later a sixth site was added.) Every year, the state provides $500,000 to each site. Among the six sites, there is a diversity in student ethnicity, school organization, instruction strategies and emphasis, and type and configuration of technology. These projects offer opportunities for a variety of research studies. They serve as demonstration and training sites, and educators can visit and adapt components of these projects to meet the needs of their own schools.

At one site, the Emery Park Elementary School (K–8) in Alhambra School District, Los Angeles County, the focus is on student-centered learning in a technologically rich environment where students have the power of self-choice, self-control, and self-monitoring of education. At Emery Park, the project, in its second year of funding, is designed to explore various technologies, including computer (home, lab, hallway, and classroom) video, telecommunications, laser discs, and satellite reception. A home-school component helps parents use computer technology. Fifteen computers may be checked out for week-long periods. Parents may check out both Spanish and English versions of LOGO Writer.

National Diffusion Network Projects

In several previous chapters, we discussed the National Diffusion Network (NDN). This nationwide program is funded by the U.S. Department of Education to help schools improve their educational programs through the adoption of already developed, rigorously evaluated, exemplary educational programs. NDN also supports two related resource projects: State Facilitators (SFS) and Developer Demonstrators (DDS). Extensive, creative programs involving the use of computers, the development of appropriate software, and the integration of modern technology with the total school program are being developed by these projects.

Many other innovative projects relating to the use of computers are supported by local school districts, by companies manufacturing hardware or software, and by minigrants financed through the Educational Compensatory Improvement Act. Progress reports are found in the *Arithmetic Teacher* in the sections dealing with computers and computer software.

CULTURAL IMPACT OF COMPUTERS ON MATH EDUCATION

Papert uses the term "cultural resonance" to explain math that makes sense in terms of a larger social context. His Turtle math made sense to children. But he felt that it would not be truly meaningful to them unless it was accepted by adults too. Papert felt that the cultural assimilation of the computer presence would give rise to a computer literacy. This "literacy" involves knowing how to use computers and when it is appropriate to use them. According to Papert, "A new world of personal computing is about to come into being, and its history will be inseparable from the story of the people who make it."

More recently, James Flanigan (1989) has raised the same question of the cultural assimilation of technologies, especially the supercomputers. In reporting on pending legislation to create a National Research and Education Network and give computer access to all, he stated that, "Technologies have withered from too few customers before." He cited the failure of the picture telephone in the 1950s as an example of poor commercial acceptance. The main aim of the proposed legislation is to support research in computer software and hardware and to bring every university in the nation into a supercomputer network by the mid 1990s. The network would provide access to such repositories as the Library of Congress and the National Centers for Disease Control. The real objectives — from innovations in computing to national growth in the information-based economy — "*would be achieved by the users, the American people.*"

The computer can expand what it is possible to do, learn, and teach in mathematics education. It influences teachers' attitudes toward mathematics and the teaching of mathematics. Its use may begin to make Papert's notion of a computer culture within mathematical microworlds a reality. Ross (1988), in an important article on the computer as a cultural influence in mathematics learning, states that "social, affective, and cultural issues are at least as interesting as the cognitive and we need to realize the potential for cultural change that the computer might bring to learning of mathematics."

According to Papert, significant changes in patterns of intellectual development will come about through cultural change. Further, he feels, the most likely cause of cultural change in the near future is the increasingly pervasive presence of the computer.

SOURCES FOR SECURING APPROPRIATE SOFTWARE AND SERVICES

One of the best sources of keeping abreast of new, appropriate software for primary-level teachers is the *Arithmetic Teacher*. Each issue of this publication has a section entitled "Technology, Views, and Reviews." Leading educators review and report on new software, giving suggestions as to grade level and making recommendations based on the appropriateness of the program and the quality of the disks.

Also, school systems using computer programs provide current information on new software that is appropriate for specific classrooms.

The main sources for information on computer software are:

1. Computer journals for education such as *Classroom Computer Learning* of Belmont, California or *The Computing Teacher,* Department of Computer and Information Services, University of Oregon, Eugene, OR
2. General computer journals, such as *BYTE,* 10 Main St., Petersborough, NH
3. Software directories, such as the Apple Software Directory, "Education," WDL Video, 5245 West Diversey Ave., Chicago, IL
4. Software clearinghouses, such as Microcomputers Educations Application Network (MEAN) 256 North Washington St., Falls Church, VA.
5. See also the article by John Greer (1988) listed in our bibliography.

We now turn to a consideration of meaningful uses of calculators in mathematical programs for young children.

MEANINGFUL USE OF CALCULATORS

In 1980 and again in 1986, the National Council of Teachers of Mathematics recommended the use of calculators in teaching mathematics. With their 1986 recommendation, they stated "that publishers, authors, and test writers should integrate the use of the calculator into their mathematics materials at all levels."

In a comprehensive report of 79 different studies of calculator use, Hembree (1986) concluded that "use of calculators can improve the average student's basic skills with paper and pencil, both in basic operations and problem solving." His recommendations apply to all grades K–12. He concluded that calculators applied across all grades and abilities made two major contributions: (1) students using calculators in testing produced much higher achievement scores than those doing paper and pencil work, both in basic operations and in problem solving; and (2) students using calculators have a better attitude toward mathematics than students without calculators.

Through the years, there has been much controversy over the use of calculators. The main area of disagreement has been the effect of calculator use on the learning of basic skills. This controversy will continue, as Thomas Dick (1988) reports.

Marilyn Suydam (1983) prepared the first definitive report on the desirable use of calculators in mathematics education. She began by pointing out the need for children to learn basic mathematics skills and operations before they begin intensive work with calculators. She went on to say, however, that after young children have learned certain basic facts and can apply operations to these facts, they can and should use calculators. Instruction in using the calculator should follow the continuum of mathematical content, concepts, and skills. It is the teacher who guides calculator use to fit the objectives established for specific lessons.

Following Suydam's work, an Instructional Affairs Committee of the NCTM (1988) prepared a list of suggestions for the desirable use of calculators. We summarize here those recommendations that apply to the teaching of young children. The calculator can be used to:

- Encourage students to estimate, experiment, and be creative
- Assist in making wise decisions as a consumer
- Reinforce basic arithmetic operations
- Develop an understanding of computational algorithms
- Verify the results of computation
- Promote independence in problem solving

In this book, we have used most of these recommendations. For example, we suggested that the calculator be used for:

- Adding and subtracting on worksheets, where children make their own facts with + or −
- Counting patterns, such as by 2s and 5s
- Demonstrating the commutative property, with children making their own examples
- Demonstrating the associative property in beginning work in addition and multiplication
- Estimating and then checking
- Finding a missing addend
- Finding three numbers to make sums of 10 (7, 2, 1) or 15 (8, 2, 3, ?)
- Problem solving involving buying, using a local newspaper and a given amount of money to spend
- Determining children's bills for purchases at a classroom or school store
- Making change and playing games using play money
- Counting with eyes closed after entering a number and estimating an answer after repeated entries.

In every instance, we recommended that the calculator be used appropriately to fit the objectives of the lesson or activity for a particular age level. The classroom teacher is responsible for presenting learning activities with the calculator that require children to think, explore, solve problems, and secure information meaningful to them. (Suggestions for calculator exercises are given later in this section.)

As the basic algorithms are developed and children begin to understand them, teachers can eliminate paper and pencil work to solve them and allow children to use calculators. The calculator will produce a quick, accurate answer. Instruction can then concentrate on ensuring that children understand the meaning of the operation and its use in problem solving.

Experiences with physical manipulatives and concrete, hands-on materials to represent math concepts must be continued while children are working with the calculator and computer. They need to use these materials in order to *generate their own math problems* and then to use the calculator or computer to help in solving or exploring these problems.

In the next section, we present some appropriate calculator exercises. The examples show how the calculator can help children with mental operations, speed, accuracy, and understanding of basic math concepts. They are not labeled by age or grade level.

CALCULATOR EXERCISES

The following calculator exercises are extensions and expansions of the suggested uses listed earlier in this chapter.

Addition and Subtraction Exercises

1. Find out how the calculator is used to compute simple basic operations.
   a. Work simple addition games.

4	6
8	5

Start at 4 and add around the rectangle, 4 + 6 + 5. . . . When the sum is obtained (23), subtract the numbers 23 − 8 − 5 . . .

   b. Use the number in the center of the circle and add each of the other numbers to it; start with 8.

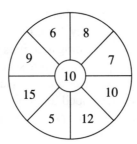

2. Add: Odd numbers   and   Even numbers

series	sum
1 . . .	1
1 + 3 . . .	4
1 + 3 + 5 . . .	
1 + 3 + 5 + 7 . . .	
1 + 3 + 5 + 7 + 9 . . .	

series	sum
2 . . .	2
2 + 4 . . .	
2 + 4 + 6 . . .	
2 + 4 + 6 + 8 . . .	
2 + 4 + 6 + 8 + 10 . . .	

3. Add:

$$
\begin{array}{cccccc}
48 & 38 & 59 & 129 & 382 & 240 \\
+\ 51 & +\ 27 & +\ 67 & +\ 36 & +\ 156 & +\ 100
\end{array}
$$

4. Subtract:

$$
\begin{array}{cccccc}
75 & 382 & 565 & 291 & 472 & 400 \\
-\ 25 & -\ 61 & -156 & -\ 88 & -\ 126 & -\ 281
\end{array}
$$

Multiplication and Division Exercises

1. For each multiplication problem, find two related division sentences.

   $4 \times 6 = 24$ $24 \div \underline{\ 4\ } = \underline{\ 6\ }$ and $24 \div \underline{\ 6\ } = \underline{\ 4\ }$

   $5 \times 7 = 35$ $\underline{\ \ } \div \underline{\ \ } = \underline{\ \ }$ and $\underline{\ \ } \div \underline{\ \ } = \underline{\ \ }$

   $4 \times 8 = 32$ $\underline{\ \ } \div \underline{\ \ } = \underline{\ \ }$ and $\underline{\ \ } \div \underline{\ \ } = \underline{\ \ }$

2. Tell how multiplication works for each example:

$$
\begin{array}{ccccccc}
25 & & 20 & & 5 & & 3 \times 5 = 15 \\
\times\ 3 & = & \times\ 3 & + & \times\ 3 & \text{or} & 3 \times 20 = 60 \\
& & & & & & 75
\end{array}
$$

$$
\begin{array}{cccc}
10 & 50 & 100 & 100 \\
\times\ 2 & \times\ 2 & \times\ 2 & \times\ 3
\end{array}
$$

3. Use the operations given to complete each problem:

$\times$	$+$	$\div$		
6	2	4	8 $=$	2
8	8	6	5 $=$	
10	5	10	6 $=$	
100	10	100	100 $=$	

4. Show division as repeated subtraction:

$$
\begin{array}{r}
25\,\overline{)\,250} \quad 1 \\
-\ \ 25 \\
\hline
225 \quad 2 \\
25 \\
\hline
200 \quad 3 \\
25 \\
\hline
\end{array}
$$

Fractions

Common fractions must be changed to decimal fractions when using the calculator to perform basic operations on them. This work should be taught in fourth and fifth grades.

Money and the Calculator

Children will have many opportunities to purchase needed items at a grocery store or supermarket. The calculator is useful for determining the amount of money spent for a party, change to receive after a purchase, unit costs for an item, and comparing savings by buying at several stores.

1.

Item	Cost	Totals
peanut butter	$1.19	$1.19
bread	1.05	2.24
cake	2.50	
ice cream	2.89	
napkins	1.10	
paper cups	.85	
punch	1.50	

The child has $12.00.
What will the change be?

_____

$11.08

2. A child has $20.00 to spend for groceries. Use a newspaper (shopping specials for week) to see what items can be purchased so that the total will be exactly $20.00.

3. Use the same procedure to purchase items from a catalogue (Sears) with exactly $20.00.

4. Make a list of grocery items. Use the weekly paper with specials for the week.
   Which store should you buy from? _____
   Which store has the highest prices? _____
   Which store is next to the highest? _____

Item	Store 1	Store 2	Store 3
eggs, 1 doz.	$ .93	$1.02	$1.19
sugar, 5 lb.	1.29	.97	1.32
lettuce	.39	.49	.47
milk, 1 qt.	.58	.56	.57
bananas, 1 lb.	.39	.38	.37
potatoes, 10 lb.	1.84	1.89	2.01

SUMMARY

In this chapter we introduced the use of calculators and computers within the framework of the standards prepared by NCTM. We discussed the characteristics of computers for the benefit of those using them for the first time.

We reviewed basic research on the use of computers to point out important findings that will help primary-level teachers understand recent developments in computer instruction.

We discussed Papert's use of Piaget's developmental theories of learning in preparing new software. The creative work of Papert shows how children can control computers and act on software to make things happen. The creative development of "microworlds" by Papert was used by Haugland and Shade to prepare ten criteria for identifying software that is developmentally appropriate for young children. Suggestions were given for selecting and using appropriate computer software.

Finally, we summarized the recommendations of the NCTM for the desirable use of calculators and applied them to a variety of practical classroom activities. Calculator exercises were presented as examples for math instruction for young children.

ACTIVITIES FOR TEACHER INSIGHT

1. Plan a visit to an elementary school in your neighborhood to observe young children using a computer. If possible, have a child show you how to use a particular software program. List some of the important skills, vocabulary, and concepts involved in using the software.

2. Arrange an interview with parents who have a computer in their home that is used by one or more young children. What instruction did they give the children for its use? What programs do they use? What suggestions do they have for helping young children use computers?

3. Contact a school district office near you to arrange for one or more visits to primary-level classrooms where calculators are used in connection with teaching math. As you observe, see if the teachers are using some of the criteria listed in this chapter. What suggestions would you make to improve the use of calculators?

4. Secure admission to a primary-level classroom (third grade) and interview several children and the teacher to find out how children use a calculator at home. Do parents help the children use the calculator? How are children using calculators at home?

REFERENCES

BEESON, B. S., & WILLIAMS, R. A. (1985). The effects of gender and age on preschool children's choices of the computer as a child-selected activity. *Journal of the American Society for Information Science, 36,* 339–341.

BINDER, S. L., & LEDGER, B. (1985). *Preschool computer project report.* Oakville, Ontario, Canada: Sheridan College.

BUCKLEITER, W., & OLSON, K. (August 1989). Kids at the keyboard. *Child Care Exchange, 11,* 37–41.

CLEMENTS, D. H. (1985). Logo programming. Can it change how children think? *Electronic Learning, 28*(4), 174–175.

———. (1987). Computers and young children: A review of research. *Young Children, 40,* 4–44.

CORBITT, M. K. (Ed.). (1985). The impact of computing technology on school mathematics. NCTM Conference. *Arithmetic Teacher, 32*(8), 14–18.

D. C. Heath and Company. (1988). *Heath mathematics book three.* Lexington, MA: Author.

DICK, T. (1988). The continuing calculator controversy. *Arithmetic Teacher, 35,* 37–41.

FLANIGAN, J. (September 13, 1989). U.S. could give computer access to all. *Los Angeles Times.*

GREER, J., & GREER, B. (1988). Public domain software. *Arithmetic Teacher, 36,* 26–30.

HAUGLAND, S. W., & SHADE, D. D. (1988). Developmentally appropriate software for young children. *Young Children, 43*(4), 37–43.

HEMBREE, R. (September 1986). Research gives calculators a green light. *Arithmetic Teacher, 34,* 18–21.

HOOVER, J., & AUSTIN, A. M. (1986). *A comparison of traditional preschool and computer play from a social/cognitive perspective* (ERIC Document Reproduction Service, No. ED 27220).

LAWLER, R. W. (1982). Designing computer based microworlds. *Byte Magazine, 1,* 138–160.

LIPINSKI, J. M. (1986). The effects of microcomputers on young children: An examination of free-play choices, sex differences, and social interaction. *Journal of Educational Computer Research, 2,* 147–168.

LUND, C. (1983). *Computer math activities.* New York: Addison-Wesley.

MCLANAHAN, T. F. (Winter 1984). Software for young children. *Day Care and Early Education,* 26–29.

National Council of Supervisors of Mathematics. (1988). *Essential mathematics for the 21st century.* Minneapolis, MN: Author.

National Council of Teachers of Mathematics. (1988). *Curriculum and evaluation standards for school mathematics.* Reston, VA: Author.

National Materials Advisory Board. (March 1988). *The impact of super-computing capabilities on U.S. materials, science, and technology.* Springfield, VA: National Technical Information Service.

National Science Foundation. (1983). *Educating America for the 21st century: A report to the American people and the National Science Board.* Washington, DC: Authors.

PAPERT, S. (1980). *Mindstorms: Children, computers, and powerful ideas.* New York: Basic Books.

REID, J. M. (1975). *Metrics for everyday use.* Peoria, IL: Chas. A. Bennett, pp. 1–24.

ROSS, R. (1988). The computer as a cultural influence in mathematical learning. *Educational Studies in Mathematics, 19,* 251–268.

SHADE, D. D., & WATSON, J. A. (1987). Microworlds, mother teaching behavior and concept formation in the very young child. *Early Childhood Development and Care, 28,* 97–114.

SPIKER, J., & KURTZ, R. (1987). Teaching primary-grade mathematics skills with calculators. *Arithmetic Teacher, 34,* 24–27.

SUYDAM, M. (November 1983). Research report on achieving with calculators. *Arithmetic Teacher, 31.*

THOMPSON, C. S., & RATHMELL, E. C. (1988). NCTM's standards for school mathematics K-12. *Arithmetic Teacher, 35,* 17–19.

TSANTIS, L., WRIGHT, J., & THOUVENELLE, S. (January–February 1989). Computers and preschoolers. *Children Today, 18,* 21–23.

WALKER, D. F. (1988). *Reflections on the educational potential and limitations of microcomputers.* Bloomington, IN: Phi Delta Kappan.

WILSON, P. S. (1987). Microcomputer use in the elementary school. *Arithmetic Teacher, 35,* 33–34.

CHAPTER 10

Planning for Instruction, Classroom Organization, and Resource Materials

SCOPE AND SEQUENCE FOR MATH

Determining the mathematics content (scope) and when to present this content (sequence) is an important task faced by those who prepare textbooks and courses of study and by teachers who must plan and implement the program.

The publishers of textbooks for elementary schools take into consideration modern theories of learning; the important aspects of child growth and development; recommendations of the National Council of Teachers of Mathematics, including those regarding social aspects; and the basic components of mathematics. The content thus determined is organized around topics or strands. These were identified in Chapter 1. Emphasis is placed on understanding math concepts, problem solving, using hands-on materials, and using visual models that relate to real-world situations.

Once the mathematical content has been determined, the topics are sequenced for each learning level. The sequence is determined based on research findings and the recommendations of the National Council of Teachers, and then tried out in a variety of schools. Textbook series generally agree on the grade placement of topics. However, differences in approach arise in these series as publishers try to provide for advanced learners or slower learners, or try to change the presentation of mathematical concepts.

Some states, such as California, adopt mathematics textbooks for the entire state. Publishers must prepare textbooks for these states according to the state guidelines. Thus, many different textbooks are used among and within states. If there is no state-adopted math textbook series, or several are adopted, the choice of textbooks is left to the local school systems.

Classroom teachers are faced with using adopted textbooks and following a proposed course of study as they plan their instruction. Nevertheless, teachers must decide for themselves what content to use and when to present it for a particular group of children. The classroom teacher is the one who determines what to teach and when to teach it. This is a professional responsibility, and primary-level teachers are noted both for their ability to make these decisions and for their understanding of young children.

A NEW SCOPE AND SEQUENCE FOR MATHEMATICS FOUR-YEAR-OLDS THROUGH EIGHT-YEAR OLDS

In this book, we have taken a new approach to determining the mathematics program for young children. We believe there are three interrelated parts to such a program: (1) the components of children's environment (their real-world aspects); (2) the structure of mathematics, including language, vocabulary, and symbols; and (3) evaluation, with specific objectives for each aspect of the program.

With this approach, children learn mathematics using the everyday components of their environment. They use mathematics daily because it helps them learn other school subjects. Their everyday life at home and school involves the use of mathematics. Within this environment, mathematics makes sense to children, and thus they build their own understanding of each new mathematical concept.

The mathematical aspects of this new approach include most of what is found in modern textbooks in terms of concepts, skills, and basic operations. Content, however, must be selected and presented so that it is appropriate for the learner. In addition, a continuum must be developed for each main operation based on the structure of mathematics, a base ten system. Individual learning must follow this continuum—although children will progress at different rates according to their stage of development and their understanding of each new mathematical topic or concept.

The development of language enables children to: express mathematical ideas, communicate with other children in discovering new concepts, and show their understanding of mathematical work. A section on language development is provided for each age group in Chapters 3–7 that helps to show the synthesizing of the three basic strands of the program.

Evaluation is an integral part of the teaching-learning process, helping children discover and learn new math concepts with understanding as well as with satisfaction. The teacher uses evaluation procedures with each learning activity to promote children's self-evaluation and to enable them to demonstrate their understanding and exhibit readiness for new learnings.

The outline of content and strands that follows should help teachers identify the interrelated aspects of the math program just described.

Content and Strands

COMPONENTS OF CHILDREN'S ENVIRONMENT (real-world daily living applications)

- time
- money
- measurement (surface, linear)
- size, capacity
- patterns
- seasonal events
- calendar of events
- problem solving that involves mathematics
- estimating
- predicting

NUMBER (language, vocabulary, terms, symbols)

- classifying
- numeration
- addition
- subtraction
- multiplication
- division
- fractions
- place value
- technology
- estimation

EVALUATION

- behavioral objectives
- understanding concepts during instruction
- unit assessment, semester, year
- recording progress

In the following sections, we briefly outline the procedures needed to carry out the math program. We cover yearly planning, weekly planning, basic materials needed, and sample floor plans for arranging the classroom, and we make suggestions for managing class activities.

Teachers in one school need to plan together so that content strands flow smoothly and overlap where appropriate for review.

YEARLY PLANNING OF MATH PROGRAM

Content and Strands	4-year-olds		5-year-olds		6-year-olds	
	Mo.	**Wks.**	**Mo.**	**Wks.**	**Mo.**	**Wks.**
COMPONENTS OF CHILDREN'S ENVIRONMENT						
MATHEMATICAL CONCEPTS, LANGUAGE, VOCABULARY						
EVALUATION						

This outline for yearly planning allows teachers to estimate the amount of time that will be needed for each part of the program. The teacher must decide which topics to select from textbooks and the school system's course of study and approximately how much time to spend on them. Adjustments will be made as the school year progresses — as individual differences arise due to varying rates of maturity and achievement, for both individual children and groups of children.

WEEKLY PLANNING

Using the yearly planning chart as a guide, teachers must also plan weekly, making adjustments as needed. Again, consideration must be given to children's needs, their understanding of each math concept, and their readiness to move on to the next new aspect.

The following is an example of a weekly organization chart that teachers can use with the scope and sequence charts. The time shown must be adjusted for each learning level, four through eight years of age.

Time	M	T	W	Th	F
Whole class:	Number concepts	Number concepts	Number concepts	Whole class (variety of class organization)	Whole class (variety of class organization)
20–30 min	combining separating place value problem solving			Measuring Money	Using calendar Holidays: Easter Hanukkah Christmas
Small groups: 20–30 min	Independent practice games choices			Time Creative problems	Seasons Creative surprises

In this weekly plan, emphasis is placed on concept development. Components of children's environment, special events, and seasonal events are incorporated into concept development and on Thursdays and Fridays specific lessons are planned around them.

Sample Weekly Plan

In the following paragraphs, Jane Shimotsu, a teacher at the Mirman School for Gifted Children in Los Angeles, describes her math program for six- and seven-year-olds. Her weekly planning chart could be used in a regular classroom.

> Students work individually, in small groups, and as a class during the math period. For the first ten minutes of the period, students work on problem solving such as brain teasers, figural analogies, and Dale Seymour problems (1984). The problems are presented to the class as a whole. Students then work individually on the problems for approximately five minutes. When they are finished, they turn the problem sheet in to the center of the table and begin to work individually in their departmentalized Addison-Wesley math books. Students are encouraged to complete the problem sets on their own (to try their best) without assistance from the teacher. The following day (problem-solving days alternate with discussion days), during the same period of time, students are given back their corrected problem-solving sheets. At this time, the class discusses the processes involved in solving the problems. Individual students explain the methods and procedures they use to solve the problems to the whole class.
>
> After problem solving is done for the day, students continue to work in their Addison-Wesley books for forty-five minutes. The class is divided into four groups based on the students' levels of progress in the books. During this forty-five minute block of time, the

Time	Monday	Tuesday	Wednesday	Thursday	Friday
8:20	Brain Teaser (relating to specific math modules)	Problem solving	Discuss answers to Tuesday problem solving	Problem solving	Discuss answers to Thursday problem solving
8:30	Departmentalized Addison–Wesley Math Program				
	(STUDENTS MOVE AT AN INDIVIDUAL PACE. STUDENTS ARE ASSIGNED "STOP SIGNS.")				
	Meet with Blue Group	Meet with Green Group	Meet with Blue Group	Meet with Green Group	*Test Days*
	Meet with Orange Group	Meet with Red Group	Meet with Orange Group	Meet with Red Group	Pretests
					Posttests
					Cumulative test
					Fact drill tests
	Meet with INDIVIDUAL STUDENTS				Diagnostic tests
9:15					9:00–9:15 GAME DAY

teacher meets with two of the four groups while other students work individually. Students work at their own pace but are assigned a "stop sign" as a work goal for the week is completed. The following day, the teacher meets with the other two groups. Each group meets with the teacher twice a week. Fridays are reserved for tests, drills, and games.

SAMPLE CLASS SCHEDULES AND ROOM ARRANGEMENTS

Preschool

Some preschool programs are combined within a child care center where children stay all day. Usually, the early arrivals can use the activity centers until the majority of the children arrive. In the afternoon, after a rest/nap time, activity centers are open again, but the pace is more relaxed. Young children cannot take the stimulation of fast-paced activity time all day long.

9:00   Entry (parents sign child in, adult greets, and general health check)
Activity centers are open inside classroom
      (choice of centers/materials depends on number of adults in room)

Centers requiring little adult help include:

*blocks
  table toys (open shelf child choice)
  pens and paper
*playhouse area
  puzzles
  science table exploration of materials such as magnets, cornmeal
  playdough

Note: Each day three activities are out on tables in addition to areas always available (*)

9:30   Circle time
       fingerplay
       song
       tell special activities for day

9:45   Activity time begins, areas * above open plus:
       special art activity
          and/or
       snack preparation activity
       science or math activity

*1 or 2 days per week substitute science activities or special day project such as holiday preparation.

Sample Preschool Classroom

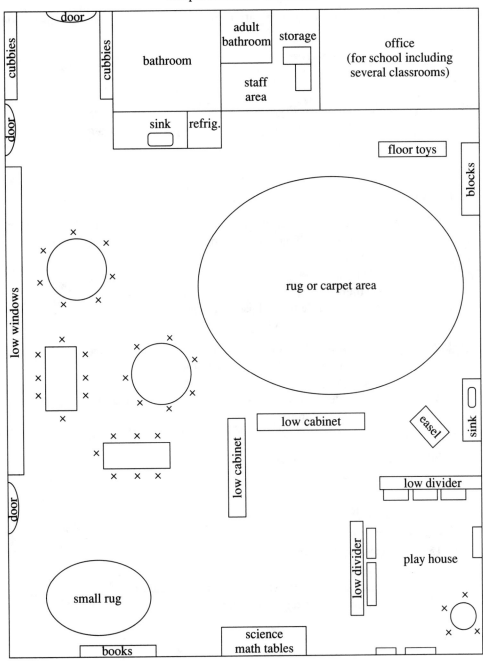

10:30   Clean up and snack

10:50   Outside play with coordination maze, or art, or science on an outside table

11:35   Clean up and toileting

11:40   Circle time
        fingerplay
        movement activity
        story (divide group by age or size if possible to promote discussion)

Kindergarten

9:00   Entry   (Bell rings and children line up from playground. Some kindergartners are on a separate playground.)
        Group circle
            calendar
            weather
            sharing/other whole-class language activities
            presentation of activity groups

9:20   Activity groups (children choose or are assigned)
            math station activities 3 tables 3 or 4 days/wk*
            small-group language activity (1 table)
            independent project/choice when finished (2 tables)
            art, science, language

10:00   Snack time

10:20   Free choice of manipulatives
            playhouse
            blocks
            painting

10:50   Recess

11:15   Carpet, whole group
            story
            music action activity, science, or math graphing
            culmination-of-day discussion

11:55   Dismiss

*1 or 2 days per week substitute science activities or special day project such as holiday preparation.

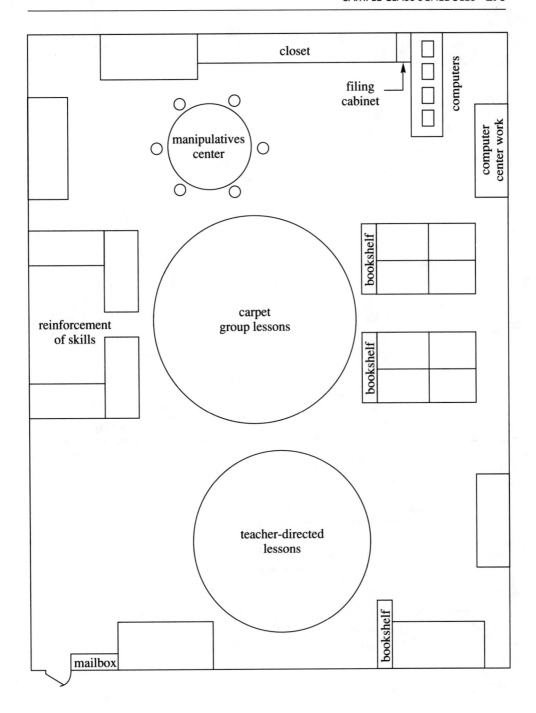

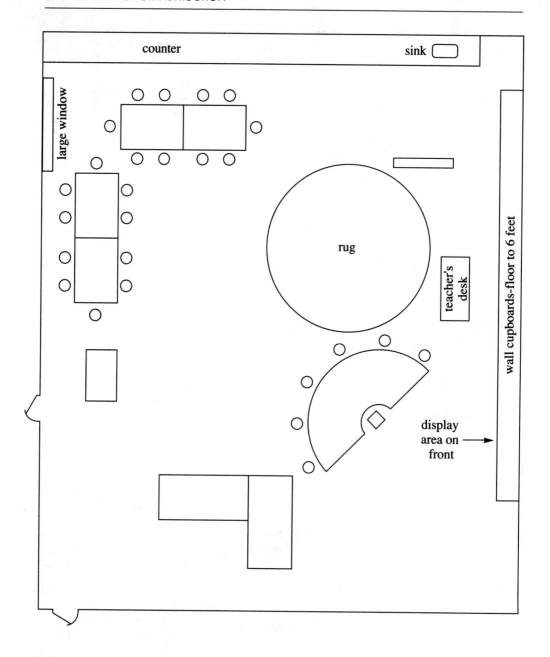

Math station activities could include places for children to work individually or in small groups. Each table could contain an activity on each side or several activities. Math station activities should be designed to be self-correcting, hands-on work with materials and need little adult help. The teacher circulates around the room checking on children's progress. Children report on their progress during the culmination discussion.

ESSENTIAL CLASSROOM MATERIALS

Blocks	Unit blocks in several sizes; small, soft wood, colored or plain; hardwood set of 70 or more pieces, and large hollow blocks: for preschool, kindergarten, optional for grades 1–3. Unit blocks fit together in precise multiples, facilitating building and beginning knowledge of fractions.
Colored rods (Stern or Cuisennaire)	Ten separately colored types of rods: a unit cube, and 2, 3, 4, 5, 6, 7, 8, 9, and 10 rods in multiples of the unit cube. The 5 rod would be five times as long as a unit cube. These may be used to show the properties of the counting numbers, fractions, and numerous patterns. Colors are used to identify each rod—for example, the red rod represents a 3.
Wood or plastic base ten components	The sets should contain 100 unit cubes, 10 rods showing tens each, 10 flats for 10×10 (100), and one large cube to show 10×100 (1,000).
Flannel board	Felt-covered masonite or tagboard for use in circle time and as individual child activity.
Manipulative objects	Assorted things for use in counting, classifying, grouping—for example, lima beans, buttons, old keys, beads, attribute blocks.
Manipulative toys	Multiuse toys that develop small muscles as well as spatial reasoning skills and other problem-solving skills: "Leggo" type toys all sizes depending on the age of the children; Fisher Price Cash Register (preschool, kindergarten), Bristle Blocks; cars, people, animals for block play.
Place-value holders	For teacher demonstration and for children to use leading to the use of number trees (first through third grade).
Sand, water	Inside in tubs, on trays, or commercial water table. Outside in large tubs, water table (or sandbox for preschool and kindergarten). Use

	with cups, cans, old kitchen materials, plastic containers, water wheels, pvc (sprinkler) plastic pipe and connector pieces. Use for measuring, estimating, and predicting results.
Storage containers	Easy to set up and clean up containers with lids, including plastic trays, tubs, shoe boxes. Leads to independent child use and clean-up. (See Burk, Snider, and Symonds, *Box It or Bag It Mathematics*, 1988).
Trays	Various sizes, used to visually focus materials on tables for children's use and assist in easy clean-up. *Source*: Office or restaurant supplier for used trays.

MANAGING CLASS ACTIVITIES AT WORK STATIONS

Planning for and directing learning activities within the classroom is a real challenge for teachers. They must establish procedures for using work stations and materials and plan a variety of techniques for helping children become familiar with these at the very beginning of the year or semester. With this help, children will be able to move from one area to another; they will become accustomed to following certain routines each day. The way materials are arranged and used has a direct bearing on successful, enjoyable learning activities.

The following suggestions will provide some guidelines for teachers in preparing their own rules and procedures based on the particular age group of their children and the program they wish to carry out (kindergarten through third grade).

1. Begin with the organization of whole-class activities. Will children come to this center at the beginning of the day, before and after recess, at closing time? Will they sit on the rug, at tables, or combinations of these? What kinds of participation will be expected: raising hands, all responding, using individual papers or chalkboards, free discussion? Will the children select centers or activities at will?

   Movement to and from the whole-class center is important. The teacher can check to see if children know where they are to go, the materials to use, the need to clean-up, and so on. To avoid confusion, one group at a time may be dismissed to go to a center.

2. The movement of children from one center to another (rotating) must be planned for. Having children leave one area and go to the next involves cleaning up and storing children's work, and checking to see if the area is ready for another group.

Pupil participation in activities involves reviewing established rules, and occasionally stopping the activity to remind pupils of their responsibilities. More importantly, the learning centers must be organized and used to promote specific instructional purposes, including allowing children to teach each other and to solve problems. Some teachers can tolerate more movement and noise than others. Consistency, purposeful learning, and pupil enjoyment are important considerations.

3. Planning for the use of materials and supplies is very important. Materials must be set up beforehand for each learning area. A teacher's aide may be available to help perform this important task. Gradually, the teacher can involve children in some of this work. Paint brushes must be washed and ready for use. Felt pens must work. Paper has to be ready and appropriate for the learning activity. New books must be introduced and placed in the reading area.

Passing paper, returning papers, and distributing other supplies must be done quickly and efficiently. Donna Burk and others (1988) suggest having fun during this process; for example, play Upset the Fruit Basket with the children's papers, passing them out hurriedly and randomly so that children must redeliver the papers to each other. A variation is to play Upset the Fruit Basket without talking.

Children like to participate in passing out materials. Table monitors can be selected for each week. Materials should be ready before the activity starts in appropriate quantity for each table or area. Rules must be established for using paper and supplies. Without some restrictions, a child could use up many pages of paper, break several crayons, and mix up enough paints and paint brushes to make any day costly and one big headache for the teacher.

MATH CONCEPTS IN CLASSROOM ACTIVITIES

Many hands-on activities selected by teachers as art, games, science, or cooking activities also have math aspects. The following list shows the math aspects of activities described later in the chapter:

Comparisons
> Body Puzzles
> Graphing
> Magic Potions
> Marble Tracks
> Word Touching Trays

Concepts

space	*	Bear in a Box
		Body Puzzles
		Coordination Maze
		Mirror Blots
estimation		Colored water
		Fist Full
		Inventor's Corner
		Sandbox River
patterns		Monster Tracks
shapes		Kaleidoscope Creations
		Monster Tracks
		Shape Pictures
		Snacks: Circles & squares,
		Quesadillas,
		Shapes to Eat

Measuring

Individual portion cooking
Juice Bags
Three Bear Porridge

Number Recognition

Going Fishing
Mixed-up Numbers

Problem Solving

Inventor's Corner
Coordination Maze
Juice Bags
Magic Potions
Marble Tracks
Sandbox River

Memory

* Find the Trick
Mixed-up Numbers
* What is Missing?

Counting

Fist Full
Going Fishing
Straw Box Counting

Activities marked with an asterisk * are suitable for group time/circle.

BEAR IN A BOX

AIM

To gain awareness of space
To learn description words: *over, under, beside, inside*
To learn body part names

MATERIALS

Milk carton ($\frac{1}{2}$ pt.), washed, dried, top opened
Counting bears (Milton Bradley), four colors, plastic, one for each child

PROCEDURE

1. Each child has a bear and a box.
2. Give group directions:
   Put your bear in the box, then
                   on top of the box, then
                   under the box, then
                   behind the box, then
                   on the side, then
                   under your leg, then
                   behind your neck.
3. Let children give the next direction.
   (*Note:* Four-year-olds may need help with front and back of the box.)

VARIATIONS

1. Give a series of directions for older children: on your knee, then under your chin, and so on, gradually increasing the number of directions to remember.
2. For six-year-olds, give all four color bears to each child and give four directions at one time: green bear under leg, blue bear on your head, yellow bear on your knee, red bear in your fist.
3. Let children give the directions.
4. Put four bears on tray, cover with cloth and take one away. Children guess which one is gone (as in the What Is Missing game). Then use boxes from the original activity and put each bear in a different position. Take one bear away. Children must say which one is gone—for example, the blue bear *behind* the box.

BODY PUZZLES

AIM

To increase children's awareness of body parts and proportions, space
To compare growth at the end of the year
To enhance self-esteem

MATERIALS

Butcher paper
Felt pens or crayons or tempera paint
Scissors

PROCEDURE

1. Trace each child's body outline on butcher paper while the child is standing against the wall or lying on the floor.
2. Let the children color the face and clothes.
3. Cut out the body (teacher needs to do this for four-year-olds).
4. Put them up around the room for a week.
5. Later, cut into three pieces or more as a puzzle (for four-year olds).

COLORED WATER

AIM

To improve small muscle skills used in pouring
To estimate volume and check answer by measuring

MATERIALS

Tray
Clear glass jars of various shapes, sizes (or clear plastic)
Measuring cup with handle/spout (plastic)
Colored water (food coloring) in bowl

PROCEDURE

1. Put glass jars on the tray (with sponge for spills).
2. Let the children pour water into jars and dump it back into the bowl.
3. Ask which jars hold the same amount.

VARIATIONS

1. Four-year-olds will just like to pour.
2. Give them small measuring cups ($\frac{1}{4}$ and $\frac{1}{2}$ cup) and ask the same question.
3. For eight-year-olds, ask which containers hold exactly one cup (estimation of volume beyond this level should wait until children are ten).

COORDINATION MAZE

AIM

To develop large muscle skills, problem solving
To coordinate muscle/perception skills

MATERIALS

Tires or hoops
Balance beam and stand

Planks

Barrels

Ladders with hooked ends, tripod ladders, boxes

Saw horses in different heights

PROCEDURE

1. Arrange seven or more of the materials into a maze, using flat surface, inclines, places to climb or slide.
2. Let children help design the order of the pieces making up the maze.

VARIATIONS

1. Attach the maze at one end to a climbing tower.
2. Ask older children to change things to make it different.
3. Ask a group of children to set one up for the whole class.
4. Five-year-olds can plan a maze with the teacher's help in groups of two or three children.
5. Seven- and eight-year-olds can time themselves going through the maze and try to decrease needed time.
6. Visit an adult "Par Course" and try the stations.

FIND THE TRICK

AIM

To check for the missing part, memory

To use teamwork to do hands-on activity with language

MATERIALS

Eight box lids, inside top covered with felt or flannel (shirt box)

Paper or felt numerals 1, 2, 3, 4 (four sets) 40 paper circles of felt pieces (in four sets)

PROCEDURE

1. Children sit in pairs at the table and place under each numeral on the lid cloth that number of circles.
2. Children take turns removing one button/circle while partner looks away.
3. The child finds an error and states it in a sentence, such as "The number 4 needs another circle."
4. For five-year-olds, increase to 10.

FIST FULL

AIM

To estimate quantity

To count to check answer

MATERIALS

Things to grab a "fist full" of that will be large enough to make 10 or less: colored cube blocks, cotton balls, small rocks, small seashells

Four trays and counting dishes

PROCEDURE

1. Put materials in piles or in bowls in the middle of the table.
2. Ask children to take a fist full of one item and guess how many are in their hand, or drop them into the counting bowl to guess.
3. Have them count to check the answer.

VARIATIONS

1. For older children who can count beyond ten, add smaller items: bottle caps, lima beans, nails, garbanzo beans, and so on.
2. Draw around each child's hand on a piece of construction paper and glue large beans or cotton balls to cover the hand. Count and write the corresponding numeral (teacher will do this part for four-year-olds).
3. For eight-year-olds, ask them to guess how many 1″ squares will be needed to cover a shape drawn on a piece of 9″ × 12″ construction paper. How many would be needed to cover the outside of the shape?

GOING FISHING

AIM

To develop eye-hand coordination

To have dramatic play using fishing

To identify color, recognize number, count

MATERIALS

Construction paper

Paper clips

Sticks or dowels

String

Magnets

PROCEDURE

1. Have children draw a fish, including eye, mouth, number, and dots.
2. Have them cut out the fish and cover it with contact paper or laminate.
3. Children then punch a hole in the nose and put a paper clip through the hole.
4. They catch the fish from the floor, or rocking boat, or covered 5-gallon ice cream round carton or basket.

VARIATIONS

1. Have them catch the fish in numbered order, by color and check the number on the tail to keep or throw back.

2. Add "junk" items as foolers that children can catch while fishing, such as, a shoe, can, or sock.

GRAPHING

AIM

To see relationships
To develop sorting, classifying, describing skills
To estimate which is more, less

MATERIALS

Objects in the classroom: children, children's shoes, blocks, playhouse dishes, any real object

PROCEDURE

1. Line up side by side objects/items to be compared — for example, blue eyes, brown eyes.
2. Have children guess which is more (then check the answer by counting).
3. Repeat with other categories: pants or shirts/dresses, long or short hair, and so on.

VARIATIONS

1. Make a symbolic graph on paper to show one of the above categories, such as blue circles for blue eyes, and glue them on white paper.
2. Children vote for their preferences — who likes chocolate chip cookies or peanut butter, their favorite ice cream flavor, and so on — by pasting their photocopied pictures from a class photo on a chart under their choice, or by writing their names in a box.
3. Add items with three categories, such as shoes with laces, with buckles, or slip-ons, and repeat original activity.
4. Transfer information to the symbolic graph using boxes, cubes, or sticks to represent votes or counting.

INVENTOR'S CORNER

AIM

To use materials to create original ideas
To figure out ways to construct their own invention ideas (with adult suggestions, questions), do problem solving

MATERIALS

Shallow plastic container
Scrap paper in variety of sizes (print shop end cuts), shapes, and colors
Felt pens

Scissors
Stapler
Construction paper available

PROCEDURE

1. Place materials near or on a table available every day. Introduce their use and possibilities, then let children create (adult just sitting at table showing interest and offering help is enough).
2. Give minimum help but show interest; possibly help with construction techniques.

VARIATIONS

1. Add foil scraps and toothpicks for older children.
2. Add sticky dots occasionally (children use the dots for focus or as heads for people, animals).
3. Put out only long 1″ wide strips with $8\frac{1}{2}$″ × 11″ base sheet.
4. Add cardboard base pieces (encourages children to build up).
5. Add newspaper tubes rolled diagonally and taped; structures can get large and can be painted, and also used as group projects.
6. Add small boxes.

EXAMPLES OF ACTIVITY:

1. A five-year-old child made an alligator, a replica of a toy used in the block area for several weeks. The child measured equal size pieces for legs and for head/mouth that opened with a tape hinge.
2. A four-year-old child created stop signs with letters for bikes and repeated the activity for four days, showing other children how to make it.
3. A four-year-old made a two-story cube house with rooms and doors.
4. A four-year-old made an instrument panel for a spaceship from large hollow blocks and boxes.
5. Six-, seven-, eight-year-olds sculpted animals using foil, paper, and toothpicks.

JUICE BAGS

AIM

To explore the origins of juice and how it gets out of the fruit or vegetable
To measure
To develop small muscle skills

MATERIALS

Fruit assortment or one particular fruit: grapes, orange sections, pineapple slices
Zip-lock sandwich bags
Small paper cups
Tray for under each child's space

PROCEDURE

1. Place one or two pieces of fruit in a plastic bag.
2. Press the zip-lock closed.
3. Have children pinch the fruit until juice comes out.
4. Have them open the bag and pour the juice into a paper cup.
5. Measure the liquid in the cup.
6. Ask questions:
   Where did the juice come from?
   How did the _____ change?

VARIATIONS

1. Use pomegranates and wrap the seeds inside a small piece of cotton cloth (white) before putting into the plastic bag. Juice will come out, leaving white seeds and a stained red cloth.
2. Substitute vegetables such as tomatoes, cucumbers, cooked carrots (vegetable juice needs a little salt).

KALEIDOSCOPE CREATIONS

AIM

To create original geometric designs
To copy another design, matching shapes (six-, seven-, eight-year-olds)

MATERIALS

Colored construction paper cut into small shapes: squares, triangles, circles (approximately 1 inch or smaller)
White butcher paper, 12″ × 18″
Paper paste pots

PROCEDURE

1. Children work alone on the table to create a design, gluing colored shapes onto the white butcher paper.

VARIATIONS

1. Put the design on the wall or in the center of the table and ask the child to copy it to make one to take home.
2. Repeat with children working in pairs; have each make a reproduction of their design to take home.
3. Put a large piece of butcher paper on a table or the floor and make a larger design over a two- or three-day period.
4. Repeat with larger pieces of construction paper (approximately 2 inches).

MAGIC POTIONS

AIM

To see cause and effect

To solve problems, predict

To measure

MATERIALS

Vinegar in measuring cup (glass with handle and spout)

Baking soda in a dish

Spoons to stir

Clear plastic glasses (5 oz.)

Measuring cup ($\frac{1}{4}$)

Measuring spoons

Plastic knives

Large bowl

SET-UP

Trays on table for work spaces

Glass with spoon on each tray

Baking soda, vinegar, spoons, and cup on a tray in the middle of the table

PROCEDURE

1. Let children pour $\frac{1}{4}$ cup of vinegar into the cup.
2. Then have them add 1 T. of baking soda.
3. Then dump it out and repeat several times using varying amounts of soda.

VARIATIONS

1. Add water and flour as choices to mix, letting children figure out what combination fizzes (to help, add green color to the water).
2. Add eight raisins to the vinegar, then add baking soda. The raisins will rise to top and then dive to bottom.
3. Pour vinegar into small pop bottle, put baking soda into a balloon with a funnel. Put the balloon over the mouth of the bottle and tip it up so the baking soda falls into the bottle. The reaction will blow up the balloon.

MARBLE TRACKS

AIM

To develop eye-hand coordination and small muscles

To make comparisons

To mix colors

MATERIALS

Cake pans, round (perpendicular sides)
Cake pans, square
Paper cut to fit bottoms of both size pans
Marbles
Tempera paint (two or three primary colors)
Small dishes for paint
Plastic spoons

SET-UP

Cake pans at work stations
Tempera paint in bowls at the sides of each pan
Marble in each paint bowl with spoon

PROCEDURE

1. Children spoon one marble into a pan (lined with a sheet of paper that will lift out).
2. They tip the pan so the marble rolls across the paper several times.
3. They return the marble to the paint bowl.
4. Ask children to compare the lines made in the square pan with those made in the round one. Also ask each child as they come to the table which paper and pan they want: the circle or square.

VARIATIONS

1. Add glitter to the paint.
2. Substitute rectangular boxes and use cars instead of marbles.
3. Add large marbles.
4. Use only white paint on black paper.
5. Stamp a print on the paper just before adding marbles that are dry.

MIRROR BLOTS

AIM

To see cause and effect
To see "duplicate" images, space
To mix colors

MATERIALS

Tempera paint mixed (three primary colors)
Muffin pans
Eye droppers or Q-tips
Construction paper folded in half

PROCEDURE
1. Have children drop dots of color on one side of the paper.
2. They fold the top over and press or smooth it down to spread the paint.
3. They open and repeat with other colors.

VARIATIONS
1. Cut construction paper into shapes: butterflies, bears, and so on. Ask children to start with one dot, then two dots of another color, then three dots of the third color.
2. Try the same process, but sprinkle salt on the paint after blotting.
3. Try on black paper with white paint.

MIXED-UP NUMBERS

AIM
To recall proper order
To guess what is wrong

MATERIALS
Flannel board
Felt numbers 1–9
Dish towel or light cloth

PROCEDURE
1. Have children arrange the numbers in order or tell what number comes next.
2. They cover the board with cloth and remove one number.
3. Children draw the missing number in the air with a finger.

MONSTER TRACKS

AIM
To identify shapes
To repeat patterns

MATERIALS
Construction paper
Tempera paint (eight colors)
Flat pans or dishes
Plastic animals and wooden clothes pins (tracks)

PROCEDURE
1. Have children dip animals' feet or the end of clothes pin into paint.
2. To print, they move the animal or clothes pin across the paper as if walking.

VARIATIONS

1. Use other utensils. Ask the children to guess which were used.
2. Make a large group paper of tracks on butcher paper.
3. Use butcher paper and have children foot-paint across. Write names by each child's first foot print and let children criss-cross each other's tracks. Put the design on the wall and help children follow their own tracks.

SANDBOX RIVER

AIM

To solve problems, estimate, do probability
To check ideas

MATERIALS

Hose to reach in sandbox
Shovels
Boards
Boats or small pieces of wood that float

PROCEDURE

1. Let the hose run into the sandbox.
2. As water begins to flow, dig channels. Children will follow teacher's lead and then take over the digging.
3. Ask, "What can we do to keep the water from going that way?"

VARIATIONS

1. Use boards for dams and bridges.
2. Reinforce the banks with boards to make the water flow faster.
3. Make branches off the main river.
4. Add leaves and other things to see the way the river flows.

SHAPE PICTURES

AIM

To use shapes in designs
To draw and cut out own shapes (grades K, 1, 2, 3)

MATERIALS

Construction paper cut into geometric shapes, including long thin rectangles
Glue or paste
Scissors
Contrasting color base sheet

PROCEDURE

1. Children put geometric shapes onto the base sheet, working at a table (or turn table)
2. They glue the pieces in place.

VARIATIONS

1. Give children six circles, three squares, two rectangles, four right angle triangles, and ask them to make a form of transportation.
2. *K, 1, 2, 3*:
   The children trace patterns to use in cut and paste (instead of ditto lines).
   They work in pairs to trace patterns on one sheet and fit in what both children need (problem solving).
   Give children each half a sheet of construction paper so they have to work to fit all their patterns on the sheet.
   They draw shapes free hand from the example and cut out.

STRAW BOX COUNTING

AIM

To show place value in daily use (K, 1, 2)
To count days of school: (K, 1, 2; preschool counts days of week)
To see the numbers that represent the straws (K, 1, 2)

MATERIALS

Two half-gallon milk cartons cut and covered with contact paper, attach to wall
1–200 straws
Rubber bands
Pocket chart
Number cards, three each of 1, 2, 3, and two each of 4, 5, 6, 7

PROCEDURE

1. Begin on the first day of the week, and put one straw into box and a number card 1 into the pocket chart.
2. Add one straw to the box each day and count them; change the card each day.
3. When nine straws are in the box, explain that tomorrow, when there are ten, we will band them. (Count only school days and begin again at a new month.)
4. For the year, band ten straws, then move the band to the tens box and count tens packages by tens (10, 20, 30).

VARIATIONS

1. String a strip of adding machine tape with the numbers 1–200 around the room and circle the 10s in red.

WHAT IS MISSING?

AIM

To learn description words
To increase memory skills

MATERIALS

Tray and dish towel to cover
Assortment of easily identifiable objects (start with four, then increase)

PROCEDURE

1. Let children look at all the objects and name them.
2. Cover the tray and take one away.
3. They guess which one is gone.
4. Then take two away.

VARIATIONS

1. Use several classes of objects at a time and take a whole class away (for example, buttons, or round things, or blocks, or blue things).
2. Use all the same object and position in different places on the tray. Take away the middle one, and so forth.

WORD TOUCHING TRAYS

AIM

To provide tactile and visual base for description words

MATERIALS

Tray (cat litter trays work well)
Materials to touch
Cards with Touch and Tell words printed on them (one per card)
Touch and Tell Words

bumpy — corrugated paper scraps
ridges — same as above for third grade
smooth — shaving cream
smooth/bumpy — add rice to above
slippery — cornstarch and water (thin mixture)
stiff/smooth — cornstarch and water (thick mixture with surface tension)
steep — hot wheel car and block wedge
flat — same as above with flat board
glide — colored tissue squares, tweezers to pick up

PROCEDURE

1. Put a tray on the table with a word card on it.
2. Let children touch materials and guess the word.
3. In preschool, children will play a long time with the materials.
4. Ask what other words could go with it.

VARIATIONS

1. For kindergarten put two trays on the table and mix the word cards (draw a picture of the correct answer on the back of the cards).

MATHEMATICS ACTIVITIES FOR GROUP CIRCLE

Group story time in preschool, kindergarten, and first grade can include mathematics if the subject is integrated into the story or activity. Stories that are interesting and also have math aspects can be used to introduce or reinforce math concepts. When a book is used as a part of group story time, the math points discussed should be brief to help the story flow. In the following section, we list some books that involve math concepts and note the grade level for each.

Fingerplays or poems can be used in circle time for both math, language, and muscle coordination. Many fingerplays are written to count backwards, but they can be changed to count forward since young children cannot easily reverse their thinking to count backwards until they are five or six years old. The following examples emphasize counting forward.

Fingerplays – Counting Forward (can be used for flannel board stories also)

Elephants (also a song)

One elephant went out to play
On a spider's web one day.
He had such enormous fun,
He asked another elephant to come.

Two elephants went out to play.
On a spider's web one day.
They had such enormous fun,
They asked another elephant to come.

Speckled Frogs on a Log (Use with flannel board first.)

Four little speckled frogs,
Sitting on a speckled log,
Eating the most delicious bugs . . . yum, yum.
One jumped into the pool
Where it was nice and cool.
Now there is one little speckled frog
IN THE POOL.

Three little speckled frogs,
Sitting on a speckled log,
Eating the most delicious bugs . . . yum, yum.
One jumped into the pool
Where it was nice and cool.
Now there are two little speckled frogs
IN THE POOL.

(Continue until all are in pool.)

Counting Bees

Here is a bee hive.
Where are the bees?
Hiding away where nobody sees.
(Make a fist.)

Soon they come creeeeping out of the hive.
(Fingers slowly come out and crawl.)
One, bee, bzz
Two bees, bzz
Three bees, bzz
Four bees, bzz
Five bees, bzz

Five Little Fishes

Five little fishes swimming in a pool.
First one said, "The pool is cool."
Second one said, "The pool is deep."
Third one said, "I want to sleep."
Fourth one said, "Let's dive and dip."
Fifth one said, "I spy a ship."
Fisherman's boat with a line ker-splash,
Away the five little fishes dash.

Finger Lines

Draw a circle, draw a circle,
Round as can be.

Draw a circle, draw a circle,
Just for me.
(fingers in air, circle)

Draw a square, draw a square
Shaped like a box.
Draw a square, draw a square,
With a bottom and top.

Draw a triangle, draw a triangle
With corners three.
Draw a triangle, draw a triangle,
Just for me.

Fingerplays with Counting

Five Little Birds

Oh, there's one little bird
In the one little tree,
He's so alone and he doesn't want to be.
So he flew far away,
Over the sea,
And brought back a friend to live in the tree.

(Repeat for the next four numbers.)

Fish Alive

One — two — three — four — five
    (Count with fingers, keep hand up.)
I caught a fish alive.
    (Close hand in catching motion.)
Why did I let it go?
    (Open hand.)
Because it bit me so!
    (Shake fingers.)

One, Two, Three

ONE is a cat that says meow.
TWO is a dog that says bow-wow.
THREE is a crow that says caw-caw.
FOUR is a donkey that says hee-haw.
FIVE is a lamb that says baa-baa.
SIX is a sheep that says maa-maa.
SEVEN is a chick that says cheep-cheep.
EIGHT is a hen that says cluck-cluck.

NINE is a cow that says moo-moo.
TEN is a rooster crowing COCK-A-DOODLE-DOO!

Five Little Birdies

One little birdie
Rocking in a tree.
Two little birdies
Splashing in the sea.
Three little birdies
Hopping on the floor.
Four little birdies
Banging on the door.
Five little birdies
Playing hide and seek.
Keep your eyes closed tight now,
Until I say PEEK!

CHILDREN'S COOKING ACTIVITIES

Preparing food, especially individual portion cooking, interests many children and presents hands-on math learning. Measuring and reading recipes are important. Cutting with a knife or cutter is often a geometry as well as a shape recognition experience. Food preparation can be set up as a work station with direction cards. After they are introduced to this experience, even four-year-olds can do it successfully. Simple recipes often need very little supervision after the initial introduction. Begin this kind of activity with a recipe that has only three or four steps. Gradually increase the number of steps required. An excellent resource is *Cook and Learn* (1981) by Bev Veitch and Thelma Harms. Many recipes do not need an oven; some require an electric skillet for heat. In the following recipes, children make their own servings.

SHAPES TO EAT

loaf of bread
biscuit cutters or animal cookie cutters
peanut butter and/or cream cheese
alfalfa sprouts
raisins
unsalted sunflower seeds

Cut a bread shape and spread with peanut butter or cream cheese. Decorate the animal with sprouts, raisins, seeds. Cut a circle shape to make a face.

VARIATION

Using a smaller biscuit cutter, cut three circles and stack them. Talk about what the child has in the middle, on the bottom, on the top.

THREE BEAR PORRIDGE

3 T. rolled oats
1 T. raisins
1 T. chopped apple
1 T. powdered dry milk
½ c. hot water

Mix ingredients in paper cup (5 oz.). Use low heat in covered electric skillet 15 min. (Most electric skillets hold 20-24 five-ounce cups.) As a variation, specify the actual number of raisins and chopped apple pieces to be used (for kindergarten children).

TRAIL MIX

4 almonds
8 raisins
6 peanuts
2 T. Cherrios

Mix in paper cup (5 oz.).

Snack Recipes Good for Math

The following recipes are snacks that allow children to talk about shapes and parts as they eat.

QUESADILLAS (24 children)

1 lb. jack cheese
2 dozen snack size flour tortillas
½ stick margarine for frying

Cut tortillas into pie shapes with plastic serrated knives on a cutting board. Grate cheese, sprinkle in middle of tortilla. Put top on and bake or lightly brown on Teflon griddle with margarine. (Put circle attribute blocks on nearby table to compare shapes.)

CIRCLES AND SQUARES

1 box Ritz Bits
1 box Wheatsworth Crackers
baskets
Ask children to find small, middle, and large size circles in Ritz Bits or ask them to take 2 of each size. Bite edges off square cracker to make a large circle.

SQUARES TO TRIANGLES (24 children)

2 pkg. wonton skins
melted margarine
Filling: just brush with margarine, or use raisins, cooked chicken, or grated cheese
Peel off a single wonton skin. Put filling in middle or just brush with melted margarine. Fold corner diagonally. Brush top side with melted margarine and bake at 400° for 5 minutes.

CHILDREN'S BOOKS WITH MATH APPLICATIONS

LEVEL	*BOOK TITLE*
P,K,1	*Bears in Pairs* by Niki Yektai. (1987). New York: Bradbury Press. Concepts, language, opposite, rhymes. First-graders can read it.
P,K,1	*Changes, Changes* by Pat Hutchins. (1971). New York: Aladdin Books, Macmillan. Concepts with people and blocks. Can be used to stimulate table block play.
P,K,1	*Moongame* by Frank Asch. (1984). Englewood Cliffs, NJ: Prentice-Hall. Concepts, counting.
P,K,1	*Round, & Round, & Round* by Tana Hoban. (1982). New York: Greenwillow Books, Morrow. Concepts of things that are round, photographs.
P,K,1	*Giggly, Wiggly, Snickety-Snick* by Robyn Supraner. (1978). New York: Parents Magazine Press. Concepts: hard-soft, bumpy-smooth, tickly-smooth, sharp, sticky, stretchy, cold-hot, and so on.

P,K,1   *Push-Pull, Empty-Full* by Tana Hoban. (1972). New York: Collier Books. Guessing about shape and predicting answers.

P,K,1   *Shapes, Shapes, Shapes* by Tana Hoban. (1986). New York: Greenwillow Books, Morrow.

P,K,1   *Things That Go* by Anne Rockwell. (1986). New York: E. P. Dutton.

POSTER PHOTOGRAPHS WITH MATH APPLICATIONS

P,K,1,2,3   Pictures on classroom walls are part of the overall learning environment that encourages children to try activities. The following color photograph posters from NAEYC (Washington, DC) show children (from many cultures) involved in math-related activities.

- "Future Physicist? Tomorrow's Engineer?" (shows child using construction manipulatives)
- "Trust Children to Succeed" (shows child cutting fruit)
- "Childhood Challenges" (shows child climbing on aluminum ladder)
- "Everyday Math" (shows children in many activities)

SUMMARY

We began this chapter with a discussion of the scope and sequence for mathematics programs for young children. After we examined the standard approaches used to determine content and its sequencing, we presented an alternative approach. In the new approach, three interrelated parts are necessary to determine an appropriate developmental program: (1) the components of children's environment (their real-world aspects); (2) the structure of mathematics, including language, vocabulary, and symbols; and (3) evaluation, with specific objectives used for each aspect of the program.

The discussion of scope and sequence led to a discussion of the importance of planning: yearly planning, weekly planning, and daily lesson planning. The classroom teacher is the one who must decide what to teach and when to present new mathematical tasks. Children must be presented with learning experiences that are within their cognitive grasp. Then, given careful guidance, they will move along the developmental continuum, extending their mathematical learning.

In this chapter, we gave examples of daily programs, room arrangements, and essential classroom materials, as well as making suggestions for managing class activities.

The last part of the chapter contains a variety of mathematical activities that have been cross-referenced to show how they can be used with various mathematical topics.

ACTIVITIES FOR TEACHER INSIGHT

1. Obtain permission to visit an elementary school in your neighborhood. Select one grade or combination grade and study its use of mathematics textbooks and other supplementary materials. How is an adopted textbook used? Is a workbook used? Are all children expected to complete the work in one textbook during the year? What provisions are made for individual differences in learning abilities and rates of learning?
2. Select two modern mathematics textbook series. Study the scope and sequence for mathematics (one grade level) for each series. Most publishers have a scope and sequence chart for the whole series K–6. How do the two series differ? When are major math topics presented? What provision is made for individual differences?
3. Arrange for a conference with a primary-level teacher to look at a weekly lesson plan book. Does anyone review or approve the weekly plans? What is done when teachers are absent? What provisions are made for substitute teachers? What is the role of the teacher's aide in lesson planning or in using the teacher's plans?
4. With the help of your instructor, prepare a lesson plan for one whole-class math lesson (levels 1, 2, or 3). Take into consideration the need for the new concept, children's readiness for the lesson, materials needed, introduction to the lesson, pupil participation, closing the lesson (evaluation), and the next steps to take (follow-up, another lesson, and so on).

REFERENCES

ASCH, F. (1984). *Moongame*. New York: Prentice Hall.

BARATTA-LORTON, M. (1976). *Mathematics their way: An activity-centered mathematics program*. Menlo Park, CA: Addison-Wesley.

BROWN, M. (1985). *Hand rhymes*. New York: E. P. Dutton.

BURK, D., SNIDER, A., & SYMONDS, P. (1988). *Box it or bag it mathematics*. Salem, OR: Math Learning Center.

California State Department of Education. (1987). *Mathematics: Model curriculum guide K–8*. Sacramento, CA: Office of State Printing.

CHARLESWORTH, R. (1987). *Understanding child development: For adults who work with young children* (2nd ed.). Albany, NY: Delmar.

Flint Public Library. (1981). *Ring a ring o' roses: Games and finger plays for pre-school children*. Flint, MI: Author.

HENDRICK, J. (1988). The whole child: Developmental education for the early years (4th ed.). Columbus, OH: Merrill.

HOBAN, T. (1972). *Push-pull, empty-full*. New York: Collier Books.

———. (1982). *Round, & round, & round*. New York: Greenwillow Books, Morrow.

———. (1986). *Shapes, shapes, shapes*. New York: Greenwillow Books, Morrow.

HUTCHINS, PAT. (1971). *Changes, changes*. New York: Aladdin Books, Macmillan.

IMMERZEEL, G., & OCKENGA, E. G. (1988). *Problem solving workbook*. Lexington, MA: D. C. Heath.

KAYE, P. (1987). *Games for math: Playful ways to help your child learn math K–3*. New York: Pantheon.

National Association for the Education of Young Children. (1986). *Position statement on developmentally appropriate practice in programs for four- and five-year-olds*. Washington, DC: Author.

RICHARDSON, K. (February 1988). Assessing understanding. *Arithmetic Teacher, 35,* 39–41.

RIEDESEL, C. A. (1985). *Teaching elementary school mathematics*. Englewood Cliffs, NJ: Prentice-Hall.

ROCKWELL, A. (1986). *Things that go*. New York: E.P. Dutton.

SCHULTZ, K. A., COLARUSSO, R. P., & STRAWDERMAN, V. (1989). *Mathematics for every young child*. Columbus, OH: Merrill.

SEYMOUR, D. (1984). *Problem parade*. Palo Alto, CA: Dale Seymour Publishers.

SITARZ, P. G. (1987). *Picture book story hours—from birthdays to bears*. Littleton, CO: Libraries Unlimited.

STERN, M. (1988). *Experimenting with numbers: A guide for preschool, kindergarten, and first grade teachers*. Cambridge, MA: Educators Publishing Service.

SUPRANER, R. (1978). *Giggly, wiggly, snickety-snick*. New York: Parents Magazine Press.

SUTHERLAND, Z. (1986). *Children and books* (7th ed.). Glenview, IL: Scott, Foresman.

VEITCH, B., & HARMS, T. (1981). *Cook and learn: Pictorial single portion recipes*. Rev. ed. Menlo Park, CA: Addison-Wesley.

YEKTAI, N. (1987). *Bears in pairs*. New York: Bradbury Press.

APPENDIX A

Physical, Cognitive, and Social-Emotional Traits and Needs of Children Four Through Eight Years of Age

We believe that the main determinant of the quality of mathematics programs for young children is the extent to which child growth and development are defined and implemented in these programs.

The careful study of the physical, cognitive, and social-emotional traits and needs of young children will help teachers understand the importance of the development viewpoint in guiding the learning activities of young children. Some principles gleaned from studies in this field are:

- Children at different developmental levels think and learn in qualitatively different ways.
- Age is an important factor, influencing the kind of cognitive structures available and the appropriateness of instruction.
- Children who do not have the required cognitive structures may not learn certain basic math concepts.
- The math curriculum must be within the cognitive development of children.

Thus, the teacher must diagnose the level at which a child is functioning in mathematics and then adjust instruction to that level. The outlines of child growth and development that follow will help teachers make this diagnosis.

FOUR-YEAR-OLD CHILDREN

Readiness for school and concern over the unmet needs of children in the early years have become major issues in planning instruction for four- and five-year-old children. Considerable attention, therefore, has been given to planning exploratory learning activities, language development, reading readiness, and appropriate materials to use with this age group.

During the early years of life, the child is susceptible and responsive to environmental influences that are stimulating and enjoyable. All who work with young children must be sensitive to the development of their physical, cognitive, and social-emotional traits and needs. A safe, challenging educational environment will have a positive effect on the development of a child's intelligence, motivation to learn, concept of self, relationships with other children, and health.

Not only are these traits interrelated — cognitive development and social-emotional development, for example, are closely aligned — but they provide clues to learning activities that are in keeping with specific growth patterns. In the following outline of characteristics of the typical four-year-old, many traits have been identified that will enable teachers to study an individual child, guide effective mathematical learning, and communicate with others about children's growth and development.

Physical, Cognitive, and Social-Emotional Traits and Needs for the Four-Year-Old Child

PHYSICAL

- Develops at child's own unique rate and according to child's own unique pattern of size
- Shows increased competence in moving about
- Tests out growing abilities — strength, agility
- Climbs as high as possible (equipment, trees)
- Masters the three-wheeler, stunts, and speeds
- Likes fantasy play as a car, rider, driver, and so on
- Develops more upper arm strength; can saw, swing, and climb
- Coordinates hand use and handles objects and materials
- Pulls or wriggles into clothing; needs help with buttons, laces
- Runs and jumps easily; balances on one foot

COGNITIVE

- Extends capacity for mental symbols that represent things
- Uses and manipulates mental substitutes for the real thing
- Imitates mentally and makes internal symbols
- Uses language as a tool for thinking
- Experiments with words and gradually refines their meaning
- Begins to use longer sentences, including specific word or structure

- Begins to count without understanding sequence
- Shows interest in how things work but not "why"
- Develops concepts of space as shown through words used: "way up there," "next to," or "under"
- Develops beginning concepts of time through regular experiences at home or school and by repeated references to time
- Makes distinctions between foods, friends, animals, happy times, or sad times

SOCIAL-EMOTIONAL (closely aligned to cognitive)

- Shows interest in others; is sensitive to people
- Enters into many kinds of activities, alone and with others
- Seeks exploration and asks many questions
- Experiments with a variety of different actions—putting clothing on backwards, eating different ways, trying out ways to wash or use the toilet facilities
- Is often aggressive due to testing reactions rather than animosity
- Shows frustrations and anger that may cause fights
- Becomes angered by words used such as *dope, dog, dummy*
- Likes to be with small groups
- Enjoys birthday parties and invites friends
- Expresses feeling of happiness and sympathy for others

NEEDS

- Needs frequent daily provision for: activity and rest, food and drink, going to the bathroom, outlets for emotions
- Needs help in learning new ways to function socially with individual or groups
- Needs protection (health and safety) and learns to protect self
- Needs wide variety of opportunities to explore at own interest rate

FIVE-YEAR-OLD CHILDREN

Five-year-old children are at an impressionable age in their growth and development. They are ready to do things. Teachers must be concerned about providing an environment for living and learning that builds confidence, self-assurance, and a positive attitude toward self and school.

To provide this desirable learning environment, the teacher must understand the main characteristics of this age group so that learning experiences will be appropriate for their stage of development.

Physical, Cognitive, and Social-Emotional Traits and Needs for the Five-Year-Old Child

PHYSICAL

- Is active and usually not willing to sit for long periods of time; may tire easily
- Enjoys outdoor play, using large muscles to manipulate toys and materials
- Coordinates skills for jumping, running, climbing efficiently
- Develops improved eye and hand coordination
- Cuts with scissors, copies shapes, folds paper, and begins to make letters and numbers — some reversals appear
- Achieves independence in dressing
- Has improved health and is less susceptible to communicable diseases; usually has a complete set of temporary teeth

COGNITIVE

- Thinks about what is perceived/seen
- Begins to think intuitively, seeing relationships
- Acts on concrete things to manipulate, to arrange or rearrange, and classify
- Thinks in terms of immediate perceptions and by inability to keep in mind more than one relationship at a time
- Contradicts self since is unable to keep in mind more than one thing at a time
- Experiments with words; sees humor and is able to speak in sentences
- Has attention span influenced by interests as well as immediate perceptions

SOCIAL-EMOTIONAL

- Models the behavior of older children — an impressionable age
- Seeks approval, affection, and attention; tends to be self-centered
- Works or plays with small groups while interested; may seek time to be by self or to have parallel play; wants to play with children of own age
- Becomes independent and at times may be aggressive
- Accepts small responsibilities and can help plan activities of interest
- Requires that activities be changed frequently, according to attention span and interests

NEEDS

- Needs activities that alternate active and quiet, large and small muscles, indoor and outdoor play
- Needs guidance in developing group interaction skills

- Needs approval and encouragement in endeavors and protection from over-exertion

SIX-YEAR-OLD CHILDREN

Beginning the first grade in school is important to the six-year-old child. The child will have lost much of the fear and trauma surrounding entrance into kindergarten. Friends will make going to school a happy experience.

Once established in school, the child experiences pressures and expectations from teachers as well as from parents. The child has to work at organized tasks longer than was required in kindergarten. The child must learn to write numerals and letters as well as to begin reading these symbols. Finally, the child must remember many things connected with school and new learning activities.

The teacher needs to be aware of these expectations and pressures, and carefully determine the stage of development the child has attained. With these data, the teacher can plan appropriate learning activities as well as inform parents of the child's stage of development.

Physical, Cognitive, and Social-Emotional Traits and Needs for the Six-Year-Old Child

PHYSICAL

- Is active and inclined to be noisy and boisterous
- Tires easily in large motor activities and may become out of breath easily due to increased exertion and strength level
- Continues to develop immunity to communicable diseases
- Coordinates skills for running, jumping, climbing efficiently
- Learns to throw and to catch a ball with the use of the hands rather than with the chest
- Uses small muscle ability to form letters and numerals with the use of models
- Reverses some letters and numerals and makes some large and irregular forms
- Requires continued guidance in small muscle skills
- Uses preferred hand (about 85 percent will be right-handed, 10 percent left-handed, and 5 percent not determined or ambidextrous)
- Recognizes other children and interacts with others by size, sex, attractiveness, or other physical features

COGNITIVE

- Continues to think in the preoperational stage, relying on preconceptual or intuitive thinking, gradually moving toward next stage
- Becomes aware of space relationships such as left, right, across
- Begins to relate oral language to reading symbols and pictures
- Increases attention span in individual and group activities
- Begins to understand and use time relating to work and play to the hour and then half hour
- Distinguishes well between fact and fantasy in everyday situations
- Shows interest in stories, songs, dramatic play, sense of humor

SOCIAL-EMOTIONAL

- Experiences some difficulties in "growing up"; may have regression, such as tears and wanting "mother"
- Loses baby teeth, an event very important to the child
- Acts in somewhat self-centered and demanding way
- Seeks recognition, praise and approval; rejects criticism, blame, punishment
- Acts pleased when own ideas are accepted
- Takes responsibility for a variety of duties
- Shows inconsistent behavior at times
- Exhibits rivalry with younger siblings; may use a variety of attention-seeking actions

NEEDS

- Needs activities that emphasize creativity, making choices, and decisions
- Needs alternating quiet and active time periods
- Needs help in developing learning habits
- Needs social situations that develop followership as well as leadership skills
- Needs experiences that involve humor and laughing, singing, listening to music and poems, and opportunities to talk about these interests

SEVEN-YEAR-OLD CHILDREN

Seven-year-olds are ready for a wide variety of new learning activities. This readiness is due to improved coordination of hand and eye movements and the ability to use large and small muscles; an increased attention span and thinking that is not dominated by perceptual factors; and the development of reading skills so that they can discover the meaning of new mathematical vocabulary.

Physical, Cognitive, and Social-Emotional Traits and Needs for the Seven-Year-Old Child

PHYSICAL

- Develops strong immunity to disease; has fewer colds than at six
- Works in sudden bursts of energy; is not as active as at six
- Uses large muscles quite well and shows increased skill in use of small muscles
- Improves coordination of hand and eye; develops own expectations of perfection
- Sprawls on floor or carpet, even desk top, rather than sit
- Requires activities using eye concentrations that are brief
- Acquires six-year molars
- Grows more slowly than at four, five, and six, but steadily
- Engages in many kinds of large and small motor activities

COGNITIVE

- Increases attention span
- Uses dramatic play to play-act stories
- Begins to interpret vicarious experiences in terms of past experiences
- Begins to understand time relationships
- Begins to make mathematical operations in thought; thinking is not dominated by perceptual content
- Evaluates own performances but may expect too much of self
- Reads independently
- Uses picture dictionary
- Uses more descriptive and action words

SOCIAL-EMOTIONAL

- Works and plays with others or alone
- Observes actions of others carefully
- Wants to erase mistakes and is concerned about errors
- Worries over minor problems and may be pensive
- Assumes responsibilities
- Interprets parents' and teachers' demands as unfair

- Develops and shows close personal feelings toward teachers
- Demonstrates some independence of mother, father
- Seeks a place in family and may continue to be jealous of siblings
- Demands to have private ideas, and may not want to show others
- Shows interest in short- and long-term projects
- Begins to want to produce, not just create

NEEDS

- Needs activities that include use of large and small muscles
- Needs short work periods involving reading and writing, with time to make adjustments or to complete tasks
- Needs assistance in recognizing a reasonable point at which to stop an activity or learning task
- Needs experiences fostering learning by doing — in groups and alone
- Needs opportunities to learn leadership and followership skills in a group
- Needs opportunities for self-expression — orally and written, in music, art, dramatic play
- Needs understanding and friendship from teachers
- Needs to be liked

EIGHT-YEAR-OLD CHILDREN

Active mathematical learning takes place when the emotional energies of children are concentrated on an interest of real worth and when intellectual maturity supports this interest.

We are concerned with the maturing of mental abilities that form the basis for favorable physical and mental experiences in mathematical learning. Teachers need to recognize this maturity in order to plan and guide mathematical activities that are satisfying and appropriate for children.

Eight-year-old children have entered one of the most important stages of mental and physical growth and development. To provide for optimum growth in mathematical learning, we must adjust both the demands we make on children and the type of concepts we present.

The following outline presents the most important characteristics and traits of the eight-year-old child. Teachers must study and work with these traits in order to establish an environment and instructional procedures that are appropriate as well as fulfilling to eight-year-olds.

Physical, Cognitive, and Social-Emotional Traits and Needs for the Eight-Year-Old Child

PHYSICAL

- Has good health; has had many communicable diseases; tonsils begin to shrink in size
- Plays or works to the point of exhaustion; has much physical energy
- Uses smaller muscles and shows good manipulative skills; has developed good eye-hand coordination; may be careless and have accidents
- May be going through a stage of rapid growth in length of legs; bodily movements are generally easy and with some skill
- Has mature digestive system and can tolerate more unusual foods; less regularity in eating times
- Has marked increased ability to focus eyes at near and far distances; can focus on microscope
- Dental defects begin to develop

COGNITIVE

- Concentrates for longer periods of time than the seven-year-old child
- Combines consistently the skills and information learned
- Increases ability to distinguish fact from fiction
- Shows interest in defining own problems
- Develops some patterns of logical thinking
- Acquires some understanding of space and time
- Puts own ideas into words, including emotions

SOCIAL-EMOTIONAL

- Tends to project self into dramatic situations
- Shows capacity to accept some criticism and to evaluate own actions
- Enjoys working and playing with others, including mixed groups of boys and girls
- Begins to accept responsibilities in a group
- Shows an interest in being a member of an identified group (soccer, scouts); has special friends
- Begins to enjoy competition
- Responds easily to praise, feels more self-confident than at six and seven
- Expresses ideas and takes part in activities
- Exhibits some fears — real or imaginary
- Has some difficulties getting along with siblings, sees self as "grown up"; wants to be treated in a more mature way

- Seeks close relationship with mother and is interested in family
- Assumes responsibilities at school and at home
- Begins to appreciate the worth of others as well as of self

NEEDS

- Needs to participate in games, activities, and vigorous exercises
- Needs real and vicarious experiences related to understanding environment
- Needs challenging instructional program

APPENDIX B

Individual Evaluation Techniques: Piagetian Concepts

The following are suggestions for individual interviews using Piagetian concept tests. The items covered include: one-to-one correspondence to make equivalent sets (three tests); ordination with objects of different lengths; part-whole relationship with color (two tests); conservation of liquid; conservation of length; and conservation with solids (clay).

I. One-to-one correspondence to make equivalent sets

   A. *Materials:* 18 to 20 counters, same color and shape; two dolls or puppets. Numbers 1 and 2 to designate these dolls will be used in all following test items.
     Vocabulary: as many as, more than, less than, fewer than

   B. *Procedure*
     1. Put counters in front of child being tested. Have a 8½" × 11" cardboard on which to place counters. Have circles the same size as counters drawn on the cardboard.
     2. "Help me put counters on each circle on this card (1)."
     3. "Can you give this other doll (2) as many counters as this one (1)? Put them here."
     4. "Has doll (2) as many counters as this one (1)? Tell me how you know that."

   C. Move the counters close to doll (1) and cluster them together.
     1. "Has this doll (1) as many as this (2)? Why do you think that?"
     2. Spread doll (1) counters so they cover more space.
     3. "This doll (2) thinks that there are more counters over here." Point to (1). "What do you think? Why do you think that?"

II. One-to-one correspondence to make equivalent sets

A. *Materials:* 18 counters, same color and shape; two dolls: (1) and (2).

B. *Procedure*
1. Place counters in one pile between the two dolls (2) (1).
2. "This doll (1) wants as many counters as this doll (2). Can you give them as many as each other? Use all of the counters."
3. "Now (after dividing) do they have as many as each other? How do you know?"
4. If child completes task (equal groups), spread (1's) counters to cover more space. "Does (1's) have more counters than this doll (2)? Or as many as? Why do you think that?"
5. Move doll (1's) counters still farther apart and doll (2's) closer, bunched.
6. "This doll (1) thinks there are more counters here because they are spread out. What do you think?"

III. One-to-one correspondence to make equivalent sets

A. *Materials:* 6 small cups and spoons placed in a row between dolls (1) and (2).

B. *Procedure*
1. "Can you put a spoon under each cup? Are there as many spoons as cups? How do you know that?"
2. Move spoons apart so there is no direct alignment.
3. "Doll (1) thinks there are still as many spoons as cups. What do you think? Why do you think that?"
4. Move spoons so they form a straight (horizontal) line under the cups. "Are there still as many spoons as cups? How do you know that?"
5. Other arrangements to use if needed:
   a. Put cups in a line. Put spoons in a line parallel to and under the cups.
   b. Stack cups on top of each other and the spoons in a line underneath.

IV. Ordination with objects of different lengths

A. *Materials:* dowels ¼″ in diameter and of different lengths.

B. *Procedure*
1. Place dowels in random order between dolls (1) and (2).
2. "Can you build a staircase starting from this one?" Place shortest dowel in a vertical position on the table.
3. After child arranges them, ask "Are the sticks in the right place? How do you know that?"

4. Interchange two sticks, such as fourth and sixth. "What do you think? Why do you think that? Can you put them in the right place?"

5. Ask child to put head down. Play a game. Remove a dowel such as the fourth. Keep the fourth dowel out of sight. Then interchange the second and third. "Now heads up."

6. "Can you put them back in the right places?" Then bring out the fourth dowel. "Can you put this in the right place? Why did you put the dowel there?"

V. Part-whole relationship with color

A. *Materials:* 5 plastic circles and 4 plastic squares. Same size of shapes within each group.

B. *Procedure*
1. Put the 9 counters, random order, between (1) and (2).
2. "Can you show me the ——— square the ——— circle (child shows the color asked for and the shape)." "What is the same about all the counters (square, circles)?"
   If child cannot do this, show a square. "What is this?" Show a circle. "What is this?" Then, "What is the color of this?"
3. Rearrange counters, mixed, random. "Are there more green ones or more circles? Why do you think that? This doll (2) thinks there are more green ones than circles? What do you think? Why? This doll (1) thinks there are more circles than green ones. What do you think?"

VI. Part-whole relationship with color

A. *Materials:* 10 dual-colored counters (disks or circles).

B. *Procedure*
1. Place counters 3 red and 7 blue randomly in front of child and between dolls (1) and (2). "Here are some counters, red on one side and blue on the other."
2. "Can you show me a red counter? Show me a blue counter. Can you put all the circles here?" Show a space between the two dolls. "What is the same about these counters?"
3. "Are there more circles or more blue ones? Why?"
4. "This doll (1) thinks there are more circles than blue ones. What do you think? Why?"
5. "This doll (1) thinks there are more red ones than circles. What do you think? Why?"

6. Move counters around. "Now are there more circles or more blue counters? Why?"

VII. Conservation of liquid

A. *Materials:* 3 sets (two each set) of containers 1, 1', 2, 2', 3, 3'; sand or water, newspapers, and tray to catch spills.

B. *Procedure*
1. Place same size containers before (1) and (2). Fill the container in front of (1). Then pour this sand into the container of (2). Fill (1's) container again. "Do they have as much sand as each other? Why do you think that?"
2. Take containers 2 and 2' (which are low and wide). "This doll (1) wants me to put the sand in this can." Pour it. "Does this doll (1) have as much sand as this doll (2)? Why?"
3. Move containers side by side. "This doll (2) thinks that this container (points to larger, low C) has less sand because the container (1) is not as high as this. Do you think (1) has less than (2)?"
4. "Doll (1) wants me to put the sand into these cups. Does (1) have as much sand as he had before? Why? Doll (2) says there is more sand in (1's) because there are more cups. What do you think? Why?"
5. Pour sand from the cups into wide and low container. "Do doll (1) and doll (2) have as much sand as each other now? Does (1) have more sand than (2)? Why?"

VIII. Conservation of length

A. *Materials:* 2 chains or rope, same length.

B. *Procedure*
1. Place chains in a heap before (1) and (2). "Here are two chains, one for each doll (1) and (2). Can you see if they are both the same size? As long as each other? Are they the same length? Why?"
2. Pull one chain to the right so that the ends do not coincide. "Are they still the same length? Why?"
3. Loop one chain over your finger. Hold the other chain full length. "This doll (1) thinks the chain is still as long as this. What do you think?"
4. Hold one chain vertically. Stretch the other chain on the table horizontally. "(1) thinks his chain is shorter. What do you think?"
5. Take one chain and wind it around (1); part of the chain is obscured because it is behind the doll. "(2) thinks his chain is longer. What do you think?"

IX. Conservation with solids (clay)

    A. *Materials:* one small container and modeling clay.

    B. *Procedure*
       1. Place ball of clay in front of child, the small container between (1) and (2). "The dolls need some clay. Can you find a way to give each the same amount of clay?" Child divides clay into 2 balls, giving one ball to each doll (1) and (2). "Do they have as much clay as each other? How do you know?"
       2. Squeeze one ball into a cylinder-like shape. "(1) thinks that there is as much clay as (2) has. What do you think?"
       3. Break (2's) clay into 3 balls. "Now (2) thinks there is more clay. What do you think?"
       4. Roll the other ball into a cylinder longer than 10 cm. Place the 3 balls close together and alongside the cylinder. "Now (1) thinks that (2) has more clay because it is longer. What do you think?"

GLOSSARY

Abacus Device used for calculating, in which beads are slid along wires to show place value.

Addend Any number that is added — for example, in $4 + 2 = 6$, the 2 and 4 are addends.

Algorism or algorithm A step-by-step procedure for solving a mathematical problem, such as one of the basic operations.

Approximation A result that is not exact but sufficiently accurate for a certain purpose.

Area The numerical measure (in unit terms) of a plane region, including a closed curve; contains a number of unit squares.

Array Orderly grouping of things in rows or columns. An addition table or multiplication table is an array of numbers.

Associative Law of Addition A principle that states: When adding three or more terms, the way in which the terms are grouped does not affect the sum — for example, $(2 + 3) + 3 = 8$ and $2 + (3 + 3) = 8$.

Associative Law for Multiplication A principle that states: When multiplying three or more terms, the way in which the terms are grouped does not affect the product — for example, $(a \times b) \times c = a \times (b \times c)$.

Base A place-value system of numeration, such as base ten; also applies to the exponential form when a number is multiplied by itself several times: $10 \times 10 \times 10 = 1,000$ when the base is 10.

Binary operation A rule that assigns to each pair of elements a, b, a unique defined third element, c.

Calculator Small, often hand-held machine that performs mathematical operations mechanically.

Cardinal number A number that specifies the number of elements in equivalent sets. Cardinal numbers are a set of simple counting numbers $(0, 1, 2, 3, 4, 5, \ldots)$ and/or an ordered set of numbers such that $0 < 1 < 2 < 3 < 4 < \cdots$

Circle The set of points in a plane that are the same distance from a given point to the center. The circle itself is a closed curve called the circumference.

Closed curve A curve that has no end points and encloses a plane region.

Column A vertical array of numerals (used in column addition).

Colored rods See Rods.

Commutative Law of Addition A principle that states: The order in which two numbers are added does not affect their sum.

Commutative Law of Multiplication A principle that states: the order in which two numbers are multiplied does not affect their product.

Computer A computing machine that consists of three subunits. A modern computing system consists of a central processing unit (CPU) and one or more input and output devices.

Computer-assisted instruction (CAI) Instruction that uses the computer as an educational tool, providing children with a unique way to deal with information.

Congruent figures Two figures that have the same shape and size but a different location and orientation.

Conservation The principle of: *number* — the cardinal number of a set remains the same when its elements are rearranged; *length* — the length of an interval is unchanged when it is bent, or when it is cut and rearranged; *area* — the area of a surface is unchanged when the surface is cut and rearranged; *volume* — the volume of a fluid is unchanged when the fluid is poured into different vessels; *weight* — the weight of a substance is unchanged when the shape is changed.

Counting numbers or natural numbers The set 1, 2, 3, 4, which is ordered such that $1 < 2 < 3 < 4 < 5 \ldots$

Cube A prism with square bases and square lateral faces.

Cuisenaire rods See Rods; a trademark name with many varieties available.

Curve A term used in geometry to express the idea of a path that may turn in any manner as it proceeds indefinitely in either direction.

Decimal A numeral in which a decimal point is used to indicate the denominator, which must be a power of ten.

Degree A unit of measurement of angles. The symbol for degree is °. There are 360 degrees in a complete revolution.

Denominator The number named by the term below the horizontal bar in a fraction.

Diameter (of a circle) Line segment whose end points lie on the circle and that passes through the center of the circle.

Digit A basic symbol used in a numeration system to write a numeral. The digits of the Hindu-Arabic system of notation are 0,1,2,3,4,5,6,7,8,9.

Discrete objects Separate or individually distinct objects.

Distributive Law of Multiplication over Addition A principle that states: When an indicated sum is to be multiplied by a number, each addend is multiplied by that number and the products are added.

Dividend A number to be divided.

Divisor A number by which a dividend is divided.

Element One of the things that forms a set or collection; a member of a set.

Empty Set (or null set) The set that has no elements.

Equation A mathematical sentence stating a relationship of equality between two numerical expressions; the relationship may be true, false, or open statement.

Estimate A numerical value that is assigned, based on incomplete evidence or general considerations and not by exact mathematical procedure.

Evaluation A process for identifying a child's progress toward the mastery of measurable objectives established for specific skills.

Even number An integer divisible by 2: 4, 6, 8 . . .

Expanded form or notation A numerical expression that shows the number represented by each digit in a place-value numeral, such as $364 = 300 + 60 + 4$ or 3 hundreds, 6 tens, 4 ones.

Factor Any of the integers that, when multiplied together, form a product.

Figure Any set of points: lines, curves, surfaces and solids; also, a symbol that represents a number; a drawing used to assist in explaining a topic.

Fraction A numeral that represents a rational number. It may be a common fraction or a decimal fraction.

Function A set of ordered pairs such that each first element appears in one and only one ordered pair.

Graph A representation of a number relationship in pictorial or figure form.

Hindu-Arabic Numerals The digits 0, 1, 2, 3, 4, 5, 6, 7, 8, 9 used in the decimal numeration system.

Identity element for addition and multiplication Addition: The number 0 is the identity element under addition since for all numbers a, $a + 0 = a$ and $0 + a = a$; multiplication: The number 1 is the identity element under multiplication since for all numbers a, $a \times 1 = a$ and $1 \times a = a$.

Integers The numbers $-4, -3, -2, -1, 0, +1, +2, +3, +4$ . . .

Interval (line interval) May be a line segment. The portion of a (straight) line lying between two points on that line.

Inverse An operation that "undoes" another operation.

Law of closure A principle that states: For every pair of numbers, a and b, there exists a unique number $(a + b)$ called the sum of a and b. For multiplication, the product of two natural numbers is a natural number. Thus $2 \times 3 = 6$.

Length The quantity that has been measured along a single dimension such as a line or curve.

Line (straight line) An undefined term used in geometry to express the idea of an unturning path indefinitely extended in both directions. In elementary math we use the term *number line*.

Mathematical model A mathematical expression or statement that represents a physical object or event and that can be used to predict information about the object or event.

Measure A number assigned to an object or event that indicates its size compared to a standard or chosen unit.

Measurement Comparing some object or event with a standard unit.

Multiple of a counting number The product of that counting number and any counting number.

Multiplication A binary operation on two numbers to obtain a third number called the product.

Notation The use of signs or symbols to represent an aspect of mathematics. Symbols are the letters and marks from which mathematical expressions and formulas are built.

Number A property of a set, representing quantity, as the number of things in a set. We think with numbers. We cannot see numbers. A distinction is made between number and numeral.

Numeral A symbol used to represent a number.

Numeration A system of numerals for naming numbers.

Odd number An integer not divisible evenly without a remainder.

One-to-one correspondence Pairing between the members of two sets.

Operation A way of obtaining an element from one or more other elements.

Percent A fraction whose denominator is 100. Percent is shown by the symbol % written to the right of the numeral for the numerator, such as 5% (five percent).

Placeholder A symbol in a mathematical expression that stands for a numeral, an operation sign, or a relation sign.

Place Value A property of a numeration system that gives digits a different value according to the position the digit holds in the numeral.

Plane An undefined term in geometry for a set of points that can be considered as the extension of a flat surface — for example, a table top.

Point An undefined term in geometry that indicates a position.

Polygon A closed curve figure.

Product The result of the operation of multiplying a pair of numbers.

Quotient A number that results from the division of the dividend by the divisor.

Rate A comparison between two quantities that may be of different types, such as miles per gallon or miles per hour.

Rational numbers A number that can be expressed in the form $\frac{m}{n}$, where m and n are integers and n is not 0; a number represented by a fraction, such as $\frac{1}{2}$.

Ray (half line) A straight line that begins at a point and is continued indefinitely in one direction from that point.

Rectangle A parallelogram that has one angle a right angle, and therefore with all four angles right angles.

Region A plane region is all points of the interior of a sample closed curve and the points on the curve; a solid region is all points of the interior of a closed surface and all points on the surface.

Regrouping A term that replaces the older expressions of *carrying* and *borrowing* in addition and subtraction.

Rods Set of unit blocks cut in proportion: The 2 size equals two of the 1 size; the longest equals 10.

Scale For a map, the ratio of a distance on a map to the actual distance it represents.

Sentence A formula that shows the relations between the elements of a set of numbers; may be true, false, or open.

Set An undefined term in math for any collection of elements.

Space An undefined term in geometry, usually referring to three-dimensional space in which solids can be measured for length, breadth, and height.

Structured objects Materials designed to show some aspects of base ten, such as colored rods representing numbers 1 through 10.

Sum The result of the operation of addition of a pair of numbers; for example, the sum of 4 + 5 is 9. The 4 and 5 are addends.

Surface The area that corresponds to a plane surface.

Whole numbers (0, 1, 2, 3, 4, . . .) Used to describe sets of whole objects. See also Cardinal number.

I N D E X

Wilbur H. Dutton

Professor Emeritus of Elementary Mathematics Education, Curriculum, and Instruction at the University of California, Los Angeles, Wilbur Dutton received his A.B. and M.A. degrees in Elementary Education from Colorado State University, Greeley, and the Ed.D. degree in Elementary Curriculum and Instruction from Stanford University.

He has been an elementary school teacher, supervisor of student teaching, Principal of Ira D. Payne Elementary School in Tempe, Arizona, Curriculum Coordinator K–12 in Eugene, Oregon, and Director of Elementary Supervised Teaching (UCLA).

His writings include *The Modern Elementary School, Arithmetic for Teachers, Evaluating Pupils' Understanding of Arithmetic, Essential Modern Math Book C, Attitudes of Teachers Toward Arithmetic,* and *Comparative Studies of Primary-Level Mathematics* (England, Japan, Australia).

He was director and teacher for an experimental program in Mathematics (Piaget-based TRIAD I) with sixty four- and five-year-old children at the Corrine A. Seeds University Elementary School, UCLA.

Ann Dutton

A Child Development Instructor at Modesto Junior College (1979 to present), Ann Dutton works with student teachers and three- to five-year-olds in the laboratory school and teaches Early Childhood Education theory courses. She received a B.A. degree in Kindergarten-Primary Education from San Jose State University in 1957 (Child Development minor) and an M.A. degree in Human Development from Pacific Oaks College in 1979. Prior to 1979 she was, for nine years, the teacher/director of a Parent Participation Preschool which focused on activity-based learning. She taught first grade for four years. She is a member of the California Community College Chancellor's Advisory Committee for Child Development Instruction and Services. Currently, she is serving as the president of the California Community College Early Childhood Educators.